David Fiorazo has an uncompromising, hard-
ing with compassion for all people, and his per
the truth of God's Word. His sense of urgency
silence cannot be overstated. He is one of my
consider him one of the best "watchmen on the

Jan Markell
Founder of Olive Tree Ministries

The Cost of Our Silence should be required reading for high school and college students, professing Christians, and perhaps most importantly, our pastors and church leaders. This book will open people's eyes and motivate them to action.

Rob Pue
Publisher, *Wisconsin Christian News*

David Fiorazo is an eloquent and excellent writer, challenging Christians to speak out and take action against the growing secular culture infiltrating our nation. His new book, *The Cost of Our Silence*, builds to a powerful conclusion and is a clarion call to all those concerned about the direction of our nation as well as the church in America.

Mike LeMay
Stand Up for the Truth

I appreciate David Fiorazo's thoughtful and passionate analysis concerning the moral and spiritual decline facing believers today. While many in the church waver under the pressures of secularism and unbiblical thinking, David is counted among the clear voices, enunciating God's truth in these troubling times.

Eric Barger
Take A Stand Ministries

We live in dark times disguised as enlightenment. David Fiorazo not only identifies the reality of the underlying problem, he also gives his audience real hope in a world filled with false hopes. David is a modern day "voice in the wilderness."

Dr. James Langteau
Director of SE Asia, Wycliffe Associates

David Fiorazo lives his faith. His new book communicates biblical truth with an uncompromising passion and takes aim at the many "professing" Christians who refuse to acknowledge or oppose the evils ravaging society – and the church – in America today. A MUST READ.

Alan Scholl
Executive Director, Freedom Project Education

David Fiorazo is a rare and refreshing voice for truth in an age of apostasy and deceit.

Joe Schimmel
Good Fight Ministries

The Cost of our Silence

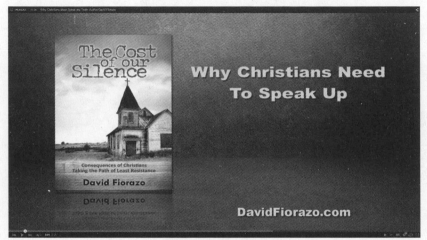

Introduction Video: https://youtu.be/ow4Hn-5IW7I

The Cost of our Silence

Consequences of Christians Taking the Path of Least Resistance

David Fiorazo

ANEKO PRESS

Cover Design: Amber Burger

Cover Photography: Tania A/Shutterstock, Sascha Burkard/Shutterstock

Editors: Sheila Wilkinson, Charlotte Graber

Printed in the United States of America

Aneko Press – *Our Readers Matter*™

www.anekopress.com

Aneko Press, Life Sentence Publishing, and our logos are trademarks of

Life Sentence Publishing, Inc.
203 E. Birch Street
P.O. Box 652
Abbotsford, WI 54405

RELIGION / Christian Life / Social Issues

Paperback ISBN: 978-1-62245-271-2

Ebook ISBN: 978-1-62245-272-9

10 9 8 7 6 5 4 3 2 1

Available wherever books are sold.

Share this book on Facebook:

Contents

Thank you, Jesus, for saving me and for giving me hope in this life and the next; may this book point people to You and glorify Your name. And thank you, Rosanna, for your support and patience throughout the lengthy research, writing, editing, and publishing process. I love you.

INTRODUCTION

America has over 300,000 churches, but few would contest that our Christian influence is decreasing as the nation becomes more secularized. Our biblical values are no longer being consistently demonstrated and promoted and therefore, do not translate out from behind church walls and into culture. Why are there so few speaking up for Jesus Christ and for righteousness in public anymore? Hope for revival remains, and a remnant of committed leaders and believers are doing their part, but because of the posers and pretenders, American Christianity has almost become a joke. People in the Middle East look at Hollywood, the Internet, and our government. They see our education system, media, and the people we elect. They observe our greed, idolatry, and society as a whole and refer to us as "The Great Satan."

The country has strayed so far from where we used to be morally, economically, politically, and spiritually, that the United States is hardly recognizable when you read our true, unedited history. Yes, we have been under heavy attack by the enemy of our souls and the battle is raging. But too many of us stopped caring and too many churches have been on a diet of cotton candy instead of steak. Christians must take responsibility and change course before it's too late.

How are we contributing to the collapse of this great country? Unless we admit the truth and act accordingly, this nation is toast. Evil began knocking centuries ago, but in the last hundred years – and particularly in the last fifty – we thrust the door wide open and invited evil in! Rather than resist the sin that used to repulse us and cause us deep remorse, we have warmed up to it and have welcomed godlessness with open arms. Tolerance, grace, and a "judge ye not" attitude are the norm in many churches, while repentance and holiness have practically become four-letter words.

It is time to *wake up and strengthen what remains and is about to die* (Revelation 3:2 NIV). We have neglected the study and application of God's Word. We have failed to share our faith and openly discuss every human being's biggest problem – sin. We have not resisted the world's ways, and in fact, we're just like them.

The country is sick and the church is on life support; should we not call on the Great Physician to heal and save her? Why are so few willing to talk about the fact that sin seems to be celebrated rather than confessed? Are we so wrapped up in our own selfish lives or distracted by the latest technology to care? It's as if we'd rather mind our own business than help the brokenhearted. People are losing hope; many are dying without Christ and going to hell – and we're going to the mall.

Because the church is struggling, so is the nation. Instead of being a beacon of light to the world, America has paved perverted pathways into deeper darkness. Rather than be an example of godliness, we have become a stench in the nostrils of a holy God. (But we *do* have the best entertainment, sports, restaurants, and reality shows, don't we?)

What has been our collective reaction to immorality? We have chosen silence. Let's just be honest with God: We are too busy, and for the most part we have little concern for the people Jesus Christ died a horrible death to save. The truth is – Silence never saved anybody. Lost souls rarely put their trust in Jesus on their own, and indifference rarely turned a sinning Christian back to a forgiving God.

If we are truly His followers, shouldn't we be living differently? Peter asks, *what sort of people ought you to be in holy conduct and godliness, looking for and hastening the coming of the day of God?* (2 Peter 3:11-12). We are in big trouble, my friend. The world is imploding, time is running out, and the door through which people can be saved is closing. God's judgment is coming to America and it will start with the church.

Our hearts should be breaking! People all around us and across this country are feeling empty and hopeless. Just as Jesus wept for Jerusalem while acknowledging its judgment, should we not weep for America as the signs clearly point to God's impending judgment on a once-mighty, blessed nation? Do we expect God to stay His hand of judgment and continue blessing a rebellious and narcissistic people with His protection and provision?

Our country has forgotten how to blush and has cast aside all moral restraint while forgetting our Christian history. Profanity and adultery are commonplace; the murder of babies in the womb is legal and often celebrated; we have perverse parades, judicial tyranny, and a power-grabbing government with no accountability. A biased and progressive media cheers for immorality, Christ-less education, and makes a mockery of marriage.

Our land is filled with too many permissive pastors, lukewarm Christians, and sin justifiers, while same-sex promoters, godless entertainment consumers, evolution defenders, and satanic sympathizers are celebrating. We allow Hollywood to dump filthy garbage into our living rooms, and as a result, we welcome witchcraft, blasphemy, and the glorification of sin. We have become desensitized to the influence of liberalism within the church.

One might argue, "But God is still on the throne." Sure. I agree He is sovereign over all events and circumstances. He remains all-powerful, but He does not control us or force people to love Him. God was also on His throne in 1973 when we legalized abortion, and soon America will be closing in on 60 million babies murdered in the name of "choice." Christians helped elect the most pro-abortion, anti-Christian president in our history – twice. Do you suppose God cares how we vote?

God is still on the throne – and He is preparing to judge a complacent people who continue ducking the issue of sin.

I am not blaming President Barack Obama for the mess this country is in today – the decline began decades ago. But we are the ones who most recently rejected God and elected a king just like Israel once did. We chose a man who is now doing exactly what he declared he would do if elected – transform the United States of America. By now, most informed citizens understand what he meant in 2008. Obama is certainly not obeying the teachings in the Bible, nor does he care about the heart of God for America. As he tramples the Constitution, he is simply following his own heart and further weakening a nation bent on immorality.

He promised change, didn't he? Oh, I see – you failed to look into his past beliefs, associations, and history. You gave him the benefit of the doubt and didn't want to feel guilty for not voting for the first half-black president. How irresponsible. With progressives, atheists, and socialists already in our government, the pump was primed and the stage was set for Obama's America. By chipping away at the moral and spiritual foundations of the United States, he and his minions have successfully taken us further from the Judeo-Christian principles and the God who prospered us in the past. And the church is silent.

As the Eric Holder Justice Department gave states the go-ahead to ignore the will of tens of millions of Americans across the country, radical federal judges are overturning laws implemented to protect marriage between one man and one woman. The Supreme Court now leans left as well.

If you are not a Christian, I don't blame you for the condition of our country or whom you vote for, though I vehemently disagree with your worldview. I do challenge you, however, to read this book to the end as you may be surprised by the truth and history contained in these pages.

The blame is squarely on the church in America. We have failed to be effective witnesses for our Lord Jesus Christ. Too many professing believers do not represent authentic, Bible-based Christianity. We have been sold on appearing spiritual, pursuing comfort, and living for self. I speak from experience because I used to have one foot in the church and another in the world.

It is impossible to be a part-time Christian.

The word *Christian* means "of or relating to Jesus Christ" and "a diminutive Christ." This implies a person who thinks, acts, talks, serves, and speaks like Jesus. Effectiveness for the kingdom of God starts with our own individual commitment to live for His glory rather than our own. It is not complicated: Know the Lord and make Him known to others.

IDENTIFYING THE PLAYERS AND THE PROBLEMS

In the Christian camp there is quite a diverse mix of beliefs, lifestyles, and opinions.

- First, a remnant of mature Christ followers remains committed to His cause; these believers love the Lord with all their hearts, representing an authentic, vibrant faith, and have a God-fearing, biblical worldview. They love others and shine for Jesus; they share the gospel with the lost, and they are unafraid to confront sin in the church.

- Second, another category of believers profess to be saved and maybe grew up in a religious home; they make it to church and read the Bible occasionally. But they love this world, are more concerned about the approval of man, and not very passionate about the things of God. They may be considered lukewarm. It is often hard to tell the difference between their lifestyle and that of unbelievers.

- Others have no idea what the true gospel is, but say they're going to heaven and consider themselves to be "a good person." They probably do not attend church often, and their lives show little fruit. They do not think there is a literal hell and do not believe the Bible is God's Word. They have never seriously trusted in Jesus Christ.

For the purposes of this book, when I refer to "professing Christians," the general meaning is those who say they are Christians but don't believe the Bible nor do they live according to its precepts in every area of their lives. They may fall in the second or third category above. The fruit in their lives – their actions, behavior, and words – fails to reflect the teachings of Jesus Christ, and they have a limited understanding of God and His Word. Professing Christians confuse onlookers by their lives and can reflect negatively on Christianity.

Professing believers also include those who think they're Christian because they grew up in America or in a family that attended some church once a week. They may claim salvation, but have no idea what repentance and sanctification are, and they only like the parts of the Bible they agree with. Typically, they do not believe Jesus is the *only* way to God, and they often think Christianity should be more "relevant" and more like the world.

These professing believers avoid engaging in cultural battles; they criticize believers who do engage, and are more interested in what movie is playing in the theatres this weekend. This segment of America's religious population ignores the greater spiritual war manifesting in society and couldn't care less about the Left's progressive march through the major institutions toward their godless utopia.

Finally, there are enemies of Christ and of biblical truth – an unrelenting segment of people who are more active and emboldened to attack Christians than ever before. Some have masked themselves as moderates and have even crept into the church. They aim to silence the opposition and eliminate everything good and moral. They hate Jesus, the Bible, America and her history, and they fight to eradicate any influence of the Judeo-Christian God from society. They are freely and continually marketing and advancing evil with little resistance from Christians.

On *both* sides of this epic battle, some people are uninterested and unengaged, simply wanting to live and let live. They may be Christian or atheist, conservative or liberal, religious or nonreligious, but they don't speak up or fully commit to their leader's (Jesus or Satan) cause. They pretty much stay out of the battle. These players are insignificant and irrelevant, keeping to themselves. Also on both sides are people who don't know *why* they believe what they believe. This should never be the case with mature Christians.

Some people have made up their minds against Christianity when they never have had the whole gospel explained to them. They must be challenged with the question "If the Bible were true, would you believe it?" Are we prepared to have such conversations or debates? This is one of the reasons you and I are still alive today.

> But sanctify Christ as Lord in your hearts, always being ready
> to make a defense to everyone who asks you to give an account
> for the hope that is in you, yet with gentleness and reverence
> (1 Peter 3:15).

This is a spiritual battle that manifests in the physical realm as *the devil prowls around like a roaring lion seeking someone to devour* (1 Peter 5:8). Even if it were possible to avoid conflict, shouldn't our love for sinners move us to action, and doesn't our love for Jesus compel us to speak and do what He commands?

With America heading for destruction and judgment, now more

than ever, disciples must be established in the faith as we seek to make more disciples. Dedicated followers are to stick close to the Leader and obey His teachings, and true witnesses are to *publicly* testify to the grace of God and hope in Christ alone. We are not to accept, accommodate, ignore, or approve of people's sin. We are called to tell them the truth and do our best to live as examples of that truth.

America has more Christian churches and more resources than ever before – more than any other country in the world – so why do we look less and less like a Christian nation every day? We have more Bibles, seminaries, Christian music, and Christian entertainment than ever before. We have the fanciest churches, the finest Christian colleges, countless ministries and non-profits, and we have an abundance of Christian radio, television, and Christian bookstores across the country. Now consider the dwindling amount of Christian influence in our culture today. Something is drastically wrong.

With all of these resources, why are most kids falling away from God by the time they reach junior high school, and over 80 percent of Christian youth leaving the faith by their second year in college?

Christians in America are facing indoctrination from a multitude of directions. Schools instruct our children in evolution, environmentalism, and earth worship. Later they learn about Freudian psychology, social justice, and homosexuality. We are deluged with secular entertainment, promiscuity, and promotion of the abortion business. Society is inundated with Marxism, socialism, and secularism. Our lives are bombarded with atheism, witchcraft, false religions, and liberalism. Even in some church denominations, liberals (some may refer to them as religious "progressives" or the "Christian Left") have gained power and introduced theological heresies including New Age philosophies.

We must now define what it means to be Christian because the hypocrisy of some can be confusing to a watching world. In addition to loving the Lord our God with all our hearts and loving our neighbor as ourselves, mature Christians must:

1. Preach the gospel to all creation (Mark 16:15) and make disciples of all nations (Matthew 28:19); preach the Word in

season and out of season (2 Timothy 4:2) in order to reach the lost, hopeless, hurting, and afflicted with the good news.

2. Teach others to observe everything Jesus commanded (Matthew 28:20); encourage, train, and restore by calling to reconciliation (2 Corinthians 5:20) *believers* who have conformed to this world and are struggling with sin. When necessary, confront, correct, and rebuke (2 Timothy 3:16).

3. Contend for the faith (Jude 1:3) and be prepared at all times to defend the truth while giving a clear, convincing answer, explaining what we believe and why we believe it (1 Peter 3:15). Rather than approving of or participating in sin, expose it (Ephesians 5:11), always pointing people to the saving truth of Jesus Christ.

Can we accomplish any of these things by being silent? Can we avoid the spiritual warfare every Christian must endure? The world often interprets the silence of Christians as our approval, indifference, or both. Francis Schaeffer said:

> "We as Bible-believing evangelical Christians are locked in a battle. This is not a friendly gentleman's discussion. It is a life and death conflict between the spiritual hosts of wickedness and those who claim the name of Christ."

Opposition is guaranteed. Most of us understand in today's culture that living our faith in public will attract resistance, ridicule, and even hatred. If we remember *our struggle is not against flesh and blood* (Ephesians 6:12), we will not take it personally when people come against us. Their problem is with Jesus Christ, not us.

If we are serious about our faith, others will know. In contrast, if we are living for this world and acting like the world, why should unbelievers place their trust in God? We're not much different than them.

The primary message of Jesus and John the Baptist was, *Repent, for the kingdom of heaven is at hand* (Matthew 3:2; 4:17). The message has not changed. One big problem we have today is fewer believers are willing to talk about God's law, sin, the cross, and repentance. Evangelist and author, Leonard Ravenhill, once said, "There's one thing we need above everything else; it's something we don't talk about these days. We need a mighty avalanche of conviction of sin."

Let's acknowledge there are gaping holes in the armor of American Christianity. We are not as strong as we think we are, and the church is a far cry from the spotless bride for whom Christ will return. Too often we get worn down and end up compromising our biblical convictions. I was compelled to write this book to address our indifference and investigate solutions to the lack of salt and light in society. Throw in the anti-Christian agendas and we have a dangerous combination. We are instruments chosen by God to be messengers of truth. We must speak for Him regardless of the consequences. No, it's not hip and popular. Yes, we will be verbally attacked and ostracized at the very least. But who are we trying to impress?

> *For am I now seeking the favor of men, or of God? Or am I striving to please men? If I were still trying to please men, I would not be a bond-servant of Christ* (Galatians 1:10).

God needs more watchmen on the wall to warn the church to repent. Some may respond, "but if I say anything about people's sin, they'll accuse me of judging." Is it too much to ask to help a backslidden believer or to save someone for eternity when Jesus sacrificed everything? Because He died for us and rose again to give us life, the least we can do is speak up.

The choice is ours. We have the right to remain silent. We have the right to keep our faith to ourselves and go about our own business. We have the right to avoid confrontation, coast through life, and ignore the evidence of a collapsing culture. We have the right to stay out of politics and public debates and deny the signs of the times. We have the right to live in comfortable complacency in the privacy of our own homes and limit our church activity to Sunday mornings.

We have the right to allow people around us to go to hell. But can we honestly love others and not share with them the most important, wonderful, life changing, lifesaving truth about salvation through Jesus Christ? God has committed to us the message of reconciliation (2 Cor. 5:19). We have the most urgent, vital message in the world, one by which God miraculously transforms hearts and lives. What a privilege that He uses broken vessels like you and me!

It's time to sound the alarms, rally the remnant of committed believers, and take our positions. God's love and mercy endure forever and His patience means salvation (2 Peter 3:15). We must act quickly for the salvation of sinners, while there is still time. God is not finished with us yet and there's hope for America, but His judgment will not be held back much longer.

You will hear this theme throughout the book: Without addressing the issue of sin and without the preaching of the gospel, there can be little conviction leading to repentance. As a result, fewer hearts and lives will be changed for Christ, and our culture will remain on its current pace and path of deterioration.

I pray this book may be a wake-up call and your response will be one of action rather than hitting the snooze button and rolling over. Christians are one of the only preserving influences on culture and what's left of morality. One goal of this book is to encourage more believers to take this faith seriously. I also hope to inform younger Christians by equipping them to face the hostilities of an anti-Christian culture.

When culture is darkest, light shines the brightest. We have the Word of God to renew our hearts and minds. Impacting culture for Christ starts with you and me. It is not easy, but God promises it will be worth it. With persistent prayer, anything could happen.

Imagine getting this message out to the church. Imagine more converts and better follow-up with new believers. That impact could result in bolder disciples, stronger Christians, thriving churches, faithful witnesses, a national revival, and a culture transformed for Christ.

As Christians go, so goes America. There is a cost and there are consequences to our silence, but there are rewards for our faithfulness to the gospel and obedience to God's Word. The choice is ours to make.

> *But having the same spirit of faith, according to what is written, "I BELIEVED, THEREFORE I SPOKE," we also believe, therefore we also speak, knowing that He who raised the Lord Jesus will raise us also with Jesus and will present us with you. For all things are for your sakes, that the grace which is spreading to more and more people may cause the giving of thanks to abound to the glory of God. Therefore we do not lose heart, but though*

our outer man is decaying, yet our inner man is being renewed day by day. For momentary, light affliction is producing for us an eternal weight of glory far beyond all comparison, while we look not at the things which are seen, but at the things which are not seen; for the things which are seen are temporal, but the things which are not seen are eternal (2 Corinthians 4:13-18).

CHAPTER 1

WHAT'S HAPPENING TO OUR HERITAGE?

"Being thus arrived in a good harbor and brought safe to land, they fell upon their knees and blessed the God of heaven, who had brought them over the vast and furious ocean, and delivered them from all the perils and miseries thereof, againe to set their feete on the firme and stable earth ... Having undertaken, for the Glory of God and advancement of the Christian Faith and Honor of our King and Country, a Voyage to plant the First Colony."
—William Bradford, *Of Plymouth Plantation*[1]

In the earliest days in this land, when Christians experienced hard times, their desperation caused them to rely on God. Conversely, when things are going well, we often choose to rely on ourselves. Throughout history, the Lord often allowed persecution in order to turn people back to Him. Men came to these shores hoping to establish a God-fearing settlement that would flourish on faith and freedom.

Devout Christian, Mayflower Pilgrim, and Plymouth Colony Governor of thirty-one years, William Bradford died in 1656. Near the end of his life, an entry in Bradford's chronicle of the colony reveals evidence of how difficult it can be to avoid subtle moral erosion in a society. He saw similarities in the material success achieved at the Plymouth Plantation and the wealth enjoyed by England, both of which came at the price of spiritual decline.

Historians disagree about the reasons for Bradford's disdain over

---

1   William Bradford: History of Plymouth Plantation, c. 1650, http://www.fordham.edu/halsall/mod/1650bradford.asp.

prosperity and sin, but here is one of the final entries in his journal lamenting the dispersal of the original church community:

> O sacred bond, whilst inviolably preserved! How sweet and precious were the fruits that flowed from the same! But when this fidelity decayed, then their ruin approached. O that these ancient members had not died or been dissipated (if it had been the will of God) or else that this holy care and constant faithfulness had still lived, and remained with those that survived ... But (alas) that subtle serpent hath slyly wound himself under fair pretenses of necessity and the like, to untwist these sacred bonds and ties ... I have been happy, in my first times, to see, and with much comfort to enjoy, the blessed fruits of this sweet communion, but it is now a part of my misery in old age, to find and feel the decay and want thereof (in a great measure) and with grief and sorrow of heart to lament and bewail the same. And for others' warning and admonition, and my own humiliation, do I here note the same.[2]

Bradford was grieved about their apparent failure to meet or live by the high biblical standards expected of them because in the early days, Christians took their faith seriously and were committed in their pursuit of holiness as individuals and as a community. Do we experience that kind of grief, sorrow, and heartache over our own sins and the spiritual condition of our culture?

On April 8, 1630, nearly ten years after the Pilgrims landed at Plymouth Rock, a fleet of eleven ships left England from the Isle of Wight. Carrying more than 700 Puritans, plus livestock and provisions, they hoped to begin a new colony in Massachusetts Bay, free from religious persecution by the Church of England. Understanding the dangers of such a journey and aware that half of the Pilgrims who settled in Plymouth had died, many Puritan leaders were so concerned England was declining spiritually they believed the chance for religious freedom in the New World outweighed potential hardships, including death!

Sailing west on the ship Arbella, an English Puritan lawyer by the name of John Winthrop was part of the first large wave of immigrants

---

2   William Bradford, *Of Plymouth Plantation*, 1620-1647, p. 33.

and a leading founder of the Massachusetts Bay Colony, the first major settlement in New England. Winthrop would serve as governor for the first twelve years, settling in the Shawmut Peninsula and founding what is now Boston. An estimated 200 people died from disease and a variety of other causes in the first several months, including Winthrop's son Henry. Encouraging other colonists to trust in God and work hard, Winthrop is said to have joined workers and servants in manual labor to set an example so that "there was not an idle person to be found in the whole plantation."

It's interesting to note years earlier in England, Winthrop was first tutored at home and was regularly exposed to religious discussions between his father and clergymen, resulting in his knowledge of spiritual things at a very young age. This led to his admission to Trinity College when he was just fifteen years old. His strong religious upbringing and education would help set the tone for America for many generations.

> You are the light of the world. A city set on a hill cannot be hidden; nor does anyone light a lamp and put it under a basket, but on the lampstand, and it gives light to all who are in the house (Matthew 5:14-15).

During the journey to America, Winthrop wrote and delivered a lay sermon to the people based on the above Scriptures. Entitled "A Model of Christian Charity," he envisioned a unified new colony ordained to build "a City upon a Hill" dedicated to God. This famous work originally inspired the idea of American exceptionalism. With an emphasis on individual responsibility, integrity, and group discipline, his writing described how to keep the colony strong in faith and committed to God in the endeavor of creating a holy community.

Politicians as diverse as John F. Kennedy, Ronald Reagan, Michael Dukakis, and Sarah Palin have quoted or referred to John Winthrop in speeches. He seemed to know the Massachusetts Bay Colony would be "watched by the world," and the Puritans would either set an example of righteousness and "find that the God of Israel is among us," or if they failed to uphold their covenant with God, "we shall be made a story and a by-word through the world" and could incur God's judgment. Winthrop's Bible-inspired writings dominated the development and growth of New England and influenced the government of neighboring colonies.[3]

Though Winthrop's godly influence can be seen in the first couple hundred years in America, we now know it is much easier to slide down to the world's ways than to stay close to God and pursue holiness.

Millions of religious people today have not had in-depth teachings on the Bible and spiritual things. How many can name all Ten Commandments or perhaps books and authors of the Bible? How many can share the whole gospel including the need for redemption through the blood of Christ? What we have is increasing ignorance of the Word of God and American history, as well as a disinterest in Christianity and spiritual things.

For many decades, the truth about our Christian heritage has been downplayed or worse, forgotten. Moreover, how can we avoid repeating the most disappointing parts of our history if cautions from our founders and warnings from Christian leaders are no longer taught and remembered?

> Resolution One: I will live for God. Resolution Two: If no
> one else does, I still will.
> —Jonathan Edwards

One of America's greatest theologians was Jonathan Edwards (1703-1758), a Congregational preacher and missionary in New England and grandfather of Aaron Burr, the third Vice President of the United States. Edwards was a man of hard preaching with a heart for God's glory above all things, which is what drove him. This led him to compose a set of resolutions to guide his conduct in all areas, from his battle against sin to the use of his time.

Edward's famous sermon, "Sinners in the Hands of an Angry God," is credited for starting the First Great Awakening in America. He wrote about the previous decade, saying it represented a far more "degenerate time" than ever before. Preaching in Northampton, Massachusetts, and Enfield, Connecticut, in 1741, Edwards delivered strong words to the Puritans at that time by saying:

> Yea, God is a great deal more angry with great numbers that

---

3   John Winthrop – Wikipedia, http://en.wikipedia.org/wiki/John_Winthrop.

are now on earth: yea, doubtless, with many that are now in this congregation, who it may be are at ease, than he is with many of those who are now in the flames of hell … The wrath of God burns against them, their damnation does not slumber; the pit is prepared, the fire is made ready, the furnace is now hot, ready to receive them; the flames do now rage and glow … and the pit hath opened its mouth under them.

Among his many riveting resolutions was this one about living with an eternal perspective:

I resolve to endeavor to my utmost to act and think as if I had already seen the happiness of heaven and the torments of hell.

Like Edwards, many dedicated, outspoken men of God wrestled with what they knew from the Holy Scriptures, concerned with the lures and perils of the secular world surrounding them. The enemy uses whatever and whomever he can to distract us and draw us away from God.

Speaking to record crowds and traveling the thirteen colonies on a revival tour at that time was the great preacher and orator, George Whitefield, with whom Edwards was somewhat acquainted. Entire chapters and books have been written about these men and others of great faith who impacted Christianity and America. God-fearing, committed men have often been used by the Lord as catalysts of repentance and spiritual regeneration in society.

One common characteristic men of God possess is the willingness to give their all for Christ, hoping to store up treasures in heaven. Edwards had asked for a loan from the trustees at Harvard during his short time as president, and Whitefield struggled with debt from orphanages he had started in Georgia and in England.

Traveling at a time when sailing was primitive, Whitefield made thirteen trips across the Atlantic Ocean. Many believe the diligence and sacrifice of George Whitefield helped turn two nations back to God. Jonathan Edwards was leading the charge in America while the great John Wesley was preaching up a storm in England. George Whitefield completed this trio of godly men who at that time were primarily responsible for waking up the church and reconciling the lost to Christ on both sides of the Atlantic.

While emphasizing salvation by God's grace alone, Whitefield presented the gospel and concluded his sermons with "Come poor, lost, undone sinner; come just as you are to Christ!"

Prior to preaching his last sermon on September 29, 1770, Whitefield looked up and prayed:

> Lord Jesus, I am weary in thy work, but not of thy work. If I have not yet finished my course, let me go and speak for thee once more in the fields, seal thy truth, and come home and die.

He was given strength for what would be his last sermon. The subject was faith and works. Although scarcely able to stand when he first arrived, he preached for two hours to a crowd that no building could have held. Whitefield died the next morning.

After these three godly men came Fisher Ames, who was born in 1758. His father died when Fisher was six years old, but his mother was determined to provide her son with a classical education in spite of her limited income. Fisher began to study Latin and when he was twelve years old, he attended Harvard College, graduating in 1774 at the age of sixteen. He went on to become a lawyer, a Founding Father, and the author of the First Amendment of the Constitution. As did most of our founders, he believed the Bible to be the best source of all learning.

Having beat Samuel Adams, Fisher Ames was elected to the First United States Congress and served a total of three terms representing Massachusetts. Being concerned about a "dangerous trend" taking place in education and around 1800, Ames stated:

> We've become accustomed of late to putting little books in the hands of children containing fables with moral lessons. We are spending less time in the classroom on the Bible, which should be the principle text in our schools. The Bible states these great moral lessons better than any other man made book.[4]

The spiritual battle for the hearts and minds of young children was already underway! Here is the author of the First Amendment, which includes the free exercise clause protecting public expressions of faith

---

4   Ben Kinchlow, "Get That Bible Outta Here," 10/23/2011, http://www.wnd.com/2011/10/359405/.

and religion, voicing concerns over 200 years ago. And today in government schools, a Christian can be scolded or disciplined for doing the very things our founders set out to protect – reading, studying, and quoting the Bible.

We can look back at those times and ask why religious leaders and the people seemingly failed to heed the warnings. We may also wonder how Ames and others had the commitment and insight to make such admonishments. It is as if they knew the consequences of Christian silence and inactivity would include a culture that has almost completely blotted God out of America. Signs were unmistakable all along that this country was gradually losing the battle for righteousness.

United States history indicates that prior to the acceleration of our moral decline, Christians in the 1800s were gaining converts, momentum, and influence. Some consider that century the greatest missionary century in history. Our culture, institutions, laws, and businesses were carried along and led by Christians who, for the most part, were not ashamed to live their faith publicly and discuss spiritual things.

They firmly believed America was a Christian nation and strived to live accordingly. However, the impact of the industrial revolution would soon be seen in society as well as in the church. Business, prosperity, and worldly success brought about a whole new set of problems in life. It's no wonder many past presidents and political leaders called for repentance among the people. Even the United States Congress once issued an official Proclamation of Thanksgiving and Prayer on October 18, 1780, calling on Americans "to cause the knowledge of Christianity to spread all over the Earth."

President Abraham Lincoln also recognized the nation's need for repentance in 1863 as he designated "a national day of humiliation, fasting, and prayer." Acknowledging the nation's growth and success, Lincoln was concerned the people had forgotten God so he requested all Americans abstain "from their ordinary secular pursuits, and to unite, at their several places of public worship and their respective homes, in keeping the day holy to the Lord." In gratitude for the gracious gifts of the Most High God, Lincoln was determined to move the people to confess their sins and ask for God's mercy as well as the restoration of the country:

> All this being done, in sincerity and truth, let us then rest humbly in the hope authorized by the Divine teachings, that the united cry of the Nation will be heard on high, and answered with blessings, no less than the pardon of our national sins.[5]

People enjoyed the growing prosperity of a country God had blessed with abundant natural resources. The problem was – and remains today – we cannot serve both God and money. As Jesus said regarding these two masters, *for either he will hate the one and love the other, or he will be devoted to one and despise the other* (Matthew 6:24).

During that time, a young man who would become very influential in America, evangelist Dwight L. Moody, converted to Christianity at a shoe store near Boston where he worked when he was eighteen years old. Moody had grown up very poor, but after moving to Chicago he became successful selling shoes and also started a Sunday school at the local YMCA. Moody's school quickly grew in attendance to hundreds of students with dozens of volunteers from area churches serving as teachers. The school earned such a good reputation that President Lincoln visited and spoke there on November 25, 1860.

Combining preaching with social work, Moody was president of the YMCA in Chicago for four years. During the time of the Civil War, he often visited the battlefront to evangelize the Union troops, traveling as far as Richmond with the army of General Grant. Supported by wealthy businessmen who believed in his ministry, Moody was married, had three children, and invested time in preaching, missions, and social work. When the Great Chicago Fire of 1871 destroyed his church, his home, and the YMCA, all he had left was his Bible and his family.

In His sovereignty, God used the fire to refocus Moody's ministry. Shaken by the losses, he went to New York to seek rebuilding funds, but admittedly his heart was "not in the work of begging." At that time he described the Holy Spirit overflowing in his life. He felt the strong presence of God leading him to return to Chicago to preach the kingdom of God and devote his life to evangelizing that generation.

The next year he was invited to preach in England as calls for crusades

---

5   Abraham Lincoln, "Proclamation Appointing a National Day of Fasting," 3/30/1863,
     http://www.abrahamlincolnonline.org/lincoln/speeches/fast.htm.

began to increase. Charles Spurgeon requested he preach in London in 1875, and when Moody returned home, larger crowds became the norm. On farmland he purchased in Northfield, Massachusetts, where he was born, Moody would later hold conferences attended by prominent preachers and evangelists from around the world. In America, crowds of thousands grew to tens of thousands as Moody became well known.

United States President Ulysses S. Grant and some of his cabinet members attended one of Moody's meetings on January 19, 1876. Several years later, upon meeting pioneer missionary to China, Hudson Taylor, Moody encouraged cross-cultural Christian missions. In 1886, he started his Bible work in Chicago that would later become the Moody Bible Institute.

In celebration of the 400th anniversary of Columbus discovering America, Chicago hosted the 1893 World Fair, an event that ran for six months. Moody preached the gospel to thousands of people each night, and he established locations all over Chicago for evangelistic services. With the help of visiting pastors and evangelists, Moody introduced multitudes to the Christian faith during that time. He also initiated the follow-up of converts, called an "after-meeting," to help counsel people who responded to the "altar" invitation.

Dwight Lyman Moody died six years later on December 22, 1899. Some of his final words were: "Earth is receding, Heaven is approaching! God is calling me!" Moody is said to have preached the gospel of Jesus Christ to over 100 million people worldwide.

Around the time Moody died, another Chicago-area evangelist was becoming popular. William Ashley "Billy" Sunday got saved while playing in baseball's National League during the 1880s and left baseball to preach the gospel. The Pittsburgh Pirates offered Sunday $2,000/month; Evangelist J. Wilbur Chapman hired him for $40/week.

Sunday described himself as an "uncompromising enemy of the Liquor Traffic," and opposed the secularization of society, including the increase of activities such as public dancing, card-playing, attending the theatre, and baseball games on Sunday. These things took away from church, Bible reading, and family time. Billy Sunday often asked his audiences:

Did you ever know a time in all history when the world was worse than it is now? People are passing up the Church and the Prayer Meeting for the theatre, the leg show and the movies. Oh, Lord, how we need someone to cry aloud, "Return to God!"

Sunday was an evangelist from 1893 to 1935, and one of his unique traits was his plain, straight-forward preaching. As the clergy of his day tried to impress folks with education, intellect, and vocabulary, Billy Sunday was known for his fire and simplicity. He often spoke about other preachers who were concerned about offending people with the truth about hell. He not only told unbelievers to get saved, he also preached against churches that were filled with unsaved members and those who became apathetic about the lost.

It would be a godsend if the Church would suffer persecution today; she hasn't suffered it for hundreds of years. She is growing rich and lagging behind.
—Billy Sunday

In hindsight, it's easy for us to say Billy Sunday was right. Despite the crusades, revivals, and conversions, society seemed to maintain its path toward ungodliness to the point of infecting the church in America along the way. If Christians did not awaken to this reality, which they didn't, many would soon become disinterested or apathetic.

It is indisputable men of God established this nation on biblical truth as they pursued freedom from religious persecution and "the advancement of the Christian Faith," as William Bradford stated. But since our foundations are eroding, perhaps persecution is exactly what needs to happen in order to shake us up and bring us back to God.

CHAPTER 2

FAILING TO LEARN FROM HISTORY

If the foundations are destroyed what can the righteous do?
Psalm 11:3

As the 1900s rolled around, things began changing as America experienced economic success and cultural advances. Several factors including busier lives, increased population, and worldly temptations led many believers to back out of public involvement in cultural, political, and social issues. They meant well; many just wanted to protect their families.

By 1918, all states required mandatory school attendance for children, and the public education movement in America rapidly expanded in the decades to follow, soon to be infiltrated by progressives. By more or less withdrawing from culture, Christian leaders gave humanists and secularists control of major institutions, including higher education, government, the judiciary, media, and the entertainment industry.

The results have been devastating. This spiritual war had been going on from the beginning, but suddenly it seemed as if the primary battleground and prize possession was the United States. Major conflicts were brewing within America. As you read this, you may be saying to yourself "but where were the religious leaders and why weren't more Christians taking a stand?" Can we not ask the same question today?

We must realize evil is at work all around us, and there is nothing new under the sun. When depravity and immorality appear more prevalent in society, one of the main causes can be traced to silent or inactive Christians. This environment sets the stage for emboldened agendas against God, His Word, and His people.

In 1 Chronicles 12:32, the Bible refers to the sons of Issachar, one of the twelve tribes of Israel, descended from the ninth son of Jacob – men who understood the times and had knowledge about how to use the current events to their advantage. Discernment is not just a matter of having good judgment; it is also part of biblical and cultural understanding, knowing how to apply the truths of God's Word to the issues of our day. We need more truth proclaimers and defenders today, watchmen on the wall who understand what's happening and what to do about it.

Discrimination of Christians in America is increasing and we tolerate a faulty understanding of the First Amendment, which we will investigate thoroughly in a later chapter. As culture becomes more corrupt and godless, those who hate God no longer feel the need to be subtle about it. Where they used to simply disagree with us, today they want to remove the "conservative opposition" by silencing us.

Opponents of the biblical Christian worldview are not satisfied with just denying God exists as they fight to stop our moral influence on culture. Our choice to trust in Jesus Christ rubs them the wrong way, and they now feel emboldened to go so far as to take away that option for anyone else. We are at this pivotal point in our history because Christians not only allowed the secularization of America, some have welcomed it.

The early 1900s saw an increase of industry, entertainment, liberalism, and modernism. Some churches became more accepting of secular ideas and those who promoted them. These battles would parallel the truth war – one which continues today even in the church. A major controversy over biblical doctrines had been brewing between Fundamentalists and Modernists. Many of the divisions in church denominations were caused by a debate that took place in the Presbyterian Church and would extend into the 1930s.

The primary debate was about what would come to be known as the "Five Fundamentals" of the faith. It's no wonder the truth was attacked at its roots. The very first questioning of God's Word came from the devil himself in Genesis 3:1-5, casting doubt when he asked, *Indeed has God said, "You shall not eat of any tree in the garden,"* and then that sly serpent essentially called God a liar when he claimed, *You surely will not die!*

Trouble was brewing for several years when a debate in the New

York Presbytery arose between church leaders over whether or not to ordain men who refused to affirm the virgin birth of Jesus. The majority would ordain the men, and those who disagreed with the decision filed a complaint with the General Assembly that would eventually result in the creation of a statement of faith for governing future ordinations.

The outcome was the Doctrinal Deliverance of 1910 declaring these five doctrines to be "necessary and essential" to the Christian faith:

- The divine inspiration of the Bible by the Holy Spirit and the inerrancy of Scripture.

- The pre-existence, deity, and virgin birth of Jesus Christ.

- The satisfaction of God's justice by the crucifixion of Jesus Christ (substitutionary atonement).

- The bodily resurrection, ascension, and intercession of Christ.

- The historical reality of Christ's miracles.

Those who agreed and adhered to these doctrines would be known as fundamentalists or conservatives. The controversy bled over into other denominations, and in 1928 the resolution was rejected by the Presbyterian Church of the United States.

What can we learn from this? Liberals don't give up easily in their push to adjust and conform church doctrines to the spirit of the age. They would eventually take over many Christian seminaries and produce their own disciples leading to the Emergent Church today. We'll take a detailed look at how this happened in a later chapter.

Prior to this, a 1922 sermon by Harry Fosdick, a Baptist spokesman for liberal Protestantism, fired another shot across the bow of the church. His sermon, "Shall the Fundamentalists Win?" described the differences between conservative and liberal Christians.

Clarence E. Macartney, a conservative pastor from Philadelphia, responded with a sermon published in a pamphlet, "Shall Unbelief Win?" He argued that if liberalism were left unchecked, it would lead to "a Christianity of opinions and principles and good purposes, but a Christianity without worship, without God, and without Jesus Christ."[6]

---

6   Clarence E. Macartney, "Shall Unbelief Win? An Answer to Dr. Fosdick," Presbyterian, July 20, 1922, p. 8.

Former professor of New Testament theology at Princeton Seminary for over twenty years, J. Gresham Machen was a fundamentalist Christian who left Princeton because of its liberal direction. He formed Westminster Theological Seminary in 1929 as a more orthodox alternative. The ongoing debate caused a number of conservative theologians and clergy to establish the Orthodox Presbyterian Church in 1936. Tragically, every denomination would end up accommodating liberalism to one degree or another, which helps explain why we are where we are today both as a church and a society.

This battle had to be fought. The integrity of the Word of God must be defended. Just as Jude, the half-brother of Jesus, wrote in his letter, we are to *contend earnestly for the faith which was once for all handed down to the saints* (Jude 1:3). While Christian denominations were fighting among themselves about doctrine – a necessary and worthy fight – where were the watchmen and what was happening to the culture?

That period of history seemed to be a launching pad of sorts for humanists, atheists, Marxists, progressives, and socialists such as John Dewey, Margaret Sanger, Alfred Kinsey, Saul Alinsky, and Norman Thomas (former Presbyterian minister, Princeton graduate, and member of the Socialist Party of America).

Starting in 1928, Norman Thomas ran for president of the United States on the Socialist Party ticket six times in a row unsuccessfully. He was the grandfather of Evan Thomas, who teaches journalism at Princeton and has worked for *Time* magazine. Thomas was managing editor of *Newsweek* from 1991 to 2010 and has done many hit pieces on Christianity and conservatism.

In addition to the debate over doctrine, new questions arose about the best ways to publicly express Christianity in America. Because of advances in science and technology, one particular issue came to the forefront in the Scopes "Monkey" Trial in Tennessee in 1925. The law at that time, the Butler Act, forbade any teaching that denied the biblical creation account. Even though the original verdict found John Scopes guilty of teaching evolution in public school, the media portrayed fundamentalist Christians as narrow-minded, old-school religious fools. The general public bought it, causing more Christians to sheepishly back out of culture.

The media and political liberals used the trial to criticize Christians who believed the Bible. This was a blatant move of Satan to discredit the Bible, thwart the growth of Christianity, and minimize the influence of believers. If we consider how much ground Christians surrendered, it is quite shocking for some today who thought America's problems were much more recent.

Most of our Founding Fathers would have testified to the fact that this country was based on the morals and values in the Holy Bible. Standing for truth demanded a firm foundation without abandonment of principles and standards. It is so much easier to compromise than to reverse the devastating consequences of compromise.

Perhaps one of the more known and respected Christian martyrs of the 20th century is Dietrich Bonhoeffer, a German theologian and conservative Lutheran pastor famous for his stand against Adolf Hitler and the Nazi socialist party. His beliefs and convictions ultimately cost him his life in a Nazi concentration camp days before the Allies invaded Germany in 1945. Bonhoeffer left us with a few admonishments:

> The deceit, the lie of the Devil consists of this; that he wishes to make man believe that he can live without God's Word …

> If the heart is devoted to the mirage of the world, to the creature instead of the Creator, the disciple is lost … However urgently Jesus may call us, His call fails to find access to our hearts … for they have already been given to another.

The example he set for millions of Christians lives on today, and these words should keep true believers inspired and motivated: "Silence in the face of evil is itself evil."

Christianity in Germany was considered a threat to leaders of the state, and governing authorities gradually implemented their plans to neutralize and eliminate the threat. A surprising number of young people in America today do not know who Adolf Hitler was, let alone his involvement in the Holocaust, so they cannot possibly learn from world history.

In order to enforce their evil agenda, the Nazis had to convince as many religious people as possible that the state had the good of the country in mind. Then they dealt with the unconvinced, getting them out of the way by whatever means necessary.

During the time of Hitler's rise to power, conservative pastor, Martin Niemoller, was one of hundreds of church leaders arrested for speaking out against the policies of Nazism. Just like many religious people in Germany, as well as ordinary people, it appears Niemoller originally supported Hitler for the first few years. He thought the national enthusiasm of new leadership would lead Germany to a spiritual revival. Like President Obama in his countless speeches, declarations, and press conferences, Hitler said all the right things to convince enough people to follow him, and through his charismatic delivery, many did not see the deceit.

Representing the Protestant Church, Niemoller personally met with Hitler before he became Germany's Chancellor in 1932. In a later response to questions about why he first supported the Nazi Party, Niemoller stated, "Hitler promised me on his word of honor, to protect the Church, and not to issue any anti-Church laws." Of course history proves the exact opposite; pastors were threatened, people were killed, churches were decimated, Bibles were replaced with Hitler's *Mein Kampf*, and crosses were removed to make room for swastikas.

Early on, Niemoller said he hated the growing atheist movement, which he believed was "fostered and promoted by the Socialist Democrats and the Communists." He said their hostility toward Christianity made him pin his hopes on Hitler for a while.

As Chancellor of Germany in 1933, Hitler promised:

> The national Government will provide and guarantee to the Christian Confessions the influence due them in the schools and education. It is concerned for genuine harmony between Church and State . . . The rights of the churches will not be curtailed.[7]

While Nazi leaders worked on winning over the church in Germany, they also implemented Nazi propaganda into their schools to indoctrinate the youth and at the same time, removed all religious instruction. Their ultimate goal was to promote the National Socialist worldview and

---

7   Garnet Peet, The Protestant Churches in Nazi Germany, Clarion Volume 37, No. 22-24, http://spindleworks.com/library/peet/german.htm.

eradicate Christian teachings in the schools. By the time WWII began, they had replaced religious textbooks with Nazi-approved books, and teachers had been promoting the new policies in obedience to government instructions.

Two hundred years earlier, a great patriot was born in America who warned us about this. As a signer of the Declaration of Independence, Benjamin Rush (1745-1813) said:

> The great enemy of the salvation of man, in my opinion, never invented a more effectual means of extirpating [extinguishing] Christianity from the world than by persuading mankind that it was improper to read the Bible at schools.

Sadly, we have chosen to ignore the wise and insightful wisdom of Rush and other men of God.

Looking back in regret for not opposing Hitler years earlier, Niemoller admitted he was betrayed. Laws were passed preventing churches from interfering in politics, and the Nazis systematically limited church influence in society. Talk about bullying. Special courts were established to convict Christian pastors for opposing Hitler's policies, but that would not stop Niemoller and others from eventually speaking up.

In the 1930s, one of the first things the German socialist government did was remove crucifixes and Bibles from public schools and replace them with more secular books.

In the 1960s, the United States government essentially removed crucifixes and Bibles from public schools, brought in more secular books, and eliminated prayer. Since that time, sex education, environmentalism, evolution, paganism, and socialism have been promoted; fornication, adultery, and secular music glorified, abortion legalized, and homosexuality normalized.

In Germany, the churches were kept quiet by force; in America, the churches have been silent due to self-inflicted apathy (for now). Germany was already heading in the direction of nationalized health care before Hitler came to power, while American government is now enforcing ObamaCare on people who were never given a say.

How long will true Christians and freedom-loving Americans allow a power-hungry, corrupt government to bully and intimidate us? How about when activist judges overrule the people – should we be silent? Governing authorities in Germany had the same agenda in 1935 as radicals and the left in America have today: Eliminate all Christian influence over public life.

As part of his plan to prevent Christianity from affecting politics, Hitler attacked the Catholic Church first by closing down any institution that wasn't strictly religious. Catholic schools, programs, and newspapers were shut down, and Catholic youth were corralled into the Hitler Youth brain-washing machine. Catholics could attend mass and hold other rituals, as long as they kept their faith inside the church. They were not allowed to be involved with German society. From Rome, Pope Pius XI condemned the new Nazi paganism, but his words had little effect outside Vatican walls.

Even though Christian leaders such as Dietrich Bonhoeffer opposed and resisted Hitler and Nazism from the start, it was Martin Niemoller who sent a letter to all German pastors inviting them to join the "Pastor's Emergency League." He asked church leaders to pledge themselves to be bound to Christ as Lord. The League would become the "Confessing Church" of which Bonhoeffer played a key role. The movement grew to over 6,000 pastors who recommitted themselves to the Scriptures. This was their creed:

1. To renew their allegiance to the Scriptures.

2. To resist those who attack the Scriptures.

3. To give material and financial aid to those who suffered through repressive laws or violence.

4. To repudiate the Nazi cause.

In the face of growing persecution, a group of Christian conservatives split from the Protestant Church and from the ranks of "German Christians" who were submitting to Hitler. Protestant ministers in Germany headed up by Pastor Martin Niemoller agreed upon a written proclamation opposing Hitler's regime, warning the people of idolatry. They believed the religion of Nazism threatened their nation with mortal danger, so they aimed to strengthen efforts to put God, Jesus, and the Word first. The Confessing Church warned:

> The church has by order of its Master to see to it that in our people [nation] Christ is honoured in a manner befitting the Judge of the world . . . The First Commandment says, "Thou shalt have no other gods before me." The new religion [Nazism] is a rejection of the First Commandment.

The Pastor's Emergency League decided to read protests from their pulpits in response to Hitler rallying the duped German Christians during a massive gathering at the Sports Palace in Berlin. His charisma helped convince them that if they joined his movement, reformation and renewal would come to Germany.

The remnant of faithful Christian leaders believed the true church would be held accountable "if the German nation turns its back on Christ without being forewarned." After a sermon he gave in June of 1937, Martin Niemoller was arrested for abusing the pulpit and for treason. He preached that believers had a sacred duty to address the evils of Nazism no matter the consequences.

> We have no more thought of using our own powers to escape the arm of the authorities than had the Apostles of old. No more are we ready to keep silent at man's behest when God commands us to speak. For it is, and must remain, the case that we must obey God rather than man.[8]

Nazism sought to transform the attitudes, beliefs, and values of the German people into a united national community. Hitler believed they needed to replace people's loyalty to class, religion, and geographical identity. Even he seemed to understand National Socialism and Christianity would not be able to coexist, but he believed he could placate most religious people while eliminating any opposition.

Germany is said to have had approximately 17,000 pastors when Hitler came to power. Estimates suggest over 800 pastors read parts of the declaration from their pulpits and over 500 were arrested. During Hitler's dictatorship, more than 6,000 clergymen were imprisoned or executed. That was more than a third of Germany's religious leaders.

A few years ago, I read a powerful book, *Fire Breathing Christians,*

---

8   William L. Shirer, *The Rise and Fall of the Third Reich* (New York: Simon and Schuster, 1960), 239.

by Scott Alan Buss in which he emphasizes this fact: Whenever God is removed, something or someone has to take His place. He imagined what it must have been like growing up in Germany in the 1930s and what caused the people to love such a man as Adolf Hitler, even worshipping him as some sort of messiah. After the war, when some of the German people were led through the death camps, they went in smiling but came out horrified and shocked by what they saw. Buss writes:

> How could such a thing as Hitler's Nazism rise to dominance in a once Christian nation on the very cutting edge of civilization? Why would an imminently rational, scientifically inclined people come to embrace a worldview so overtly evil and utterly devoid of positive philosophical substance? How could a people so renowned for their intellect and work ethic find themselves so completely enslaved to group-think and plunged into oblivion?

> Why did the purpose of life come to require the pursuit of death? These are questions that I contemplated … for many years … Today's United States of America holds all of the answers to what I once considered the dark mystery of history that was Nazi Germany. I now know how it is that a nation flush with pride over its technological advancement and material accomplishment can enthusiastically surrender its humanity for the sake of bettering mankind.

> I now know that it is a relatively simple and easy thing to define the inconvenient or unattractive life out of existence figuratively and rhetorically so that it might one day be done away with literally. I now know that a nation that is Christian in name only is no farther from hellish barbarism than that which openly professes allegiance to a pagan god or no god at all.

> I now know that the paths of historic Germany and contemporary America are founded on a solid, clear, and powerful line of logic. It all begins with one simple, all-encompassing and worldview defining principle: There is no God.[9]

---

9   Scott Alan Buss, *Fire Breathing Christians*, 2010 Revolution Press, Seattle, WA, pp. 195-196.

America has not been far behind Europe in many aspects of society. If there was ever a time for Christians to shout from the rooftops and warn others, that time is now.

Author and radio host, Jan Markell of Olive Tree Ministries, said it is human nature to allow compromise to get the best of us. In a 2014 newsletter, Jan explored a question many Christians fear but for some reason rarely discuss: What happens when we are seduced by government?

After the devastation of WWI, Germans in the early 1930s were promised a return to the "glory days." Government started to paint a picture of the good life returning, but only if government could become their god.

The people thought that was a great idea, hanging onto every promise of "hope and change." They simply had no idea Hitler's change would cause the swastika to be burned across the very fabric of Europe. Once Germany began its transformation, they looked the other way as the supposed "good life" was going to return for them — or so they thought. Hope and change agents always promise utopia, and America presents some haunting comparisons to Nazi Germany.

Keep in mind this is but a set-up for the Antichrist. What is happening in America and around the world is paving the way for the ultimate government that will be god to the people. The "man of lawlessness" is waiting in the wings, but Jesus Christ will ultimately bring godly government to the world during the millennium.

Here's a partial list of haunting comparisons between Nazi Germany and America:

- The demise of capitalism was complete and the rise of socialism was accepted.
- Few blinked when prayer was taken out of school in 1935.
- Daycare raised the children of Germany in the 1930s and 1940s.
- Christmas and Easter were taken out of the German public schools.
- Socialized medicine ruined the German healthcare system. The elderly and handicapped were marginalized.

- Abortion became the new normal and was even expected.

- Private education was gone by 1938.

- Government spending skyrocketed and no one said a word. Taxation soared to 80 percent.

- First there was gun registration followed by gun confiscation by the Nazis.

- Free speech gradually faded. The newspapers and other media proclaimed the pro-government side of a story.

- The green agenda was adopted as it was steeped in paganism; Hitler loved paganism.

- Government spying went off the charts.

- Children sang songs of praise to Hitler.

- Germans were spellbound by the great oratory skills of Hitler. He couldn't possibly have been lying to them.

- The church in Germany did not want to make waves; it did not want to tackle controversy. Pulpits would never address serious issues or politics.

- The church in Germany was steered into mysticism, including various meditations and other deceptions. Hitler knew this would weaken the church and make it ineffective. Most, but not all churches in Germany, were riddled with compromise.

- Many pastors in Germany wanted to be popular and find favor with the government. They did not want to offend anyone.[10]

Do you notice any similarities in America today? Markell added, "Political correctness today is, indeed, a mirror of the beginnings of Hitler's reign circa 1933," and many citizens of Nazi Germany accepted Hitler's tactics and anti-Semitism because they saw it as a means to an end. America and the world are heading toward exactly what the Bible predicted.

---

10   Jan Markell, "Hope and Change: Haunting Comparisons," May 13, 2014, newsletter; www.olivetreeviews.org.

We did not want to believe the U.S. government could become god, but that time is here. God's people must be on high alert. Placing government or politics or people above Him is idolatry. A disease-like apathy is infecting many of our hearts as more churches close down worldwide.

I came across a news report about England which mentioned that Queen Elizabeth, during her coronation in 1953, promised to maintain the laws of God and the true profession of the gospel, but the report claimed, "Britain today is at war with the gospel – and with itself." A massive move to privatize religion encompasses the country. In other words, you can have your faith as long as you don't bring it into the workplace and affect other people; just keep it to yourself. If you are vocal about your Christian faith, you risk being demoted or fired. Sound familiar?

The report continued with the grim reality:

> By some estimates, it has only taken ten years to almost completely undermine Britain's Christian heritage. Barring a sudden move of God, it's likely to take far longer to restore it.[11]

Is what we're seeing in Britain inevitable in America? And if so, how much time do we have? We know God can do all things and He will determine the outcome, but is there a point we will conclude the decaying culture is beyond repair?

With all that is happening around us, especially with the 24/7 news cycle, we could get overwhelmed with all the bad news and immorality. Some Christians even become immobilized as a result of this spirit of heaviness that is so prevalent today. Has God removed His hand of protection and providence from our nation? Many pastors believe so.

By the power of the Holy Spirit however, God can do a great work through available vessels – a work that may even surprise us if we each simply say, "Here I am, Lord, send me." He is looking for Christians who are heartbroken over the lost, spiritual state of people today; believers who are not fazed by a weak church; those who are willing to serve God knowing He couldn't care less about our resume, outward appearances, and worldly accomplishments. The Lord can use Christians with the

---

11   "Britain's War on Christianity: America's Future Fight," CBN
     News, July 8, 2010, http://www.cbn.com/cbnnews/world/2009/july/
     britains-war-on-christianity-americas-future-fight/.

heart of Bradford, Edwards, Lincoln, Moody, Bonhoeffer, Whitefield, or Sunday. God simply wants you!

Proverbs 14:34 (ESV) states, *Righteousness exalts a nation, but sin is a reproach to any people.* America will either advance toward a God-sent revival or an irreversible decline; it depends on the course Christians choose. Will we stand for righteousness in culture?

For hundreds of years, historians and scholars have studied and evaluated factors that have caused the destruction of great empires. Revival preacher Al Whittinghill, of Ambassadors for Christ International, declared that the following cannot be refuted by an honest person:

> Scholars like Edward Gibbon, who wrote the classic *"The Decline and Fall of the Roman Empire,"* and Arnold Toynbee, who wrote *"A Study of History,"* have set forth in great clarity and detail that twenty-one of the last great empires on earth all showed the same common signs of decline just before they dissolved and disappeared from world history.

The Social Symptoms:

1. An increase in lawlessness and promotion of the wrong people.
2. A loss of economic discipline and self-restraint; greed.
3. Rising government taxes and regulations and a growing bureaucracy.
4. A decline in the relevance and quality of education.

The Cultural Symptoms:

1. An increase in materialism and selfish luxury.
2. The weakening of the foundational principles that built the nation and made it great.
3. Policies based on feelings and not moral discipline.
4. A loss of respect for established authority.

The Spiritual Symptoms:

1. A rise in immorality and perversion.

2. The lure of alien gods and the exaltation of man.

3. A decline in the value placed on human life as evidenced by abortion, brutality, loss of natural affection, and lack of care for the elderly.

Nations ready to die are plagued by lawlessness, economic insolvency, loss of values, self-centeredness, and the breakdown of social order. Peace and order become impossible to maintain despite a deluge of "new laws" to stem the flood. The Barbarians then come and infiltrate, and the nation cannot resist. It loses its moral fiber and the will to sacrifice is no longer present. There are well-worn paths to disaster, and these are stark warnings to any nation. The lessons of history are meant to lead us to the Lord of history. It is really His story, and it practically shouts at us that every individual and nation is accountable to Him. History will end at the feet of our Risen Lord.

God repeatedly warns a nation and pleads with that nation, before He removes it, but history shows that nations seldom listen. The great hope is that God will send a mighty move of His Spirit in the nation and revive it to blessing and a right relationship to Him. In America, true revival will not come by simply becoming aware of our great need for it. It will not come even if we are successful in pointing out all our present grievous sin and error. It will not come because of multiplied meetings to encourage us and to make us want revival. We must have fresh revelation of God through His Word – Jesus Christ the Lord. Inherent in this revelation will come the glorious realization of who He wants His people to be. Then, the people of God must choose to authentically respond to Him in such a way as to allow Him to clear up the discrepancies and contradictions. Submitted to Him, the Church will once again become "salt and light."[12]

---

12 Al Whittinghill, "Herald of His Coming," March 2006, http://www.heraldofhiscoming. com/Past%20Issues/2006/March/revival_can_save_a_nation.htm.

Yes, we are surrounded by evil. Our moral and spiritual foundations have been attacked and shaken; the walls are collapsing, but our instruction from God's Word is to trust Him and go! Pray, preach, shine a light on the darkness, persevering until Christ returns or takes us home.

America's once great walls of faith, morality, and freedom are crumbling, but at least they are not destroyed to literal piles of stones. In 445 BC, the walls of the once great city of Jerusalem were in ruins; persecution soared and the Israelites were dispersed. Did God prepare an army to wipe out their enemies and rebuild the city? Nope. He raised up one man.

Nehemiah was a royal cupbearer to Artaxerxes, the king of Persia. After learning about the condition of Jerusalem including a remnant of God's people, Nehemiah became concerned. He wept and prayed and after many days, Nehemiah was compelled to take action. If we are heartbroken over the lost and upset about the condition of our own city, country, or church, are we willing to speak up?

Nehemiah knew God was leading him to take a step of faith, so he prayed for and received favor from the king. He also confessed his sins, as well as the apathy and sins of God's people. We can learn from his example. In the midst of massive opposition and ridicule, he surveyed the fallen city, rallied the remnant, and went to work on restoring the walls. Most importantly, however, Nehemiah and Ezra helped restore the people and bring them back to obedience to God.

We must overcome the temptation to seek our own comfort or worldly success. Instead, we are to love and trust Jesus Christ, and speak about our faith with confidence. Since we cannot possibly know how much time we have left, we had better be about the Lord's business – preaching the good news and calling Christians back to God.

> *Therefore say to them, 'Thus says the LORD of hosts, "Return to Me," declares the LORD of hosts, "that I may return to you," says the LORD of hosts.* (Zechariah 1:3)

CHAPTER 3

NOT ASHAMED OF THE GOSPEL

Now after John had been taken into custody, Jesus came into Galilee, preaching the gospel of God, and saying, "The time is fulfilled, and the kingdom of God is at hand; repent and believe in the gospel."
Mark 1:14-15

Now I make known to you, brethren, the gospel which I preached to you, which also you received, in which also you stand, by which also you are saved, if you hold fast the word which I preached to you, unless you believed in vain. For I delivered to you as of first importance what I also received, that Christ died for our sins according to the Scriptures, and that He was buried, and that He was raised on the third day according to the Scriptures.
1 Corinthians 15:1-4

In 1965 the epic religious movie *The Greatest Story Ever Told* was released, retelling the story of Jesus Christ from His humble birth and His teachings through the crucifixion and resurrection. The media and critics at the time gave it excellent reviews and some even raved about the brilliant and inspiring, Bible-based production. Times have changed; but the gospel has not.

The gospel, aka the "good news," is the greatest gift God has given the church, because its message is about Jesus Christ of Nazareth, the greatest treasure God has given the world. Like the apostle Paul, we are to deliver to others what we also received, because people's salvation depends on it. No one would keep the best news in the universe to themselves – would they?

As committed Christians, our priority in this life must be to consistently believe, live, and deliver to others the message about Jesus Christ and the truth about His life, teachings, death, resurrection, and ascension. For those who have believed and have confessed Jesus as Lord, our ticket is punched and our place in God's presence is reserved for eternity! Our faith is in Him and our hope is in heaven.

Every person alive today and who has ever lived will stand on one side of eternity or the other. The universe revolves around the most pivotal event in the history of the world: The resurrection of Jesus Christ; the eternal Son, one with the Father and the Spirit, and the exact representation of God's nature.

Jesus willingly left His glory and the presence of the Father to be conceived by the Holy Spirit in a virgin's womb and born into our atmosphere on earth as both God and man. He lived a sinless life in obedience to the laws of God. He was baptized, preached repentance, and taught God's Word to the people.

Jesus suffered God's wrath on the cross and died in our place. He offered Himself as an acceptable sacrifice for mankind's sins. He was buried in a guarded tomb and raised from the dead on the third day, just as He promised. He appeared to his disciples and many others – eye witnesses – over a period of forty days, and in their presence He ascended to the heavens. Knowing Jesus is alive and interceding for us at the Father's right hand, we can declare, "He lives!"

An empty tomb shouts the glaring evidence and glorious truth of the resurrection. Nothing compares to this, the most famous historical event in the world's existence and the greatest news ever told mankind. We can use many methods to reach the lost, but only one message is magnificent and powerful enough to save. In order to share the gospel most effectively, we must first understand and believe the message ourselves.

The gospel is not some formula or a simple "sinner's prayer." It encompasses the entire Bible as its framework with plenty of background setting the stage. Its truth can transform our lives and its power can save the worst of sinners.

With the increasing attacks on free speech and religious expression in America today, do you see how important it is for us to be able to preach the gospel? This basic freedom is affected by politics, laws, and government. Enemies of Christianity will not relent in their agenda to squelch the mention of sins they endorse, but when push comes to shove, we must obey God rather than man. Speak the truth and leave the results to Him.

Since we have received and accepted the gospel, we must reject the world because the two are in opposition to each other. This can present a problem for many of us. If we love Jesus, we will obey Him (John 14:15), but if we love the world, we will end up following anything else *except* Him. Because this temporary earth is passing away and we are faced with an eternity that will not wait, the choice should be clear.

THE AUTHORITY OF JESUS

Getting caught up in living for today causes us to lose our eternal perspective. Because of this, frequent reminders are necessary for us to refocus our lives and priorities. Jesus never told believers to make as much money as possible, have fun, take vacations, relax, and eventually retire. His message was to *seek first the kingdom of God and His righteousness* (Matthew 6:33), trusting the Father for everything we need in this life. Then He said "go."

Therefore go and make disciples of all nations, baptizing them in the name of the Father and of the Son and of the Holy Spirit, and teaching them to obey everything I have commanded you. And surely I am with you always, to the very end of the age (Matthew 28:19-20 NIV).

Where does Jesus get such authority? It bears repeating Jesus Christ overcame death and the grave and is seated at the right hand of the Father. His tomb is famous for what it does *not* contain. Even the Jewish leaders who opposed Jesus acknowledged His tomb was empty when they made up lies to try and conceal the resurrection.

Some of the guards came into the city and reported to the chief priests all that had happened. And when they had assembled with the elders and consulted together, they gave a large sum of money to the soldiers, and said, "You are to say, 'His disciples

*came by night and stole Him away while we were asleep.' And
if this should come to the governor's ears, we will win him over
and keep you out of trouble." And they took the money and did
as they had been instructed; and this story was widely spread
among the Jews, and is to this day* (Matthew 28:11-15).

Isn't it interesting in their attempted cover-up, the religious leaders
testified to the empty tomb? The story gets even more bizarre, because
their lie included instructing the soldiers to say they were asleep instead
of guarding the tomb of Jesus. This was not some small conspiracy,
because in those days a Roman soldier caught sleeping on duty would
have been executed.

Moreover, all other gods or religious leaders who have lived on the
earth have burial sites or memorials where their bones remain. We can
easily understand how some of their followers hate Jesus, because He is
the only true, *living* God; other gods people worship are false, dead gods.

EYE WITNESSES AND DARING DISCIPLES

Hundreds of people witnessed, testified to, or wrote about the fact Jesus
Christ was born, lived, and performed supernatural miracles. They
knew He was sinless but was crucified; He was buried but literally rose
to life again after three days and nights in a guarded and sealed tomb.
No one has ever proven Christ wrong. Why would His disciples and
countless martyrs through history endure torture or die for their faith
if they knew it was a lie?

Do we have that type of commitment to the gospel? We have the
exact same message the early church had. In fact, we have an entire Bible
they did not have! But we have the same God, same Holy Spirit, and
same central message of love and truth. The disciples did not have all
the resources and technology we have today, and yet the early church
grew in numbers day by day even in the midst of threats and persecution.

*But Peter and John answered and said to them, "Whether it
is right in the sight of God to give heed to you rather than to
God, you be the judge; for we cannot stop speaking about what
we have seen and heard."* (Acts 4:19-20)

When the disciples stood up to threats of the political and religious leaders, they were blessed. They immediately went back to their friends, and do you know what they did? They all prayed for more boldness! (How often do you and I pray for confidence to speak God's Word?)

> And now, Lord, take note of their threats, and grant that Your bond-servants may speak Your word with all confidence (Acts 4:29).

As a result, the Holy Spirit that Jesus sent during Pentecost came back on the scene to fill, empower, and strengthen them. Their prayers were answered because verse 31 says they then *spoke the word of God with boldness*. How exciting in those early times of the church when thousands of believers were added to their numbers on a daily basis. Luke added a few more details about their success.

> And with great power the apostles were giving testimony to the resurrection of the Lord Jesus, and abundant grace was upon them all (Acts 4:33).

These were the same men who days earlier cowered in a locked room as the body of Jesus lay in a tomb. These were men who lived with Jesus and were part of His ministry for three years. These were rough, ordinary, uneducated men who astonished the high-ranking religious leaders of Jerusalem by their faith, knowledge, and proclamation of Scripture to the point of causing the rulers, elders, and teachers of the law take note that *these men had been with Jesus* (Acts 4:13).

Imagine being out in public passionately discussing God's Word and overhearing someone say you must have been spending time with Jesus. What a compliment! When we invest quality time with our Lord and Savior, our character, faith, and lives will reflect His influence.

The power and truth of the gospel kept driving the disciples; it should drive us as well.

When countless Christians in America, even in the face of opposition like the early disciples, say "we cannot keep silent" and pray for boldness to share His Word in the midst of hostility, God will answer by empowering us to do His work and by covering us with the grace we need.

EVERLASTING GOD

Being one with the eternal God, Jesus created all things, including us (Genesis 1:26-27), and by His word, all things hold together (Colossians 1:16-17). He is the Alpha and Omega, Beginning and the End (Revelation 21:6). All this and more gives him the honor, respect, and right to declare: *All authority in heaven and on earth has been given to me* (Matthew 28:18).

No greater power, authority, or standard exists; Jesus is Lord. We cannot *make* Him Lord; God the Father has already done so. Jesus is not a part-time God; He is sovereign, not merely a friendly assistant in our lives. If God is your co-pilot, hit the eject button on your pilot seat and stop trying to navigate your own life! If you call him "Lord," allow Him to be your pilot.

Shouldn't we surrender every area of our existence to Him who knows all, sees all, and yet loves us unconditionally? He is Lord, Redeemer, Savior, and King of all Kings, Jesus Christ, who:

> *Although He existed in the form of God, did not regard equality with God a thing to be grasped, but emptied Himself, taking the form of a bond-servant, and being made in the likeness of men. Being found in appearance as a man, He humbled Himself by becoming obedient to the point of death, even death on a cross. For this reason also, God highly exalted Him, and bestowed on Him the name which is above every name, so that at the name of Jesus every knee will bow, of those who are in heaven and on earth and under the earth, and that every tongue will confess that Jesus Christ is Lord, to the glory of God the Father* (Philippians 2:6-11).

Please understand regardless of whether or not you have placed your trust in Jesus and bowed before Him acknowledging His majesty, a day is coming in which every human being will bow down before Him and confess this truth – Jesus is Lord. This epic event will glorify God.

Who is this Jesus we preach? He is the author and perfecter of our faith who once told His disciples, *I lay down my life that I may take it again. No one takes it from Me* (John 10:17-18 ESV). Jesus voluntarily endured hours of brutality and horrific torture ending in a public execution and took His seat at the right hand of God the Father's throne (Hebrews 12:2). Time is in His hands, history belongs to Him, and even our calendar is based on the birth of Jesus Christ. Nations have risen and fallen because of Him.

In his outstanding book *The Gospel's Power and Message*, author and preacher Paul Washer said the gospel is the great need of our day. He emphasized what we have lost and what we must regain is a passion for knowing the gospel and an equal passion for making the gospel known.

> We are Christians because we find our identity, life, and purpose in Christ. We are evangelical because we believe the gospel and esteem it as the great central truth of God's revelation to men. It is not a foreword, a byword, or an afterthought; it is not merely the introductory class to Christianity; it is the entire course of study. It is the story of our lives, the unfathomable riches we seek to explore, and the message we live to proclaim. For this reason, we are most Christian and most evangelical when the gospel of Jesus Christ is our one hope, our one boast, and our one magnificent obsession.[13]

Throughout modern history, major archeological finds have either confirmed or complimented the accuracy and historic reliability of the Bible – both the Old and New Testaments. In order to confidently explain the gospel, we must believe Scripture is infallible, perfect, and God-breathed. If our delivery of the message lacks clarity or conviction, it can affect the results.

DELIVERING THE GOSPEL: MANY METHODS, ONE MESSAGE

Leading lukewarm believers back to Jesus Christ is important. Their sins must be forgiven in order for them to turn and share the gospel. Sadly, millions of people-pleasing, world-loving, professing Christians need to be warned about their lackadaisical lives and mockery of the Holy Spirit.

How much severer punishment do you think he will deserve who

---

13   Paul Washer, *The Gospel's Power and Message*, (Grand Rapids, MI, 2012 Reformation Heritage Books), p. 5.

has trampled under foot the Son of God, and has regarded as
unclean the blood of the covenant by which he was sanctified,
and has insulted the Spirit of grace? (Hebrews 10:29)

Perhaps saving professing Christians already within the church might be more difficult than saving those outside the church because helping someone who doesn't think they are sick is hard. We do not like being convicted by the Holy Spirit, corrected by others, or confronted about sin or spiritual apathy in our lives.

If we are disobedient to God, how in good conscience can we preach the gospel of repentance to others? Talk about an internal contradiction. I have seen pride rear its ugly head in my own life as well as in various church and ministry leaders. God hates pride and some say it is a huge problem today in the church. If we are not willing to take a prescription to get healthy, why should others take it?

In order to cure a disease, a good doctor will first diagnose the problem, identify what it is, what caused it, and then tell the patient what needs to be done. This includes an explanation of how to treat the disease. A doctor doesn't hate his patients simply because he told them the truth.

What's my point? We can (and should) talk much about the love of God, but we are doing the gospel and those who hear us a disservice if we do not also talk about sin and the wrath of God.

There are many symptoms of the disease (sin), but God has provided a cure (Jesus Christ) for the cause and has given us a written prescription (the Bible) to follow. The Great Physician is always on call, so let us speak about the only remedy and keep referring people to Him!

SIN AND THE LAW: A CRUCIAL PART OF THE GOSPEL MESSAGE

I believe it's just as important to consider the bad news in order to value the good. If Jesus truly saved us, should we not understand exactly what He saved us from, so we can fully appreciate that into which we are saved? He *redeemed us from the curse of the law* (Galatians 3:13), and we are saved from the wrath of God and eternal punishment for our sins. We are no longer condemned because we are "in Christ" (Romans 8:1).

Sin separates us from the presence of God. When we sin, our

communion and fellowship with the Lord is broken. If we do not repent from our sins, God will not forgive us, but once we do turn to Him and repent, our relationship is restored. Sin is lawlessness (1 John 3:4), and God uses our feelings of guilt to warn us about violating His law. God's holiness and perfection require punishment for all sin. Before we repented and turned to God, we were held responsible. Before Christ and without Him, we were guilty as charged and eternally condemned.

Writing to Christians in Rome, the apostle Paul emphasized the fact we are all under sin:

> *There is none righteous, not even one; There is none who under-*
> *stands, There is none who seeks for God; All have turned aside,*
> *together they have become useless; There is none who does good,*
> *There is not even one* (Romans 3:10-12).

Through Jesus' death on the cross, God has forgiven our sins presently, and we have His word that we are eternally saved. We are covered: past, present, and future! Our trust must be in God *who delivered us from so great a death, and does deliver us; in whom we trust that He will still deliver us* (2 Corinthians 1:10 NKJ).

We have a bright hope and heavenly destination! How could we not tell others we will be God's people and He will dwell among us? We will forever be saved from every form of sin, trial, and tragedy because the first things will have passed away, and the Lord will wipe away every tear from our eyes; *and there will no longer be any death; there will no longer be any mourning, or crying, or pain* (Revelation 21:3-4).

You may have heard the concept that we have been saved by God *from* God, but why did we need to be saved from God? Was He *that* angry? God hates sin; sin separates mankind from Him. He gave man His law to show how sinful we are and how far we are away from a perfect God. The penalty for breaking God's requirements is spiritual death. Obviously, no one could keep all the commandments or obey God's laws, so He instituted a system of sacrifices on behalf of the people to appease His wrath. Animals were sacrificed in order to pay the penalty owed due to sin.

No wonder we needed a Savior! Charles H. Spurgeon once stated:

My hope is not because I am not a sinner, but because I am a sinner for whom Christ died. My trust is not that I am holy, but that, being unholy, Christ died for me. My rest is, here, not in what I am, or shall be, or feel, or know, but in what Christ is and must be, – in what Christ did, and is still doing as He stands before yonder throne of glory.

Some say we should get rid of the law, but *we know the Law is good* if it is used properly. *Law is not made for a righteous person, but for those who are lawless and rebellious, for the ungodly and sinners* (1 Timothy 1:8-11). Jesus came to earth not to abolish the law, but to fulfill the law as the final sacrifice for sin, once and for all people, establishing a new covenant or "testament" in his blood through the cross.

Thanks to Jesus, believers have right standing before God because *Christ is the end of the law for righteousness to everyone who believes* (Romans 10:4). God's love for us cannot be fully understood if we tell others about Christ's death on the cross without explaining sin. Being naturally prideful, we must be shown the impossibility of being good enough, and our wretchedness compared to His holiness, so we can appreciate the grace of God and the free gift of salvation that we do not deserve!

Having the understanding Jesus died in our place as a substitute and His death was a propitiation (satisfying God's law) for the sins of the world, we can not only appreciate God's love, but we can preach the gospel with even more gratitude. The theology of atonement is also important here. Atonement is the doctrine of reconciling God and mankind, which was accomplished through the sacrifice of Jesus Christ. He truly bridges the gap between a holy, righteous God and filthy, sinful man. This is all part of the good news.

What happens when we sin *after* we have trusted in Jesus and have been forgiven? *If we confess our sins, He is faithful and righteous to forgive us our sins and to cleanse us from all unrighteousness* (1 John 1:9). It's all covered. The finite debt has been paid by an infinite God once and for all. "All" means all! *He Himself is the propitiation for our sins; and not only for ours only, but also for those of the whole world* (1 John 2:1-2).

Jesus Christ became the payment that satisfied the debt of sin. Though we are commanded to resist the enemy and turn from sin, Jesus the righteous, stands between us and the Father as our Advocate. We just have to believe.

Missionary, pastor, and writer Andrew Murray once said:

> To convince the world of the truth of Christianity, it must first be convinced of sin. It is only sin that renders Christ intelligible.[14]

In Romans 6:23 the Bible states, *The wages of sin is death but the free gift of God is eternal life in Christ Jesus our Lord.* You would think people would be flocking to receive this gift, but men love darkness and hate the light because their deeds are evil (John 3:19).

In addition, the gospel seems to have lost its appeal. It is not because the meaning has diminished, but most likely because some have altered the message to fit the tolerant times in which we live. God's love and grace may seem like a more compassionate message to emphasize. When the truth about sin, the reality of hell, and the severity of God's judgment are not fully proclaimed, however, people fail to address their greatest need – salvation. They naturally continue to pursue temporary, trivial things because their lives have been built around what is seen rather than what is eternal.

Author and evangelist, Ray Comfort, often preaches about God being a fair and just Judge who equally sentences everyone who has broken the law. He shares examples from a trial such as when a criminal stands guilty before the court. It would be a mistake to first speak to a lawbreaker about the judge's compassion. Better for a criminal to see the disappointment and frown of the judge, so he might comprehend the seriousness of his crime and find a place of true sorrow and grief for what he has done. It is *then* that the mercy of the judge should be revealed, not sooner.

REPENT, AND THEN BE SAVED!

This brings us back to repentance, one of the most important messages to share with both unbelievers and back-slidden Christians. In his second letter to the Corinthian church, the apostle Paul acknowledged his

14   Andrew Murray; *The Spirit of Christ*, page 125, various publishers.

first letter was stern and had caused the church some sorrow, but he said he rejoiced in the fact they were grieved to the point they responded to God! Paul did not regret communicating the truth so strongly. Why? It produced the intended result; Christians who needed to hear and receive the message turned back to God.

> *I now rejoice, not that you were made sorrowful, but that you were made sorrowful to the point of repentance; for you were made sorrowful according to the will of God, so that you might not suffer loss in anything through us. For the sorrow that is according to the will of God produces a repentance without regret, leading to salvation, but the sorrow of the world produces death* (2 Corinthians 7:9-10).

When Jesus began His ministry on earth after being baptized, His preaching always included repentance (Matthew 4:17). True repentance includes a desire to change because of the remorse one feels for sinning against God.

If the whole gospel is not preached, we may be doing folks a disservice by telling them to raise their hand and repeat a formulaic prayer and "be saved." Getting people to respond is a start, yes, but how do we know if they are sincere and sorrowful over their sin or just reacting to the emotion of the moment? We sometimes mistakenly offer the greatest treasure on earth to those who have little concept of what it is worth. I wonder if we take salvation too lightly (Philippians 2:12).

Only God knows for sure if people were truly saved in the first place, but it seems probable some did not fully grasp what it meant to become a disciple of Jesus Christ, particularly in the spiritually anemic culture we have in America today. Also, how effective was the follow-up with those new Christian converts? Discipleship is one of the most important and most neglected works the church is responsible for doing. How effectively is the church following up with new believers today? Making strong disciples of Christ is hard work, but it is not an optional commandment from the Lord.

The early Christian churches were instructed to search their hearts and examine their own faith. Most of these believers were not brand new converts; they had already been in the church for a time. This same instruction applies to us today.

> Test yourselves to see if you are in the faith; examine yourselves!
> Or do you not recognize this about yourselves, that Jesus Christ
> is in you – unless indeed you fail the test? (2 Corinthians 13:5)

If you have a desire for evangelism or for a successful preaching ministry, be encouraged and reminded Jesus Christ didn't care about numbers. He cared about individual hearts. Conviction of sin must occur at some point for authentic conversion.

Reverend David Wilkerson (1931-2011) was the founder of Teen Challenge, Times Square Church in New York City, and author of *The Cross and the Switchblade*. He was well-known for his direct preaching style and his heart for believers to remain committed to obeying the teachings of Jesus Christ. Wilkerson stated:

> I believe the church has even taken the feeling out of conviction [of sin]. Think about it – you hardly ever see tears on the cheeks of those who are being saved anymore. Of course, I know tears don't save anyone, but God made us all human, with very real feelings. And any hell-bound sinner who has been moved upon by the Holy Spirit naturally feels a profound sorrow over the ways he has grieved the Lord.

> Have I cut short the gospel Jesus preached, the gospel of repentance? Have I essentially taken scissors to my Bible and removed the higher cost of following Christ?[15]

Yes, following Jesus carries a cost, but the rewards are plentiful. The challenge is to explain the gospel as clearly and thoroughly as possible. Our salvation was paid for in Jesus' blood. How costly the sacrifice made by Christ!

THE LAMB OF GOD TAKES AWAY OUR SINS

In Old Testament times, the high priests would enter the Holy of Holies according to Levitical law and offer animal sacrifices on behalf of the

---

15   David Wilkerson, "The Gospel of Repentance," http://davidwilkersontoday.blogspot.com/2014/03/the-gospel-of-repentance.html.

people. God required the shedding of blood in order to be cleansed from sin and forgiven. A year-old lamb or goat without blemish was a temporary substitute, dying in place of the sinner, but these sacrifices stopped when Jesus offered Himself, the perfect Son of God, as the ultimate sacrifice on our behalf.

Thank God for His great mercy. The priest's duty was to obey the law and offer sacrifices on behalf of the people. Jesus finished the work God sent Him to do by living a sinless life in obedience to the Father and laying down that life. No further blood sacrifices are needed. We now *have a great high priest who has passed through the heavens* (Hebrews 4:14). The priests in those days had to frequently offer sacrifices for the people, which foreshadowed Christ's sacrifice on the cross.

> *For it was fitting for us to have such a high priest, holy, inno-*
> *cent, undefiled, separated from sinners and exalted above the*
> *heavens; who does not need daily, like those high priests, to*
> *offer up sacrifices, first for His own sins and then for the sins*
> *of the people, because this He did once for all when He offered*
> *up Himself* (Hebrews 7:26-27).

Three years before the Lord went to the cross to give His life for us, John the Baptist saw Jesus approaching and proclaimed, *Behold, the Lamb of God who takes away the sin of the world* (John 1:29).

Jesus overcame the world, sin, death, and the grave. At the end of John chapter three, John explains that God has given all things, including power and authority, to the Son He loves, Jesus.

> *He who believes in the Son has eternal life; but he who does*
> *not obey the Son will not see life, but the wrath of God abides*
> *on him* (John 3:36).

We must believe and obey, not just believe and walk away. When people hear the gospel message leading to repentance, the result should be faith followed by obedience. You can tell how much a person truly loves Jesus by observing his life (fruit).

Regeneration must occur if our faith is to be authentic. Jesus spoke of spiritual rebirth when He told one of Israel's teachers, Nicodemus, *unless one is born again, he cannot see the kingdom of God* (John 3:3).

This, of course, might seem silly to unbelievers. Regardless, this message is true and we must share with others.

> *For the word of the cross is foolishness to those who are perishing, but to us who are being saved it is the power of God* (1 Corinthians 1:18).

COMPELLED TO SPEAK

Are we willing to preach this gospel in an increasingly rebellious culture and risk being called intolerant, narrow-minded, or worse? Are we willing to be criticized and misunderstood for delivering the truth Jesus commanded us to speak? Do we love others enough to live what we believe, expose the darkness of sin, and when necessary, confront wayward Christians?

"Preach the gospel always; if necessary use words." This quote, often attributed to St. Francis of Assisi, is memorable but faulty. Doing good works is not wrong, but I believe the idea portrayed in the quote misrepresents the gospel. It suggests we should let our actions do the talking and in an extreme case, speak ("if necessary"). Other religions teach good works as well. What if someone we knew for years died before we told them the reason we live? I know it can be difficult and uncomfortable to share our faith, but we have nothing to lose; the unbeliever has everything to lose.

Finally, the doctrine of the returning King, Jesus Christ, is part of the gospel, because those who believe are saved from the coming judgment. Right before the apostle Paul charged believers to preach the word at all times, he warned them that when the resurrected Christ returns, He will *judge the living and the dead* (2 Timothy 4:1-2). This should give us a sense of urgency.

Again, God's foreordained solution (Acts 2:23) was to send His only Son, Jesus, to give His life as a ransom for us. By believing, confessing Jesus is Lord, and repenting of our sins, we are saved and have everlasting life with God. May we not muddy up the message that we are saved by grace through faith in Him (Ephesians 2:8).

If the Bible is true, then this is why you and I live: To make sure the greatest story ever is told!

Let's represent Christ well and be faithful to Him who called us. Our aim must be to glorify His name as long as we have breath, a heartbeat, and a voice. If you and I don't tell others the good news about salvation through Jesus Christ alone – who will?

Whoever will call on the name of the Lord will be saved." How then will they call on Him in whom they have not believed? How will they believe in Him whom they have not heard? And how will they hear without a preacher? How will they preach unless they are sent? Just as it is written, "How beautiful are the feet of those who bring good news of good things! (Romans 10:13-15)

So that whoever believes will in Him have eternal life. For God so loved the world, that He gave His only begotten Son, that whoever believes in Him shall not perish, but have eternal life (John 3:15-16).

If you have not placed your trust in Jesus Christ, and if you are not sure you are saved or where you will spend eternity, please read the following gospel tract!

- In the beginning, God created the heavens and the earth, mankind, and all things. He gave man and woman stewardship over His creation and He called it "good." God is holy, just, perfect, and eternal – He the only living God! His will is for mankind to live with Him in heaven, which is our reward for trusting in Jesus Christ and obeying His Word.

- Though God is sovereign, He gave us free will, and mankind chose to disobey His laws. The Bible calls this "sin." We rejected His laws and broke fellowship with the One who made us in His image. Since God is perfect and holy, sin cannot exist in His presence. Because of this sin, all creation suffers the curse of death, decay, and separation from God. Sin requires punishment, but God loved mankind too much to leave us with no hope!

- Being a gracious God, He still wanted man and woman to be able to reclaim their relationship with Him. From the foundation of the world, He had a plan to accomplish this. Since the penalty for sin is separation from God and requires a perfect sacrifice, the only acceptable offering for sin was His own Son, Jesus Christ. As God in the flesh, Jesus freely gave His life to pay a debt we couldn't possibly pay to cover the cost and penalty of our sins. Jesus became sin and died in our place upon a bloody cross, providing all of mankind with "the way" to have right, legal standing before God.

- Because He is the only Way to the Father and the only One who can bridge the gap caused by sin, every one of us must decide: Accept Jesus or reject Him. Every one of us has sinned, and we can do nothing in our own power to be "good enough" to deserve God's love or earn His forgiveness.

- We must admit (confess) our sins to God, repent (reject & turn away from our sin nature), and put our trust in Jesus Christ. Then, we are to follow His example as we obey and share His teachings found in the Bible. Our salvation is by God's grace, through our faith in Jesus Christ. Thanks to Him, we can be forgiven and avoid eternity in hell because the shedding of pure blood and sacrifice of Jesus Christ satisfied the demands for justice and the righteous wrath of God the Father.

- The proof that our confession and faith in Jesus Christ is genuine is reflected in our new way of living. The Bible instructs us to turn from the world's ways and grow in our faith and obedience to God and His holiness. In this life, we will continue to sin, but those sins are "covered by the sacrifice of Jesus." The life of the authentic believer is now marked by godly sorrow for our sins and our heartfelt repentance.

- Life's trials and challenges will not disappear – but as

believers, we have now received the Holy Spirit, and He lives in us, empowering and guiding us daily as we strive to overcome the world through Christ who strengthens us.

- If you have never done so, confess your sins to God; ask Him to forgive you, believe in His Son and you will be saved. Ask God to help you live the life He has planned for you to grow in His grace, to know Jesus Christ better, and to make Him known to others by your actions and words. Seek the Lord every day for the rest of your life!

CHAPTER 4

DUCKING THE ISSUE OF SIN

And just as they did not see fit to acknowledge God any longer, God gave them over to a depraved mind, to do those things which are not proper, being filled with all unrighteousness, wickedness, greed, evil; full of envy, murder, strife, deceit, malice; they are gossips, slanderers, haters of God, insolent, arrogant, boastful, inventors of evil, disobedient to parents, without understanding, untrustworthy, unloving, unmerciful; and although they know the ordinance of God, that those who practice such things are worthy of death, they not only do the same, but also give hearty approval to those who practice them.
Romans 1:28-32

We are losing ground by being silent. Today when someone mentions sin in public, they often face sharp disagreement, intense debate, or accusations of hate and intolerance. Why? We simply do not hear as much about sin anymore, and fewer church leaders talk about sin and its consequences, particularly when it comes to 'social issues.' Sadly, we have been following their example. Contrast Christians today with believers in early American history when they genuinely had a great concern about holiness and a reverent fear of the Lord.

Moreover, average Christians are not as equipped to defend the faith due to limited knowledge and understanding of Scripture as well as their desire to be accepted and appear loving, tolerant, and non-judgmental. Jesus, Paul, and early church leaders were quite the opposite. We need to read and study our Bibles and be able to explain the gospel. Parents, it is your responsibility to discipline and train your children in the ways of the Lord.

We also need to hear the whole truth preached in church on Sunday. If we want to build up the body of Christ, we cannot be worried about pleasing the world or offending liberal Christians. When pastors want to attract unbelievers to church and use entertaining methods, the teaching of God's Word, including the hard truths of Scripture, often take a back seat. Jesus used parables at times, but He did not tell jokes, funny stories, or entertaining analogies to make a point. We hear much about grace and love, but without balanced teachings on *denying ungodliness and worldly lusts,* and on living *soberly, righteously, and godly in this present age* (Titus 2:11-13 KJV), many believers end up on the wrong side of the debate.

We must take another necessary step in order to ensure we are not being hypocritical: We must resist approving of certain sins regardless of their popularity. Some professing believers get themselves into a no-win situation in this area. If, for example, you support Planned Parenthood or criticize a young Christian woman who chose to give birth to a Down syndrome baby, you may want to pay close attention. The same holds true for Christians on today's "gay is okay" bandwagon who demand silent compliance from the rest of us. Others defend sin-glorifying primetime television programming and R-rated movies and say those who disapprove are too legalistic or rigid, that it's just entertainment.

> *He who justifies the wicked and he who condemns the righteous, Both of them alike are an abomination to the* LORD (Proverbs 17:15).

Either we live by the entire Book or reject the whole truth therein. Unbelievers notice the moral and spiritual confusion when some Christians say certain things are sins, but other Christians turn around and defend those sins. When confronted about this by a godly, mature believer, some professing Christians may become defensive, perhaps not fully understanding why. They have an inner contradiction, knowing, for example, homosexuality is wrong according to the Bible but wanting to defend gay marriage or their gay friends publicly.

Homosexuality is not the only sin that has gained more acceptance. Adultery, abortion, coveting, divorce, idolatry, pride, and pornography – to name a few – need to be part of the discussion. However, due to media marketing and an open disregard for God, homosexuals and their enablers seem to be the ones who are driving public opinion in America. Look at our schools, media, Hollywood, government, the workplace, our courts, and yes, look at our churches.

Christians are not being divisive when addressing sin, and homosexual activists are not being divisive by blatantly pushing their agenda. Jesus Christ is the One who said He is the only way to the Father (John 14:6). Doctrine divides, and the immutable Word of God is the line drawn in the proverbial sand just as God separated the waters from the dry land in creation (Psalm 104:9). The union of one man and one woman is by God's design; marriage is not man's idea.

PHIL ROBERTSON DOESN'T DUCK

Who can forget the eruption on both sides of this issue when in a December 2013 *Gentlemen's Quarterly* (GQ) interview, *Duck Dynasty's* Phil Robertson said the primary problem with mankind is sin? If you read the full interview, it is clear Phil Robertson is anti-sin, not anti-gay, and says we should love one another. But that's not how the media framed it. Let's look at part of that extensive interview to provide some context. The following comes after GQ writer Drew Magary's lengthy introduction to his visit with the Robertsons:

> "We're Bible-thumpers who just happened to end up on television," he tells me. "You put in your article that the Robertson family really believes strongly that if the human race loved each other and they loved God, we would just be better off. We ought to just be repentant, turn to God, and let's get on with it, and everything will turn around...

> "Everything is blurred on what's right and what's wrong," he says. "Sin becomes fine."

> [Magary] "What, in your mind, is sinful?"

> "Start with homosexual behavior and just morph out from there. Bestiality, sleeping around with this woman and that woman, and that woman and those men," he says. Then he paraphrases Corinthians: "Don't be deceived. Neither the

adulterers, the idolaters, the male prostitutes, the homosexual offenders, the greedy, the drunkards, the slanderers, the swindlers – they won't inherit the kingdom of God. Don't deceive yourself. It's not right."[16]

Robertson continued in graphic language to illustrate how illogical he felt homosexual behavior was. Though I would not have expressed it as he did, I agree with Robertson's overall point about *all* sin. But out of thousands of words in that interview, it was the graphic mention of homosexuality that got activists and bullies riled up. Somewhat because of the popularity of top-rated *Duck Dynasty* on the A&E network, the issue was breaking news.

But why? Most people know or have heard that the Bible teaches homosexuality is sinful behavior. But American Christianity has been ducking the issue of sin for decades.

So today, when a Christian has the audacity to refer to sin in public, many react with hyper-sensitivity. Due to years of perverse programming and progressive propaganda, people hit the ceiling if you say homosexuality is sin, let alone use the word "abomination." During the brief suspension, the Robertsons released this statement:

> The family is excited to keep making a quality TV show for our dedicated fans, who have shown us wonderful support. We will continue to represent our faith and values in the most positive way through *Duck Dynasty* and our many projects that we are currently working on. The outpouring of support and prayer has encouraged and emboldened us greatly.

In one corner of the battle are those who believe in the Bible as well as America's founding principles of Christianity; in the other corner are those who not only oppose us, but claim they are offended (threatened) by the presence of practicing Christians. The latter minority has the loudest voices and the support of Hollywood, the mainstream media, academia, and government. Because of this ungodly alliance, we sometimes think conservatives and people of faith are overwhelmingly outnumbered.

---

16 Drew Margary, "What the Duck?" January, 2014, http://www.gq.com/entertainment/television/201401/duck-dynasty-phil-robertson.

Nothing could be further from the truth. Less than 4% of the U.S. population is LGBT (Lesbian Gay Bisexual Transgender), and in a recent census of American citizens, less than 1% of the population consisted of verifiable same-sex couples.

The difference is great marketing! No organizations proudly and publicly fight for special rights and preferential treatment or work to change laws on behalf of adulterers, pornographers, liars, gamblers, murderers, thieves … you get the idea. No conflict is more pivotal to the heart and soul of America than the sin battle.

Bryan Fischer, director of issues analysis for the American Family Association, believes, "if the forces of sexual deviancy prevail, every part of our culture will be corrupted and contaminated beyond repair" and suggests America would fall into a moral abyss of darkness. Fischer stated:

> Religious principle, tolerance and rights of conscience mean nothing to pro-sodomy advocates. They will remorselessly crush anyone and anything that gets in their path… In their quest for cultural domination, they will relentlessly extinguish the light of sexual normalcy and morality, as well as the light of Christianity.[17]

In the *Duck Dynasty* controversy, we witnessed the political and public pressure by homosexual activists such as GLAAD (Gay and Lesbians Alliance Against Defamation) and the Human Rights Campaign to not only force suspension of family patriarch Phil Robertson, but also insist he undergo sensitivity training and tolerance education.

> "Phil and his family claim to be Christian, but Phil's lies about an entire community fly in the face of what true Christians believe," GLAAD spokesperson Wilson Cruz said in a statement. "He clearly knows nothing about gay people or the majority of Louisianans – and Americans – who support legal recognition for loving and committed gay and lesbian couples. Phil's decision to push vile and extreme stereotypes

---

17   Bryan Fischer, "The battle for gay rights is THE battle… there is no other," 3/6/2014, http://onenewsnow.com/perspectives/bryan-fischer/2014/03/06/the-battle-over-gay-rights-is-the-battle-there-is-no-other#.VDct8RaKWyI.

is a stain on A&E and his sponsors who now need to reexamine their ties to someone with such public disdain for LGBT people and families."

The popularity of homosexuality has increased dramatically, but just because the general public has accepted unhealthy, sugary soda drinks loaded with high fructose corn syrup doesn't mean they are good for us.

Often ignored when discussing Robertson's interview is the fact he also referred to many other sins people commit. We all sin and every one of us needs forgiveness. To Robertson and to most Christians, sin is sin no matter who you are. Here is the Bible passage Robertson paraphrased, in context:

> *Or do you not know that the unrighteous will not inherit the kingdom of God? Do not be deceived; neither fornicators, nor idolaters, nor adulterers, nor effeminate, nor homosexuals, nor thieves, nor the covetous, nor drunkards, nor revilers, nor swindlers, will inherit the kingdom of God. Such were some of you; but you were washed, but you were sanctified, but you were justified in the name of the Lord Jesus Christ and in the Spirit of our God* (1 Corinthians 6:9-11).

Let's glean an important truth from this passage of Scripture: Verse 11 refers to Christians as sinners in the past tense (*Such were some of you*). If we believe, the blood of Jesus Christ cleansed us from our sins, and we were justified before a holy God. It is done. It doesn't matter what your sin is; it does matter who your Savior is.

For talking about this in a public interview, Phil Robertson was viciously attacked. The LGBT community claims their activism is all about love and equality, but if you don't agree with them or approve of their lifestyle, they often resort to hateful attacks, attempting to discredit and marginalize Christians. They often go so far as refusing to permit speech that opposes homosexuality. Some consider this bullying; others call it totalitarian intolerance.

If we hate them, we'll say nothing and let them spend eternity in hell after they die. If we love them, we'll tell them the truth about God's love for them and for all sinners. If we believe the Bible is true and

Jesus is the only name by which we can be saved (Acts 4:12), but fail to warn others about the consequences of sin, we don't really care about them. The way Christians demonstrate their love for non-believers is not only by serving them, but by lovingly encouraging them to repent and receive God's free gift of salvation.

If people refuse to accept the truth that what they're doing is a sin, they should take it up with Jesus and not squelch our speech, including the message of reconciliation which is not only protected by the Constitution, but commanded by God. We answer to a much higher court.

Responding to the haters, Phil Robertson offered these words in a press release:

> "I myself am a product of the 60s; I centered my life around sex, drugs, and rock and roll until I hit rock bottom and accepted Jesus as my Savior," he said. "My mission today is to go forth and tell people about why I follow Christ and also what the Bible teaches, and part of that teaching is that women and men are meant to be together. However, I would never treat anyone with disrespect just because they are different from me. We are all created by the Almighty and like Him, I love all of humanity. We would all be better off if we loved God and loved each other."

One major issue at stake here is the First Amendment: Do all Americans, including Christian conservatives, still have legal speech protections or not? I purposely mention conservatives because there are many liberal Christians who fail to accept the Bible's authority. They don't think we should speak openly about our faith or quote certain Scriptures. In essence, they are the "live and let live" crowd brainwashed into tolerating all things under the false premise of coexisting with unrepentant sinners.

The early church all the way up to 19th century evangelists and preachers had the exact opposite worldview and would never justify indifference. The following descriptions may help explain why we are more comfortable avoiding the subject of sin. The first two apply to pastors and leaders while the third is what we see among religious folks across the nation.

First, many false teachers are in the church today. Some have slipped in unnoticed while others are publicly preaching heresy. They question absolute truth, promote ambiguity when it comes to the Bible, and justify sins that would have flipped the early church upside down. Some are not even saved and they aim to discredit God's Word. I refer to this as counterfeit Christianity.

Second, even in many good churches sound doctrine has generally been watered down. The message of the gospel has been replaced with topical teaching and sermons that sound more like motivational seminars than teaching the deeper things of God such as sanctification, holiness, God's judgment, the Holy Spirit, and the end times. Some believers are so used to the fluff they are surprised or offended when we talk about sin. This is cotton candy Christianity.

You might hear a pastor talk about being positive or raising a healthy family and he may throw in a few Scripture references to support his theme for the week. Some say this is more appropriate for a Wednesday night church meeting or a lecture at a Holiday Inn than a sermon on Sunday morning.

And third, too many religious folks and professing Christians are attracted to certain churches, pastors, and paraphrased Scriptures. They are typically not interested in Bible study, apologetics, prophecy, the Old Testament, and sola Scriptura (the sufficiency of Scripture). They love verses about love, but they don't like verses relating to holy living, righteousness, the law, or being lukewarm. They pick what they like from the Bible, and they avoid the things they do not like to hear. This is "cafeteria Christianity."

Parents, your pastor or church is not at fault if your kids are rebelling or acting like their unsaved friends; they must be taught the Bible at home. We will individually answer to God for what we did with all He gave us. Back to Phil Robertson and the TV show.

Did you know A&E's original plan and intent for *Duck Dynasty* was for viewers to tune in and watch in order to laugh at and mock a family of "backwards" Christian rednecks? Instead, due to the likeability of the

Robertsons and the family values they promote, the show became the most popular cable program in history, averaging 14.6 million viewers at its peak. Ironically, the very plan that backfired ended up making them millions. A&E knew what they were getting with the Robertsons and that includes Phil.

Sadly in today's culture, evil is considered good and good is considered evil (Isaiah 5:20), and activists will no longer tolerate those who say their behavior is sinful. Some believe we've reached a tipping point. This present darkness is not about *Duck Dynasty*, A&E, the Robertsons, or Hollywood. It is not even political; this darkness is spiritual and the battle will only intensify. We can take up our positions or hide [our light] under a table.

Author and radio talk show host, Michael Brown, suggests those of us who agree with Phil Robertson should make it clear that:

1. We are unashamed of our belief in Jesus and in biblical morality.

2. We stand against the mistreatment of all people, including gays and lesbians.

3. We will not support the radical redefinition of marriage, regardless of the cost involved, nor do we see cultural capitulation to gay activism as inevitable.[18]

God and His Word do not change. There never would have been a debate fifty years ago over redefining marriage or sin. Since *Jesus Christ is the same yesterday, and today, and forever* (Hebrews 13:8), what changed? Christians gradually became silent and inconsequential in our culture. As a result, we've reached the point where activists are forcing conformity and calling it tolerance.

The problem has been diagnosed: Believers are either not getting the message at church, not building their own foundation of faith, or are unwilling to be God's messengers in public. Perhaps it is a combination of these. When Christians fail to speak truth about the Bible, Jesus Christ, and the issue of sin, our society grows worse.

---

18   Dr. Michael Brown, "Duck Dynasty, Gay Activism, and the Clash of
      2 Cultures," 12/19/2013, http://www.charismanews.com/opinion/
      in-the-line-of-fire/42158-duck-dynasty-gay-activism-and-the-clash-of-two-cultures.

Understandably, this will present an even tougher challenge, especially for committed Christian pastors and teachers who are willing to preach the whole counsel of God and call people to repentance. Church leaders, please remain strong and resist the temptation to conform to the worldly pressures of a hyper-tolerant culture.

A godless government is also stoking the fire. Since President Obama signed into law the Matthew Shepard and James Byrd, Jr. Hate Crimes Prevention Act, churches have been vandalized by homosexual activists, and some pastors have had their lives threatened. The Bible teaches us to love our enemies and pray for them. Please remember: Not all gays are radicals, but the activists have in fact been emboldened by the Obama administration.

I realize this can be confusing when over 50 million Americans profess to be Christians. Do not be ignorant about the damaging effect of our politics. Too many people continue to vote along party lines, ignoring what the Bible teaches. We continue electing candidates who do not represent the values of most citizens, let alone biblical values. We get what we vote for and we reap nationally what we have sown politically.

Though we care enough to share our hope in Jesus Christ, we don't want to force our faith on people, and most of us strive for fairness and respect toward those who disagree with us. Pastor and evangelist, Greg Laurie of Harvest ministries, weighed in and said Christians believe in God who created the world and all its creatures, and He has provided a godly design for marriage and sex. Laurie said what is being demanded of Christians goes beyond tolerance to acceptance of and endorsement of sin, and "it would be nice if love and tolerance were a two-way street."

CAN WE LOVE SINNERS BY OUR SILENCE?

We're all in the same boat when it comes to our sin nature. God has the highest of standards for believers, and though He doesn't expect us to be perfect, He promises to complete the good work He started in us when we first placed our trust in Jesus Christ (Philippians 1:6). He expects us to become mature in our faith by learning Scripture, producing fruit, and growing in Christ. When this happens, we are more effective witnesses for the Lord. As a result, others are influenced toward godliness and culture improves.

Many conservative Christian leaders believe a nation's righteousness and morality can be measured by how its people treat the unborn. How many ways can we reinterpret God's law warning us not to murder? Abortion continues to be what many consider a necessary evil in our promiscuous, over-sexed society. The Left cleverly redefined the terms and reframed the argument, so now the words *choice, freedom, reproductive rights*, and *privacy* describe this practice. Hogwash! Abortion stops a beating heart and eliminates innocent life.

Why do some of us duck these issues? As Christians, we often struggle with many of the same sins the world struggles with but perhaps with less frequency. Since the world teaches immediate self-gratification, living for the moment, doing whatever you feel like doing, and fulfilling every crazy sexual desire, the church had better be preaching the opposite and teaching discipline, godliness, obedience, and self-control.

Christians are not immune from sin leading to addictions, so we need to do a better job of preparing, training, and warning God's people about sin and its consequences. A little harmless pornography may lead to fornication or adultery, which could lead to abortion. Teenagers may contract a sexually transmitted disease. Married adults could also face divorce. We reap what we sow.

> For the one who sows to his own flesh will from the flesh reap
> corruption, but the one who sows to the Spirit will from the
> Spirit reap eternal life (Galatians 6:8).

Sin destroys everything in its path if it is not addressed and dealt with accordingly. If we ignore this fact, we find it easy to justify lust, pornography, or sexual activity. After all, "what's wrong with two people expressing their love for each other?" How could God possibly be against that? With this kind of moral relativistic reasoning, why not add a third, fourth, and fifth person expressing their "love" for each other?

If the meaning of "demonstrating your love" is to have sex, then why not make it an orgy? Where does it then stop? How about throwing in young children or adding a few animals next time. See where this ludicrous thinking is heading if the church and culture continue down the present path of least resistance? Forgive me for using such graphic, disgusting, and reprehensible analogies. I believe it's time we clarify biblical love and openly discuss solutions to the epidemic of sin we're seeing today.

In an address to pastors and church leaders at Midwest Baptist Theological Seminary in Kansas City, the Reverend Dr. Laurence White said that while America is led down a path of destruction, the church has been silent and afraid. He called on leaders to "take a stand in this moment of crisis," and have a sense of urgency. White continued:

> To compare what is happening in America today to Nazi Germany is no mere flight of rhetorical exaggeration … Look around you and read the signs of the times. Look beyond the walls of our beautiful sanctuaries, and the comfort of our padded pews to see the chaos, the corruption, and the confusion that reigns throughout our culture.
>
> We live in a society where passions are rider-less horses, uncontrolled and uncontrollable, in which there is a desolation of decency; in which love has become a jungle emotion, lust exalted to lordship, sin elevated to sovereignty, Satan adored as a saint, and man magnified above his maker. In the face of this relentless onslaught of evil, the church of Jesus Christ has grown timid and afraid.
>
> We, as Christian pastors, seem to have forgotten that God did not call us to be popular or successful, God called us to be faithful. Faithful preaching never comes in the form of safely vague, pious platitudes. Faithful preaching must identify and denounce the false gods of this world that call upon our people to bow down before them every day. God did not call us to be successful CEOs, protecting institutional peace and tranquility, bringing in the bodies and the bucks by avoiding controversy, and telling everybody what they wanted to hear.
>
> We cannot blame the liberal media, or the corrupt politicians, or the apathetic public for that which has overtaken America. Our political leaders deal in trivialities and superficial nonsense,

practicing the feel-good politics of deliberate ambiguity, while the destruction of our families, the perversion of our most basic moral principles, and the murder of innocent, unborn children goes on, and on, and on.

The issue before us as Christians and as Christian pastors is faithfulness to the Word of God, and submission to the Lordship of Jesus Christ. To speak to the great moral issues of our day is an integral and essential part of that God-given responsibility. To fail to do so is nothing less than a denial of the Lordship of Jesus.[19]

The church must get back to influencing society for God, but in order to do this we must get back to living for God ourselves. This starts with honest, self-evaluation and perhaps for many of us, repentance, and then a decision to recommit to the cause of Jesus Christ. Again, pastors are not to blame if we remain lukewarm.

We should encourage pastors and ministers because being a church leader is not easy work and I don't want to give the impression I would do a better job. I respect anyone who had enough courage to follow God's lead into ministry, and more importantly, I respect anyone who has the heart and boldness to preach the whole counsel of God in its undiluted power and truth.

I love humble men of God who lead their flocks, tirelessly serving our King without apology or compromise. Keep fighting the good fight of faith and remember you are not alone.

Throughout history, well-known men of God as well as nameless and courageous men have made the difficult decision, the right one, to seek Jesus Christ first and speak in His name. These great people of faith understood following Jesus and preaching the Word could come at a cost. Following and obeying Jesus always comes with a cost, but the rewards are unimaginable.

SET APART MEANS SET APART

Judgment begins with Christians in the house of God. Though we are

---

19   Dr. Laurence White, "The Sin of Silence," 9/6/2000, http://www.hiswayministries.org/fdsilence.htm.

to expose darkness and sin, we are not to expect unbelievers to live according to a Book and a God they don't believe in. Let's start with ourselves and our brothers and sisters in Christ, encouraging one another to bear good fruit.

Though unbelievers accept abortion and approve of killing thousands of babies every day, Christians should stand for life. Though unbelievers are fine with pornography and sleeping around, Christians should never be fine with the same. Though the world loves money and materialism, we must love God alone as we cannot serve both. Though the world approves of and enjoys profanity, perversity, and anti-Christian entertainment, including *most* of what is on television, believers are better off avoiding the soul pollution.

Even though godly morals and values have been long removed from government schools, believers must never stop displaying biblical principles. Christians must not allow our children to be indoctrinated by a godless education system.

Though secular rap and rock music dominates the airways and schools in America, Christian kids must resist any and all music that legitimizes promiscuity, sex, abortion, drugs, satanic worship, the love of money, violence, rape, murder, and the disrespect of parents and authority. (Mom and Dad, chances are your kids won't do this without your help.)

We are seeing increased discrimination against Christians and church leaders in America as well as growing persecution around the world. This may be what the people of God need in order to wake up and turn back to God. Father in Heaven, please forgive us, restore us again and send revival to your church in America!

One last challenging and thought-provoking quote from the great conservative Christian pastor, Dietrich Bonhoeffer, about the cost of our silence:

> We the church must confess that we have not proclaimed often or clearly enough the message of the One God who has revealed Himself for all time in Christ Jesus, and who will tolerate no other gods beside Himself. She must confess her timidity, her cowardice, her evasiveness, and her dangerous

concessions. She was silent when she should have cried out because the blood of the innocent was crying aloud to heaven. The church must confess that she has witnessed the lawless application of brutal force, the physical and spiritual suffering of countless innocent people, oppression, hatred, and murder.

And that she has not raised her voice on behalf of the victims. And has not found a way to hasten to their aid. The church is guilty of the deaths of the weakest and most defenseless brothers of Jesus Christ. The church must confess that she has desired security and peace, quiet, possession, and honor to which she has no right. She has not born witness to the truth of God and by her silence, she has rendered herself guilty, because of her unwillingness to suffer for what she knows to be right.
—Dietrich Bonhoeffer, 1940

We cannot keep ducking the issue of sin and expect the church and our country to change for the better. We cannot justify the path of least resistance or the approval of sin any longer. Many lives are at stake. If we want to obey the Lord's instructions and make the biggest impact, we have only one choice: We must speak up – even if laws are passed suggesting we stay silent.

Therefore, we are ambassadors for Christ, as though God were making an appeal through us; we beg you on behalf of Christ, be reconciled to God (2 Corinthians 5:20).

CHAPTER 5

SEPARATION OF CHRISTIANITY AND STATE

"In matters of religion, I have considered that its free exercise is placed by the Constitution independent of the powers of the general [federal] government."
—Thomas Jefferson, Second Inaugural Address, 1805

"I don't care what you do in your church, I don't care what you preach in your church; I don't care what you believe in your church, as long as you keep it there. The church may belong to you [Christians], but the public square belongs to us."
—Lesbian activist, 2009

"That all may bow to the scepter of our Lord Jesus Christ and that the whole Earth may be filled with His glory."
—John Hancock, as Governor of Massachusetts, 1791

"The church must be separate from the state … politics do not belong in the church"
—Adolf Hitler, 1937

CHIPPING AWAY AT THE FOUNDATION OF FAITH AND FREEDOM

For all practical purposes, what we see in America today is the separation of Christianity and state. Nearly every other religion or expression is allowed, tolerated, and even welcomed; however, a majority of citizens share the same biblical faith as our founders and yet its expression is deemed offensive at the very least and outlawed at worst. Extensive evidence proves this tragic truth, and yet the squelching of our religious freedoms as well as overt tyranny continue with little resistance. Why is this happening and what can we do at this point?

When Democrats are in the White House, we have a virtually unchecked federal government gaining more power and exercising more control over the people. At the same time, we have a large number of uninterested and uninvolved citizens. These two factors make it easy for God haters to push Christianity out of the public square. Most Founding Fathers envisioned just the opposite of silencing people of faith; they supported strong Christian influence in government.

I am simply advocating the allowance and influence of Christianity in America again, not a takeover of government or country by the church.

Make no mistake; ours is a secular government with no allegiance to Jesus and the God of the Bible. Many judicial appointees now practically disregard both Christ and Constitution. In fact, everything we see in public policy and the implementation of laws in recent years reveals an anti-Christian government. Some good, conservative, and even Christian representatives do still grace the halls of Congress or government agencies today, but we need to face the fact that the few conservative Christians in Washington are essentially missionaries in a culture where corruption, greed, and deceit are the norm.

Does our government truly reflect "we the people"?

Many Christians have been wrongly conditioned to avoid discussions about political issues, including policies specific candidates stand for when running for election. To compound the problem, a majority of true Christians are not deciding who will represent them because they are not registered to vote, and far too many people are uninformed or disengaged when it comes to politics and current events.

The Bible is clear about opposition to the Christian faith from the beginning. But with such a strong history in America, including men who took great pains and sacrificed much to establish a free, God-fearing nation, how did we reach the low we have today?

First, the discrimination we're seeing in America today is not even close to the level of persecution our brothers and sisters around the world have suffered. However, pastors and church members alike must decide if we will exalt Jesus as Lord above all things and stand when the heat is turned up. It's coming.

Some have debated and argued over how many founders were Christians as opposed to deists, Masons, or atheists. From historical writings, documents, and public records, the answer is clear and the debate is over. The signers of our Declaration of Independence strove to discuss and protect biblical principles, spirituality, and Christianity.

We cannot allow deceivers to force us to debate whether or not every Founding Father was a perfect Christian in practice and theology. This is *not* the issue; it's an attempt to divert attention from the truth. Some will misquote our founders, minimize their intent, and rewrite history in order to wrongly apply the First Amendment.

TRUE FAITH OF OUR FOUNDERS

During the War of Independence (Revolutionary War) when the delegates were having a hard time reaching a consensus in drafting the Constitution, God intervened through Benjamin Franklin. The debates went on for a few months during the 1787 Constitutional Convention, and at Franklin's suggestion they knelt and prayed. They then proceeded to finish one of the most amazing documents in history, and from that time onward, congressional sessions began with prayer. Franklin stated:

> I have lived, Sir, a long time, and the longer I live, the more convincing proofs I see of this truth—that God Governs in the affairs of men. And if a sparrow cannot fall to the ground without his notice, is it probable that an empire can rise without his aid?

Fifty-two of the fifty-six signers of our Declaration of Independence were deeply committed, orthodox Christians as well as all thirty-nine signers of the Constitution. The others agreed the Bible was God's divine truth and that He personally intervenes in the lives of people.

Our founders continued what early American settlers set out to do – establish a society based on the morals of Christianity. This fact is backed up by letters, prayers, and official declarations. For example, going back to Carpenters Hall in Philadelphia, Pennsylvania, the first Continental Congress was opened with prayer on September 7, 1774.

Immediately after reading Psalm 35, Reverend Jacob Duche prayed to open Congress:

> O LORD, OUR HEAVENLY FATHER, high and mighty King of Kings, and Lord of Lords, who dost from Thy throne behold all the dwellers on earth, and reignest with power supreme and uncontrolled over all the kingdoms, empires and governments; look down in mercy we beseech Thee, on these American States, who have fled to Thee from the rod of the oppressor, and thrown themselves on Thy gracious protection, desiring henceforth to be dependent only on Thee; to Thee they have appealed for the righteousness of their cause; to Thee do they now look up for that countenance and support which Thou alone canst give; take them, therefore, Heavenly Father, under Thy nurturing care; give them wisdom in council and valor in the field; defeat the malicious design of our cruel adversaries; convince them of the unrighteousness of their cause; and if they persist in their sanguinary purpose, O let the voice of Thy own unerring justice, sounding in their hearts, constrain them to drop the weapons of war from their unnerved hands in the day of battle!
>
> Be Thou present, O God of wisdom, and direct the counsels of this honorable assembly; enable them to settle things on the best and surest foundation, that the scene of blood may be speedily closed, that order, harmony and peace may be effectually restored, and truth and justice, religion and piety prevail and flourish among Thy people. Preserve the health of their bodies and vigor of their minds; shower down on them, and the millions they here represent, such temporal blessings as Thou seest expedient for them in this world, and crown them with everlasting glory in the world to come. All this we ask in the name and through the merits of Jesus Christ, Thy Son, Our Savior. Amen.[20]

They prayed publicly, they taught their families from Scripture, and

---

20   http://www.usachristianministries.com/us-history-quotes-about-god-and-the-bible/#sthash.s8ZgTgmr.dpuf.

they incorporated Christian principles in their everyday lives as well as in their governing work. From the historical writings we have available to us, our most prominent founders, patriots, and leaders quoted the Bible approximately 94 percent of the time!

How many people do you know quote from the Holy Scriptures if they *don't* believe in God or the Bible? With their faith as the foundation, these men set out to form our country's systems of government, commerce, and justice.

Here are a few quotes from a handful of signers of the Declaration of Independence or the U.S. Constitution:

- "I accept the Bible as the infallible Word given to us by God." —Samuel Huntington

- "I have examined all [religions] ... and the result is that the Bible is the best book in the world. It contains more of my philosophy than all the libraries I have seen." Also, "The Ten Commandments and the Sermon on the Mount contain my religion." —John Adams

- "[T]he Scriptures of the Old and New Testaments are a revelation from God, and a complete rule to direct us as how we may glorify and enjoy him." —Roger Sherman

- "I believe the Holy Bible is the inspired Word of God. It contains the only reliable rules of Christian faith and Godly practices." —John Hart

- "I have a tender reliance on the mercy of the Almighty, through the merits of the Lord Jesus Christ." —Alexander Hamilton

- "[T]hat the knowledge of the Gospel of Jesus Christ may be made known to all nations, pure and undefiled religion universally prevail, and the earth be filled with the glory of the Lord." —Josiah Bartlett

SETTING THE STAGE TO PROTECT CHRISTIANITY

There are citizens today who still do not realize the phrase "separation of church and state" does not exist anywhere in the United States Constitution. Thomas Jefferson was part of a committee appointed to write the Declaration of Independence, and there were eighty-six changes to the first draft by various members of the Continental Congress. The final version was ratified on September 17, 1787.

Nearly two years later, James Madison proposed a religious freedom amendment to the Constitution. He was concerned church denominations were not being treated equally. He had overheard Baptists complaining about their treatment for expressing their faith while the Episcopal Church nearly became the American version of the state-supported Church of England. Tariffs were collected from the people for the church. Madison revered Christianity, but he also sought to ensure the protection and rights of all faiths.

Earlier drafts of what became the First Amendment are valuable in understanding our founders' intent. Emphasizing the fact that *denomination* was one of the words proposed when drafting the meaning of the Establishment Clause is vital to comprehending their objective. They wanted complete and unhindered freedom of religion, which to them meant Christianity. But they did not want a specific denomination to hold more power, control, or influence than any other denomination.

Over several months, the progression of the First Amendment's drafting and framing included these steps:

> "That in article 1st, section 9, between clauses 3 and 4, be inserted these clauses, to wit: The civil rights of none shall be abridged on account of religious belief or worship..."

On August 20, after debating the measure, revised it further and instead approved this substitute amendment:

> "Congress shall make no laws touching religion, or infringing the rights of conscience."

On September 3, the Senate met and considered several versions of the amendment. This amendment was offered, and rejected:

> **"Congress shall make no law establishing any particular denomination of religion in preference to another."**
> (Author's emphasis)

This amendment was finally offered and accepted: "Congress shall make no law establishing religion."

And of course, most of us know the final version that kicked off the Bill of Rights which begins with the basic freedoms of speech and of religion. The First Amendment states:

> Congress shall make no law respecting an establishment of religion, or prohibiting the free exercise thereof; or abridging the freedom of speech, or of the press; or the right of the people peaceably to assemble, and to petition the Government for a redress of grievances.

Isn't it interesting with all the historical diaries, documents, and writings available to us, not one of the ninety framers of the Constitution ever mentioned the phrase "separation of church and state"? It should amaze us that the very amendment they intended as a restraint upon *government* to keep out of religious matters is used today by activists to hinder the expression of Christianity.

Known as the Establishment Clause, this amendment was to prevent an official state religion, but this is most critical to see: It also prohibits the federal government from favoring non-religion over religion. Clearly, atheists are winning more court cases today as a result of judicial irresponsibility.

Just as fascinating due to its omission from history is the outspokenness of most founders and early patriots. For example, James Madison encouraged public officials to share their faith and Christian testimony. Madison wrote:

> I have sometimes thought there could not be a stronger testimony in favor of religion or against temporal enjoyments, even the most rational and manly, than for men who occupy the most honorable and gainful departments and [who] are rising in reputation and wealth, publicly to declare their unsatisfactoriness by becoming fervent advocates in the cause of Christ; and I wish you may give in your evidence in this way.[21]

---

21   James Madison, (September 25, 1773), letter to William Bradford in 1 James Madison, The Papers of James Madison 66 (William T. Hutchinson ed., Illinois: University of Chicago Press 1962).

The state cannot force the people to support a specific religion, but government wrongly sides with the religions of atheism and Humanism over Christianity.

Moreover, Thomas Jefferson seems to be the person that the Left cites as responsible for putting up that so-called "wall of separation" between church and state. Jefferson was not even one of the framers of the First Amendment; and yet, court cases have been built on this idea, and laws have been changed because of a false premise. He used those infamous words just one time – in an 1802 letter to Baptists in Connecticut who wrote him. They were concerned about their ability to express their faith publicly. Jefferson wrote back to ensure them that government could not lawfully get in their way. He also explained the state could not enforce or favor a single religion.

In the Declaration of Independence, God is mentioned or referred to four times: as Creator who gives us "certain unalienable rights," as a sovereign legislator (Laws of Nature and of Nature's God), the ultimate authority as "the Supreme Judge of the world," and having faith (a firm reliance on) in the guardian and protector of mankind (Divine Providence). Keep this in mind when Jefferson mentions natural rights referring to religious expression in his reply to the Danbury Baptists:

> Believing with you that religion is a matter which lies solely between man and his God, that he owes account to none other for his faith or his worship, that the legislative powers of government reach actions only, and not opinions, I contemplate with sovereign reverence that act of the whole American people which declared that their legislature would "make no law respecting an establishment of religion, or prohibiting the free exercise thereof," thus building a wall of separation between Church and State. Adhering to this expression of the supreme will of the nation in behalf of the rights of conscience, I shall see with sincere satisfaction the progress of those sentiments which tend to restore to man all his natural rights, convinced he has no natural right in opposition to his social duties.

I reciprocate your kind prayers for the protection and blessing of the common Father and Creator of man, and tender you for yourselves and your religious association, assurances of my high respect and esteem.[22]

This might be one of the only occurrences in American history where an individual's written words have not only been purposefully divorced from their context, but the same words – taken from a private letter – are now used as the primary authority for a national public policy. Our silence allows this to continue.

When honestly examining past documents, evidence indicates that most of our nation's leaders and representatives not only wanted to protect religious expression, but they went so far as to openly promote Christianity. Would any of these men have approved of using a few words, possibly uttered only one time, not in the Constitution but in a private letter to defend the anti-Christian agenda of those opposing religious expression. Their agenda has succeeded to the point where a Nativity scene can no longer sit in many public places and the Ten Commandments cannot be publicly displayed.

Knowing the faith of most founders and what they believed about education, would they have approved of the Bible, prayer, the Ten Commandments, and even the mention of Jesus Christ being banned from government schools just because a few claim they were offended? I hesitate to think of what those brave revolutionary men would do today with those considered to be traitors opposing God and religious freedom. Our Constitution presupposes principles from the Bible and Christianity.

To continue investigating what these men intended when they wrote our founding documents, let's look at what 1811 Supreme Court Justice Joseph Story, appointed by James Madison, stated on the matter:

> The first and fundamental rule in the interpretation of all instruments [documents] is to construe them according to the sense and the terms and the intentions of the parties.[23]

To construe means "to deduce, infer, explain, or give intention."

---

22   Thomas Jefferson, *The Writings of Thomas Jefferson*, Albert E. Bergh, ed. (Washington, D. C.: The Thomas Jefferson Memorial Association of the United States, 1904), Vol. XVI, pp. 281-282.

23   Joseph Story, *COMMENTARIES ON THE CONSTITUTION OF THE UNITED STATES* Vol. III, p. 383, 400 (1833).

When a contract is drafted and executed, courts and individuals must examine the original context and circumstances surrounding its execution in order to correctly and properly understand its meaning.

As it relates to the drafting of our founding documents, what were the events surrounding the people and why did they deem it necessary to specifically address the expression of religion where government is concerned? Were the records of the Constitutional convention fully examined? This process includes the examination of all known communications such as writings, memorandums, letters, diaries, etc. pertaining to the parties involved. And this is what was done and understood for nearly two centuries.

For example, in an act of Congress in 1787, Article 3 of the Northwest Ordinance states:

> Religion, morality, and knowledge, being necessary to good government and the happiness of mankind, schools and the means of education shall forever be encouraged.

In 1800, the 6th U.S. Congress approved the use of the Capitol building for Christian worship services, and by 1867 the church at the Capitol was the largest in Washington D.C. with 2,000 people attending services each week inside the Hall of Representatives. James Madison, John Quincy Adams, Thomas Jefferson, and others attended worship services there.

Though public officials and members of our government were prevented from interfering in religious expression, they willingly participated in the same. Most presidents have understood this balance, but the courts would later misinterpret the Establishment Clause. Speaking to the Alabama Legislature in 1982, President Ronald Reagan stated:

> The First Amendment was not written to protect the people of this country from religious values; it was written to protect religious values from government tyranny.

SUPREME POWER TO SILENCE CHRISTIANS?

Prior to 1947, Thomas Jefferson's letter to the Danbury Baptists was used in its proper and full context, so all we are asking of the judiciary and atheist activists today is they do the same and truthfully acknowledge that the basis of their argument comes from a private letter by an individual to a group of people.

Things were fine for 150 years when one court's decision sent a shock wave through America. In the 1947 case *Everson v. Board of Education*, the Supreme Court wrongly used Jefferson's letter to disregard history and legal tradition as well as the Declaration of Independence. The Court declared, "The First Amendment has erected a wall between church and state. That wall must be kept high and impregnable. We could not approve the slightest breach." A new law was created by the Court, incorporating the Fourteenth Amendment which deals with individual State powers.

They declared federal courts were empowered to restrict religious activities of government, the States, and the people as well. Fears once voiced by the Danbury Baptists had come true – and worse. By rejecting God's law, the Court now judges under the assumption our rights do not come from a Creator but the State. Jefferson referred to this judicial irreverence as despotic, meaning oppressive and tyrannical.

Former University of Texas Professor, Joseph A. Zavaletta Jr., emphasized we are a religious people, and when any level of government encourages religion, "it follows the best of our traditions." It then respects the religious nature of "we the people."

Zavaletta Jr. stated,

> The Court now sits in judgment of our beliefs as a national theology board and uses the First Amendment as a bulldozer of social engineering to remove all religious expression … the Court now protects the rights of "those who believe in no religion over those who do believe" by engaging in the methodical religious sanitization of our institutions and communities. The Court has guaranteed freedom *from* religion as opposed to freedom of religion.

> While our forefathers left us a legacy of faith, optimism and shared values, the Court has forced us to leave our children a

moral wasteland littered with the refuse of cynicism, despair and anarchy.[24]

Another court decision then set another undesired precedent. An atheist mother of a student in Champaign, Illinois, sued the school district because a group called the Champaign Council on Religious Education was offering voluntary religious education classes for public school students from grades four to nine. The group holding the classes on school property had obtained permission from the Champaign Board of Education for the weekly thirty- to forty-minute classes. The Circuit Court of Champaign County sided with the school, and upon appeal the Illinois Supreme Court confirmed the first court's ruling supporting religion classes.

However, in *McCollum v. Board of Education* in 1948, the Supreme Court applied the "wall of separation" myth and struck down the youth program. It was clear the Court was headed in the exact opposite direction our framers intended and would continue imposing its secular meaning of the Establishment Clause.

THE JOHNSON AMENDMENT

The next important event that led to increased muzzling of churches and religious groups was the passing of the Johnson Amendment in 1954. Some still refer to its effect today as the "self-censoring of Christian pastors." Texas Democrat, Lyndon B. Johnson, was a powerful politician running for reelection as Senator, but two anti-communist, tax-exempt groups were opposing him and passing out literature during the campaigns. He contacted the IRS and found the group's activity was legal, so he sought other options to fight them.

Johnson shrewdly appeared on the Senate floor on July 2, 1954, and offered his amendment to a pending, massive, tax code overhaul bill. The bill was supposed to modernize the tax code. Records indicate an absence of committee hearings on the amendment. No legislative analysis took place to examine the effect the bill and the amendment would have, particularly on churches and religious organizations. The amendment was simply created to protect Johnson.

---

24   Joseph A. Zavaletta Jr., "The Original Intent and the Free Exercise of Religion," 1997, http://www.earlyamerica.com/review/fall98/original.html.

The Johnson Amendment was passed by Congress in 1954 as an amendment to section 501(c)(3) of the federal tax code. The Johnson Amendment states entities that are exempt from federal income tax cannot:

> Participate in, or intervene in (including the publishing or distributing of statements), any political campaign on behalf of – or in opposition to – any candidate for public office.

The Left uses this to bully Christian pastors with threats of losing their nonprofit status should they dare talk about the Bible as it relates to cultural, political, fiscal, and social issues, which all fall under the category of moral issues. Knowing what we now know, do you think the Johnson Amendment is fair and constitutional? I don't think so either.

Erik Stanley, author and Senior Legal Counsel of the Alliance Defense Fund, explained the Johnson Amendment was a bill that got inserted into the tax code through back-room deals made by a powerful Senator seeking reelection at any cost. As a result of the bill, freedom of speech and the free exercise of religion have been trampled. Stanley stated:

> We have grown up with a generation of churchgoers that believe it is illegal for their pastor to address candidates and elections in light of Scripture or church doctrine when there is no valid justification for believing that.

Johnson knew how to use the political process to silence his enemies. The new amendment not only protected him from the conservative nonprofit groups opposing him, but many pastors stopped speaking about *any* issue from the pulpit that might be deemed political either out of ignorance of the new law or out of fear. By this self-censoring, the church has chosen to ignore open immorality in culture and in government while at the same time neglecting to call attention to those political leaders who strive to live according to Christian morals and values.

One might conclude Lyndon B. Johnson not only silenced America's churches, his legislation has turned many of them into agents of the state.

What about labor unions, liberal churches, and leftist organizations? Why have many of them apparently been allowed to not only endorse and support political candidates, but openly fund their campaigns?

This is the hypocrisy of selective law enforcement by the (in)Justice Department and the IRS, a partisan government agency recently exposed in the targeting of conservative groups. Some Christians believe churches would be more effective for the gospel if they lost their nonprofit status because rather than risk confrontation, many pastors have self-censored their speech.

Have we also hesitated to address the severe persecution of our Christian brothers and sisters around the world due to radical Islam? I have to believe we all care about Christian suffering and the fact millions have lost their lives because of their faith in Jesus Christ. What I also want to believe is that religious leaders in America are not afraid to talk about *why* this is happening.

In an article for *American Thinker*, Bill Warner wrote about persecution in Islamic nations "caused by Muslim jihadists who are following the Islamic doctrine of jihad against the Christian as found in the Koran, Sira, and Hadith." Warner points to pastors and church leaders who have become comfortable operating their churches more like 501(c)(3) institutions that have meetings on Sunday. They have a corporate mentality which he believes is one of the reasons for the denial of Christian suffering.

> If you are willing to see the doctrinal roots of the ongoing murder of Christians by Muslims, then you might have to speak about it from the pulpit, and that could be seen as political speech. In spite of the fact that there has never been a 501(c)(3) revoked because of political speech by a minister, the imagined loss silences ministers. Hmmm... if a minister is worried about the IRS revoking his 501(c)(3), then whom is the minster serving? Caesar or Christ?[25]

Are these harsh words any less true of at least a small number of religious leaders in America? If your pastor resembles more of a business person or CEO than a military leader preparing his troops for battle, it may be time to approach him in love and encourage him to address persecution, sin, and politics from time to time.

---

25   Bill Warner, "The Silence of the Pulpits" August 19, 2012, http://www.americanthinker. com/2012/08/the_silence_of_the_pulpits.html.

Because many misunderstand why politics were supposedly forbidden in church, some Christians have mistakenly assumed that the process of voting and electing America's leaders is either unbiblical or unimportant. Only about 25 percent of Christians vote in elections today. Some pastors do talk about their own obligation to impact society by equipping the saints, and do address the controversial issues of today. We need to pray for and rally around pastors such as these.

Though the Establishment Clause of the First Amendment will continue to be wrongly applied to cases involving religion, we can help by raising awareness. We can elect representatives who revere the Bible they place their hand on when taking their oath of office. Enemies of Christianity and of America have become emboldened, and people of faith need to be reminded we are provided the freedom of religion and its expression under the Constitution.

The truth is churches have a tremendous amount of freedom. From the pulpit, actual limitations include: Pastors cannot openly endorse a particular candidate, tell people whom to vote for, or contribute church money to a campaign. A pastor is absolutely free to do so as an individual *outside* the church. Pastors, churches, and nonprofits can lawfully speak in detail about all biblical issues. They may also quote any Scripture in the Bible, discuss unethical abortion funding and the protection of marriage, and distribute voter guides and information as well as register folks to vote. Churches can invite politicians to come in and speak to their congregations as long as they extend an invitation to both parties.

I do understand the concern some pastors have about mixing religion and government, but we cannot divorce our faith from our politics. If we do, we'd have to leave Jesus at home or outside when we enter the voting booth *if* that were even possible. Politics affect many areas of our lives, and the Bible has answers and instructions for every single one. Christians must have a voice when it comes to who is elected, what policies get promoted, and which laws get passed. Someone's legislation and worldview will surely be enacted and enforced in America – so will it be those who oppose Christianity or those who support it?

Are we willing to remind and inform this generation about who we are and what America once was? Are we willing to speak the truth about Christ and culture no matter how unpopular we may become? The nation has not *yet* declined to a point of total ungodliness and destruction, and our government needs our prayers and our participation to generate a revival. Concerned Christians must unite again.

Every believer should see the need to speak up with a sense of urgency whether you are a parent, a pastor, or a person in the public square.

The Reverend Don Wildmon, founder of the American Family Association, has been instrumental in fighting for the family and Christian values in our country. He wrote the following over ten years ago:

> Today, 4,000 innocent precious lives of unborn babies were snuffed out ... And 300,000 pulpits are silent ... The networks make a mockery of Christians, the Christian faith and Christian values with nearly every show they air. Greed, materialism, violence, sexual immorality are standard fare. Program after program, movie after movie contains anti-Christian episodes and plots. News articles condescendingly refer to the "fundamentalists, right-wing Christians." Those who speak out for the sacredness of life are branded as extremists. And 300,000 pulpits are silent.
>
> Teenage suicide is the highest it has ever been ... Christian morality cannot be taught in schools, but atheistic immorality can ... And 300,000 pulpits are silent. Rape has increased 700 percent in the last fifty years, and that takes into consideration the population growth ... And 300,000 pulpits are silent.
>
> Rock music fills the airwaves and our children's minds with music which legitimizes rape, murder, forced sex, sadomasochism, adultery, satanic worship, etc. And 300,000 pulpits are silent. A majority of states now have lotteries [gambling has been legalized, no longer a crime]. And 300,000 pulpits are silent.[26]

Perhaps your pastor or church leader has in fact been speaking

---

26 Don Wildmon, American Family Association, http://www.frc.org/prayerteam/ prayer-targets-will-the-church-forget-watchmen-on-the-wall-call2fall-boy-scouts.

out on these and many other problems in our society. Thank him and encourage him! You are blessed to have him and the church in America needs more like him. Our hope is for Christian leaders to do what the Confessing Church in Germany chose to do; put the Word of God above all things. We must not have any gods besides the one true God. Real faith cannot be silenced by government orders. This applies to individual Christians as well.

If we do nothing and the majority remains silent, the secular progressives win. Then, with God removed from all aspects of American society, they will be the ones to rule, deciding what is right and wrong, true and false, moral and immoral. As the great Reverend Charles Finney once said, "God will bless or curse America depending on the course Christians take in politics; they must vote for honest men and take consistent ground."

We have been losing because Christians have not first been firmly established in their faith, and second we have not been openly preaching and living the Word of God without compromise. I admit my past failures in this area and have confessed them to the Lord; how about you?

The most important thing is not winning battles for culture or country, but winning eternal battles for the kingdom of God. To win the souls of men, the whole truth of the whole gospel must be proclaimed. True Christianity cannot be confined behind the walls of any church. The unlawful silencing of believers should not be allowed, but corrupt, power-hungry men such as black-robed progressives cannot help it.

CHAPTER 6

JUDICIAL TYRANNY

For the LORD is our judge, The LORD is our lawgiver, The LORD is our king; He will save us
—Isaiah 33:22

"You seem … to consider the judges as the ultimate arbiters of all constitutional questions; a very dangerous doctrine indeed, and one which would place us under the despotism of an oligarchy … Their power is the more dangerous as they are in office for life and not responsible, as the other functionaries are, to the elective control."
—Thomas Jefferson, September 28, 1820, letter to William Jarvis

"[T]he judiciary from the nature of its functions, will always be the least dangerous to the political rights of the Constitution … [T]he judiciary is, beyond comparison, the weakest of the three departments of power … [and] the general liberty of the people can never be endangered from that quarter."
—Alexander Hamilton, The Federalist #78

WHEN GOVERNMENT POWER TRUMPS THE PEOPLE

Our founders realized if men in any branch of government violated their God-given parameters as well as constitutional limits of their office, government could become abusive. Since our founders established a system in which all three government branches were accountable to the people, they would most likely be astonished today that the people for which the Constitution was written to protect have done little about the massive growth, recklessness, and unchecked power of the United States government.

According to Webster's Dictionary, an oligarchy is defined as "a form of government in which the supreme power is [placed] in the hands of a few persons or a dominant class; a species of aristocracy." Because of the power of judges and the fact that one political party now dominates our government, we have an imbalance of influence which was never by design or intent. When both sides of a debate or issue are not allowed, our God-given rights and freedoms are in danger.

In the last chapter, we touched on some early American history, we examined the Constitution and a few amendments, and we reviewed what the founders intended. We have seen quite a contrast between actual documented history and how the country is operating today. Investigating and examining some court cases will shed light on the unprecedented power of the judicial branch in America.

The first few years in the 1960s would prove both pivotal and detrimental to the church, culture, and family values in American society. Christians had already been dealt a blow in the previous decade as the Johnson Amendment affected churches and nonprofits, but in the 60s Christianity would be targeted in the public school system.

In the 1962 landmark ruling, the Supreme Court again misused the Constitution and without citing a single precedent banned voluntary prayer from public schools. In the case of *Engel vs. Vitale*, the Court claimed that a basic, simple nondenominational prayer in New York schools established "an official state religion." That ruling against a benign, one-sentence prayer should be shocking to most fair minded citizens when all it did was recognize dependence on God and ask for blessings on the children, their parents, teachers, and country. That's it!

Justice Potter Stewart, a voice of common sense and reason, was one who disagreed with the decision, saying:

> The Court today says that the State and federal governments are without constitutional power to prescribe any particular form of words to be recited by any group of the American people on any subject touching religion...

> With all respect, I think the court has misapplied a great constitutional principle. I cannot see how an "official religion" is established by letting those who want to say a prayer say it. On the contrary, I think that to deny the wish of these school

children to join in reciting this prayer is to deny them the opportunity of sharing in the spiritual heritage of our Nation."[27]

Six liberal Supreme Court Justices including Earl Warren initiated an unconstitutional transfer of power from the legislative and executive branches of American government to the judicial branch. Our founders were rightly concerned the federal judiciary might seize powers from the states. Thomas Jefferson was one of several who warned the courts could gain power little by little, advancing like a thief "until all shall be usurped from the states." We truly do not give the Framers of our Declaration enough credit for their wisdom and foresight.

The Engel ruling would be the basis for many future decisions involving the blotting out of God and the Bible, banning the Ten Commandments, prayer, and the quoting of Scripture in public schools. Here's what many of us forget: When something good, moral, and biblical is eliminated or removed, something bad, immoral, and unbiblical will replace it. Soon after the ushering out of Christianity from government-run schools, the doors were held wide open for other religions and immoral behavior.

One year later, Pennsylvania took the next hit in the 1963 case *Abington School District v. Schempp* in which voluntary Bible reading and prayer at the beginning of each school day was abolished. (This case piggybacked on *Murray v. Curlett* in Baltimore, Maryland.) The Court said religious activities must be kept out of the schools. This ruling either displays contempt or disrespect for the founder's intent of the First Amendment.

The Supremes declared Bible reading and reciting the Lord's Prayer a violation of the Establishment Clause and teaching children to practice religion was not only unconstitutional, it discriminated against atheists.

> The Bible is the chief moral cause of all that is good and the best corrector of all that is evil in human society; the best book for regulating the temporal [secular] concerns of men.
> —Noah Webster (1758 – 1843)

The path the Supreme Court sent this nation down has been disastrous. In 1965, the Court nullified a state statute in *Griswold v. Connecticut* when Planned Parenthood's Estelle Griswold fought to repeal a state

---

27   *Engel v. Vitale* 370 U.S. 421.

law against birth control and against giving medical advice to married couples. The problem is not with repealing a state law; the problem lies with the fact the Court based its decision on a supposed "right to marital privacy" which is nowhere in the Constitution.

The Supreme Court cannot and does not make laws, but in this case it created a constitutional right. When our government ignores American citizens and refuses to allow the people to decide by voting on state issues, we end up with laws having consequences that extend far beyond the case for which the ruling was handed down.

Over thirty years ago, on September 25, 1982, President Ronald Reagan said:

> Unfortunately, in the last two decades we've experienced an onslaught of such twisted logic that if Alice were visiting America, she might think she'd never left Wonderland. We're told that it somehow violates the rights of others to permit students in school who desire to pray to do so. Clearly this infringes on the freedom of those who choose to pray, the freedom taken for granted since the time of our Founding Fathers … To prevent those who believe in God from expressing their faith is an outrage … The relentless drive to eliminate God from our schools … should be stopped.

THE LEGAL RIGHT TO KILL?

In 1973 one of the most horrific rulings was decided when abortion was legalized and made the law of the land in the case of *Roe v. Wade*. Most of us believe this issue is about the life or death of a human baby in the womb, not a clump or mass of tissue or a women's right to privacy. God's Word and His law trumps man's word and man's law – every time, in every possible situation.

Having acknowledged this, looking at the issue from a constitutional perspective, we must set aside moral arguments for a moment because that case should have been a matter of state's rights. Murder is against God's law; abortion is man's law. Scripture holds abortion to be sin and in America, it used to be illegal. Let's look at how spiritually ignorant men overruled Almighty God.

The ACLU (American Civil Liberties Union) had an agenda and represented plaintiff, Jane Doe (Norma McCorvey), to secure abortion on demand. They pushed her to get a signature on the affidavit, and since she was struggling with alcohol, drugs, and depression at the time, she was exactly what the ACLU wanted. Here was a pregnant woman in dire circumstances they could exploit to sell the court on the need for women to be allowed to kill their babies prior to giving birth if they thought their circumstances were not optimal.

The untold story is Norma gave her life to the Lord in 1995 and admitted she was used and "persuaded by feminist attorneys [such as Sarah Weddington] to lie; to say I was raped and needed an abortion. It was all a lie." Her book, *Won by Love*, as well as pro-life efforts have made a difference in recent years as more truth came out about *Roe v. Wade*.

Remember, powers reserved for states are not to be infringed upon by the federal government. The Tenth Amendment to the U.S. Constitution reads:

> The powers not delegated to the United States by the Constitution, nor prohibited by it to the states, are reserved to the states respectively, or to the people.

Just four states had legalized abortion in 1973, while forty-six states restricted abortion, but the Supreme Court decided to enforce an unwanted law on the entire country. The ruling continues to divide American families and political parties today.

Using the court's reasoning, since prostitution is legal in Las Vegas and illegal in every other state, should the Court legalize prostitution in all fifty states based on one case? Atheists and anti-Christian organizations such as the Freedom From Religion Foundation and the ACLU work the system, forcing the Court to rule by filing suits challenging the constitutionality of a statute. Their whole aim is to push their progressive political agenda.

Activists and radicals have achieved preferred rulings by feeding their cases to power-hungry courts; a runaway judicial branch has set the stage for an executive branch dictatorship in a country where this was never supposed to be possible. Let it be known, most Republicans have not pushed back enough and seem to have little power to stop the liberal locomotive leading to a godless, one-party rule in America. Democrats aren't complaining, and if amnesty gets passed, the balance of powers could well be over.

Conservatives have tried fighting the corruption, but since many of their voices are not loud enough and the media typically opposes their cause, they receive little attention.

The following are a few more examples in chronological order:

- 1980 – The Supreme Court ruled that posting the Ten Commandments in public schools was unconstitutional in the case *Stone v. Graham*. Promoting the Ten Commandments was no longer a "permissible objective" of the education system to allow children to learn and obey the moral teachings of the Ten Commandments. Do not murder, lie, cheat, steal, etc. Ironically, Moses and God's Law, the Ten Commandments, are engraved on the Supreme Court building as well as on the lower inside sections of its wooden chamber doors.

- 1984/85 – The Court ruled Alabama schools could no longer allow teachers to hold one minute of silence at the start of each school day for voluntary meditation or silent prayer. In *Wallace v. Jaffree,* Ishmael Jaffree, father and member of the American Humanist Association, sued the district on behalf of his children, arguing the allowance for [silent] prayer discriminated against his religion of Islam.

- 1992 – The Court prohibited clergy-led prayer at graduation ceremonies. In *Lee v. Weisman*, Daniel Weisman sued a middle school in Providence, Rhode Island, because a Jewish Rabbi opened and closed the school graduation ceremony with a nonsectarian prayer mentioning God. Apparently, when a person feels he is being "psychologically coerced," the activity is unconstitutional.

- 2000 – The Court banned a policy allowing student-initiated, student-led prayer at high school football games, claiming it violates the Establishment Clause. In *Santa Fe ISD v. Doe*, the Court extended the ban from the *Lee v. Weisman* case.

- 2002 – Alabama Supreme Court Chief Justice Roy Moore, concerned the moral foundation of our laws in America were being eroded, placed a Ten Commandments monument in the Alabama judicial building. You may recall the national debate that ensued. Justice Moore was brought before a federal court because he believed state officials have the right to acknowledge Almighty God. This case, *Glassroth v. Moore*, was about the authority of the Constitution, and evidently Moore had gone too far by placing God over both man and government.

Ironically, the trial opened with words acknowledging the God whose laws were in question: "God save the United States and this Honorable Court." Attorney for Justice Roy Moore, Herb Titus, declared in his opening statement the case was about religious freedom as well as censorship. He said it was part of an ACLU-backed movement going on in America to "misuse the Establishment Clause as a sword" and to prohibit the public acknowledgement of God by elected government officials. They want God censored from the public square. Titus stated:

> The public acknowledgement of God as the source of our liberties is essential if we are to preserve those liberties. As the Declaration of Independence attests, if the source of individual rights is not God, then our rights are not inalienable, and if you take God out of the equation, then the all-powerful state is unchecked by any higher law.[28]

Polls from CNN, USA Today, and Gallup showed 77% of Americans were against the federal court order to remove the Ten Commandments monument. Judge Mylon Thompson did not want to answer to a higher Authority and was comfortable rejecting God when he ruled the monument was unconstitutional, saying:

> [T]he court disagrees … that, as a matter of American law, the Judeo-Christian God must be recognized as sovereign over the state … [W]hile the Chief Justice is free to keep whatever religious beliefs he chooses, the state may not acknowledge

---

28   Trial Transcript for *Glassworth v. Moore*, 229 F. Supp. 2d 1290 (M.D. Ala. 2002), Vol. I, p. 4.

the sovereignty of the Judeo-Christian God and attribute to that God our religious freedom.[29]

Today, many people have the faulty belief or opinion that a federal judge or the Supreme Court is the ultimate power, arbiter, or authority and that something is or isn't constitutional until the Court makes a ruling. What happened to the power of the people? In every one of these past major cases affecting millions of Americans, none were decided by a majority vote or the will of the people; they were decided by a small group of unelected justices. Contrary to the beliefs of Obama-appointee, Supreme Court Justice Sonia Sotomayor, judges and courts do not make laws.

In the book *Judicial TYRANNY – the new kings of America?*, contributing author William Federer emphasized the massive effort that goes into the legislative process in America – registering voters, political campaigns, introducing and debating bills, representatives voting on bills, dealing with vetoes, etc. Federer stated, "This is all an exercise in futility if only a few unelected judges can invalidate the entire process."

We have seen this happen as more judges are emboldened to strike down marriage laws despite the fact majorities from states across the country went to the polls and voted their deeply held beliefs in favor of defining marriage between one man and one woman. At least thirty-one states have passed bans on partial birth abortion but were suspended by federal judges.

In opposition to a majority of the people, federal judges overruled every single one of the following cases: Colorado citizens voted *not* to give special rights to homosexuals (1992); Arkansas and Washington states passed term limits for politicians (1995); California voted to stop state-funded, taxpayer services to illegal aliens (1995); New York and Washington citizens voted against physician-assisted suicide (1996); Arizona voted for English as their official language (1997); Missouri passed "A Woman's Right to Know," requiring physicians to wait twenty-four hours after consulting a woman before performing an abortion (2000); and Nebraska citizens passed a traditional marriage amendment with 70% of the vote, but U.S. District Judge Joseph Batallion (appointed by president Clinton) overruled the people (2005).

---

29   Ibid. at 1310.

Fifteen thousand citizens gathered around the Missouri State Capitol on September 5, 1999, supporting a ban on partial birth abortion which Democrat Governor Mel Carnahan vetoed, but the legislature overrode the veto on behalf of the people. Federal District Judge Scott Wright suspended the law the next day when Planned Parenthood filed a challenge.

At the national level, after years of incremental efforts on a bill to ban partial birth abortion, it was finally passed by both houses of Congress and signed by President George W. Bush on November 5, 2003. Federal Judge Richard Kopf suspended the law one hour later.[30]

Giving a speech in Montgomery, Alabama, in the wake of the Court decision to remove the Ten Commandments, Ambassador Alan Keyes passionately explained the free exercise of religion means "we have the right in our families and in our schools and in our communities and in our governments and in our states to live according to the Word of God." Keyes emphasized the fact that for most of America's history it never occurred to judges to assert differently.

> Generations have acknowledged Scripture as a foundation to our lives and freedoms. Our founders believed people in their individual states have the right to live according to their faith, under institutions they put in place to govern themselves. If the people believe the Constitution was violated by a judge, they do not have to sit back and take it. The Declaration of Independence also supports the idea that "when there is a long train of abuses that are destroying our rights, the founders said that it is not only our right, it is our duty to oppose them." Against God's will, courts are imposing their beliefs on us.

But in the conclusion of his speech, Dr. Keyes declared the bottom line: We cannot live with true, responsible self-government by force of law, police, or the military. The Ten Commandments must not simply be a *symbol* of morality; they must be revered again in our hearts. When the Word of God is written on our hearts, morality in our communities will be affected the way our founders envisioned. Keyes' closing statement was: "It is the heart of such a people that fits them for a freedom that will endure."[31]

---

30   Mark I. Sutherland, *Judicial TYRANNY- the new kings of America?* (St. Louis, MO, AmeriSearch, 2005) pp. 96-98.

31   Ibid. pp. 45-53.

The people have more say than we realize, but we must unite in the hopes of spiritual revival and moral reversal. We can raise awareness, talk with friends, blog, write, use social media, volunteer locally, and be active at church as well as politically. We must not give up! Do you think the Left and the ACLU will ever stop pushing their anti-Christian agendas?

NOT EXACTLY REPRESENTING LIBERTY FOR ALL AMERICANS

Founded by Roger Baldwin in 1920, the ACLU claims to be a nonpartisan organization defending the liberties of all citizens. To understand the true worldview of an organization, we must look at its founder and its history. Baldwin, an agnostic and socialist with an elitist mindset, was given the Medal of Freedom in 1981 from President Jimmy Carter. One of Baldwin's friends was eugenicist Margaret Sanger, founder of Planned Parenthood. Indisputable links exist between the ACLU, abortionists, and progressives from their early days.

> I am for socialism, disarmament, and ultimately for abolishing the state itself as an instrument of violence and compulsion. I seek social ownership of property, the abolition of the prop-ertied class, and sole control by those who produce wealth. Communism is the goal.[32]
> —ACLU founder, Roger Baldwin

The ACLU has used the courts to enforce an agenda the major-ity of Americans still oppose. The ACLU supports the distribution of pornography in order to undermine marriage and traditional families. They have opposed any government effort to enforce obscenity laws, refusing to protect parents and children from offensive material. The ACLU defends those who abuse children but attacks those who pro-mote morality. The First Amendment was never intended to protect what is considered obscene material and sinful behavior. Because of continued efforts to devalue life, the ACLU has helped open the legal door for euthanasia, an aspect of social Darwinism.

One of the goals of the ACLU is a secularized America, sanitized

32   Peggy Lamsom, *Roger Baldwin: Founder of the American Civil Liberties Union; A Portrait* (Boston: Houghton-Mifflin, 1976), p. 192.

from the Judeo-Christian religion and biblical teachings. They seek a country in which religious speech is not only silenced but punished. With vast resources, including hundreds of millions of dollars plus millions more in donations from ACLU members such as Progressive Insurance chairman, Peter B. Lewis, they have been waging war on America virtually unchallenged for eighty years.

The ACLU may have hundreds of staff members, volunteers, a big budget and over sixty full time attorneys, but one thing they don't have is God. They may wreak havoc for a short time in our history, but the Lord Jesus Christ will have the final say.

In the book *THE ACLU VS AMERICA* Alan Sears and Craig Osten lay out the facts, the truth, and case backgrounds that few of us know or remember. The ACLU's agenda is not hidden. Look at their website, policy guides, court documents, speeches by their leaders, and what they defend. Let's take a look at some of the ACLU's [extreme] positions:

- All legal prohibitions on the distribution of obscene material – including child pornography – are unconstitutional.

- Pornographic outlets can locate wherever they please ... Tax-funded libraries should not restrict access of children to pornography on the Internet.

- Parents should have no legal recourse when it comes to shielding their children from exposure to hard-core pornography.

- Parents cannot limit their children's exposure to, or participation in, public school classes and assemblies ... except orthodox Jewish or Christian teachings.

- The military cannot stop open displays of homosexual behavior within its ranks.

- Public schools cannot observe recognized religious, historical, and cultural holidays such as Christmas, Easter, or Hanukkah, despite hundreds of years of American tradition.

- All legislative, military, and prison chaplaincy programs should be abolished.

- All criminal and civil laws that prohibit polygamy (having multiple wives) or prohibit same-sex "marriage" should be done away with.[33]

Through lawsuits filed by activists in the last few years, we've seen the government bully Christian business owners, because they chose not to participate in homosexual ceremonies. We've seen government force Christian companies to provide abortion-inducing birth control to employees as a result of ObamaCare, which causes business owners to violate their own moral conscience and, more importantly, their Christian faith. Isn't this unconstitutional? What will you and I do when a law is placed on the books requiring that we accept, embrace, and honor what God says is sinful?

Christian-bashing radicals have now convinced and recruited many homosexual activists to do their dirty work. Again, most gays and lesbians are not hateful, prideful, intolerant, activists. In fact, many would prefer to live and let live and are even embarrassed by the cultural bullying taking place in the name of gay "rights" by extremists as well as by the Obama administration. We need to pray for them because like you and me, they need the love and forgiveness of Jesus.

There are many kind, loving, and confused homosexuals who simply want to be left alone. They in turn should remember Christians want to be left alone as well, and though a small number of extremists exist on both sides, our Constitution still provides us all the right to deny God or worship God freely *and* publicly.

Sadly, the Constitution does not matter to those who have reinterpreted its meaning. Even though the majority of American adults believe Christians have the right to say no to any request for services that conflict with their religious beliefs, activists continue using the court system to further their godless agenda.

According to a Rasmussen Reports poll,[34] a whopping 85% of Americans side with the right of a Christian or any person of faith who might choose to turn away someone's business for reasons of religious

---

33   Alan Sears, Craig Osten, *THE ACLU VS AMERICA*, (Nashville, TN, Alliance Defense Fund, B&H Publishing Group, 2005) p. 3.

34   Rasmussen Reports, July 2012, 85% Think Christian Photographer Has Right To Turn Down Same-Sex Wedding Job, http://www.rasmussenreports.com/public_content/business/general_business/july_2013/85_think_christian_photographer_has_right_to_turn_down_same_sex_wedding_job.

convictions. This and other recent polls again prove that activists, bullies, extremists, media, and Hollywood are out of touch with the majority.

RECENT CASES OF ACTIVISM AND INTIMIDATION

Elaine and Jonathan Huguenin, owners of Elaine Photography, a very small business in New Mexico, were taken to court after turning down a request to photograph a lesbian commitment ceremony. Elaine politely declined to use her artistic talents to support a message opposing her beliefs. The woman, Vanessa Willock, easily found another photographer, but filed a complaint with the New Mexico Human Rights Commission who ruled against Elaine Photography and ordered them to pay $6,637.94 in legal fees to Willock (*Elaine Photography LLC v. Willock*).

The New Mexico Supreme Court upheld the ruling and one of the justices actually wrote that it's the price of citizenship and the Huguenins "now are compelled by law to compromise the very religious beliefs that inspire their lives." The business owners appealed to the Supreme Court and on April 7, 2014, they were turned down. I echo the comments of American Family Association's Tim Wildmon, who stated:

> By refusing to take up the appeal of law-abiding citizens seeking to exercise religious liberty under the Constitution, the U.S. Supreme Court has shown itself in this case to be an utterly unqualified defender of that Constitution.

Another case has developed into three separate lawsuits involving the ACLU: *Ingersoll v. Arlene's Flowers, State of Washington v. Arlene's Flowers*, and *Arlene's Flowers v. Ferguson*. In 2013, Washington State Attorney General, Bob Ferguson, sued Barronelle Stutzman, owner of Arlene's Flowers in Richland Washington, because she declined to offer her floral arrangements and participate in the same-sex ceremony of two gay men, Robert Ingersoll and Curt Freed. AG Ferguson filed a suit after hearing about the story on the news.

Alliance Defending Freedom (ADF) and other attorneys representing Barronelle Stutzman, now in her seventies, filed a countersuit to dismiss the case because Ferguson inserted himself into the matter and had no authority to do so because he never received a complaint. ADF explained that government is supposed to protect the freedom of American citizens, not use intolerance for certain viewpoints to intimidate them.

Longtime customer and homosexual Robert Ingersoll decided to sue Arlene's Flowers for discrimination even though she had not only served but employed homosexuals in past years. As Barronelle's legal battles continue, she receives encouraging letters and calls from Christians supporting her from across America as well as from other parts of the world.

"It's me now, but it's going to be you," she warned other citizens. "They're trying to bully me into something that's against my faith and they can't do that." Washington Attorney General Bob Ferguson offered to settle the case if she paid a $2,000 penalty for violating the Consumer Protection Act, and if she agreed not to discriminate in the future. Barronelle stated:

> "You are asking me to walk in the way of a well-known betrayer, one who sold something of infinite worth for 30 pieces of silver. That is something I will not do. I never imagined that using my God-given talents and abilities, and doing what I love to do for over three decades, would become illegal. ...Since 2012, same-sex couples all over the state have been free to act on their beliefs about marriage, but because I follow the Bible's teaching that marriage is the union of one man and one woman, I am no longer free to act on my beliefs."[35]

In another case, Jack Phillips, a Colorado baker and owner of Denver area Masterpiece Cakeshop, was sued and found guilty of discrimination for refusing to make a gay couple's wedding cake. The ACLU filed a complaint with the Colorado Civil Rights Division, which ruled Phillips violated state discrimination law. The Attorney General filed the complaint and Administrative Law judge, Robert Spencer, ordered Phillips to accommodate all same-sex couples. He claimed the religious views of Jack Phillips fail to take into account "the cost to society and the hurt caused to persons who are denied service simply because of *who they are*."

---

35   Todd Starnes, Fox News, Flower Power: Christian Florist rejects attorney general's offer, won't betray her religious beliefs, 2/23/2015, http://www.foxnews.com/opinion/2015/02/23/flower-power-christian-florist-rejects-attorney-generals-offer-wont-betray-her/.

Several other bakeries offered to make a cake for homosexual couple Charlie Craig and David Mullins, but they insisted on filing a complaint regardless. Mullins accused Phillips of being "offensive and dehumanizing" and told Denver Westword, "We got up to leave, and to be totally honest, I said, 'F— you and your homophobic cake shop.'" Phillips faces a year in jail, and gay activists have held protests outside his business.

A case from 2014 reveals a cold, ruthless agenda the Obama/Holder Justice Department has against religious liberty in America. Little Sisters of the Poor, an order of Catholic nuns dedicated to providing "the neediest elderly of every race and religion a home where they will be welcomed as Christ" have been around for 175 years. They had served these people faithfully until the passage of ObamaCare in which employers are forced to provide abortion-inducing drugs and other forms of birth control to their employees.

Naturally, the Little Sisters could not – biblically or in good conscience – obey the mandates, and another legal battle began. The Obama administration even asked the Supreme Court not to exempt Catholic groups from the requirement to offer contraceptive coverage. Holder's Justice Department tried to go around the issue saying they would not impose the mandate on the Little Sisters if they signed a certificate authorizing others to fulfill the new law. Facing IRS fines and penalties, the nuns were forced to choose between obeying God or government.

A brief was filed by their attorneys saying the government is blind to the free expression of religion issue, and "the Little Sisters and other Applicants cannot execute the form because they cannot deputize a third party to sin on their behalf." HHS Secretary Kathleen Sebelius had ignored the Little Sisters until October 2013, when they came into court with their Catholic Benefits provider, Christian Brothers, representing a class of over 400 organizations that also objected to the ObamaCare mandate.

The federal government has established a clear pattern of unconstitutional acts against religious groups. The tone the government has set as well as their actions have emboldened others at state and local levels to deny people of faith their constitutionally guaranteed religious liberties. Since 2009, the Obama administration has not tried to hide their attitude toward Christianity and the Constitution. Even more disturbing is the fact that despite requests from Congress, Kathleen Sebelius never bothered to consult the Justice Department to determine whether the ObamaCare mandate was constitutional.

There is some good news: When the heat is turned up on Christians, many finally respond and take action by speaking up and standing up for the faith. At this time, in nineteen out of twenty cases brought by religious nonprofits, courts have sided with the people instead of the government. The Little Sisters of the Poor received an injunction from the Supreme Court protecting them from the U.S. Department of Health and Human Services' (HHS) controversial mandate while their case is considered by the Tenth Circuit Court of Appeals in Denver, Colorado.

The Little Sisters' case is just one of ninety-four recent lawsuits filed against the HHS Mandate, including those by Hobby Lobby and Conestoga Wood Specialties. These cases involve over 300 plaintiffs and forty-seven nonprofit groups. Hobby Lobby Stores, Inc. has been owned and operated by devout Christians, the Green family, since 1970 when David Green started the business in their garage. Today, they have over 600 stores in forty-one states, and the family believes "it is by God's grace and provision that Hobby Lobby has endured." The company website states, "He has been faithful in the past, and we trust Him for our future."

Two of the statements in their mission include:

- Honoring the Lord in all we do by operating the company in a manner consistent with biblical principles.

- Providing a return on the owner's investment, sharing the Lord's blessings with our employees, and investing in our community.

For their employees, Hobby Lobby strives to build character and strong families. Their stores are closed on Sundays, as the company believes employees should have the opportunity to spend Sundays with their families. They simply desire to do business freely, live according to their faith, and for government to allow them to do so without violating their religious beliefs. For not complying with the HHS mandate, they could have faced fines of $1.3 million a day or nearly $475 million a year.

The Greens say cancelling their company's health plan to avoid obeying the mandate was not a decision government can force them to make.

The reason Hobby Lobby filed their lawsuit was they cannot fulfill their mission and pay for drugs that cause abortions at the same time. What many people don't realize is Hobby Lobby already provides coverage for sixteen of twenty preventive contraceptives required in the mandate. The Green family has moral objections to the Plan B "morning after pill," Ella "week after pill," and two others because they are possible life-threatening drugs or devices. Covering these drugs and devices would violate their most deeply held biblical belief that life begins at conception, when an egg is fertilized.

The United States Supreme Court heard oral arguments on March 25, 2014, and on June 30 narrowly decided in favor of Hobby Lobby and Conestoga Wood Specialties. The Court said families that own for-profit businesses are not forced to violate their religious beliefs just because they own a business. At the time of this writing, Senate Democrats are protesting the decision, so this may be far from over.

In 2011, the government made the disturbing claim that churches do not have special rights under the First Amendment but merely association rights, like unions. In the case *Hosanna-Tabor Evangelical Lutheran Church and School v. the Equal Employment Opportunity Commission*, a unanimous court rejected the administration's claim.

In 2012, a Kentucky t-shirt company, Hands On Originals, was accused of violating a local ordinance when they declined to make shirts for a local "Pride Festival" that openly celebrates homosexual behavior and same-sex relationships. The Gay and Lesbian Services Organization requested the t-shirts be printed, and when they were denied, filed a complaint with the county Human Rights Commission for discrimination based on sexual orientation.

Owner of the t-shirt business, Blaine Adamson, said he thinks "it's a wake-up call for Christians, for business owners, and for American citizens," and emphasized he will be held accountable by God for how he runs his business. Represented by the Alliance Defense Fund, Adamson said the reason he declined printing the order was because of the public message he disagrees with that his company would help promote had

he taken their business and printed the shirts. ADF Litigation Staff
Counsel Jim Campbell stated:

> Americans in the marketplace should not be subject to preda-
> tory legal attacks simply for abiding by their beliefs. This kind
> of bullying may be practiced in a dictatorship, but violations
> of conscience have no place in the United States.

The response filed with the Commission explained Hands On
Originals declined shirt orders in the past for various reasons, but this
time they did not want to communicate a message that people should
be proud to engage in sinful behavior, "nor did they want to promote
the ideology conveyed at that advocacy event." The t-shirt company
has a logo with "Hands on Faith" at the bottom left-hand side of its
front page; it links out to a Christian apparel portion of the Hands On
Originals business.

Gay and lesbian activists created a Facebook page boycotting the
t-shirt company, and the Fayette, Kentucky, school district placed a hold
on future orders. Even the city mayor got into the act saying, "People
don't have patience for this sort of attitude today." Common in most
of these cases is the business owners receive hate mail and threats for
simply voicing their religious convictions. These persecuted business
owners also receive overwhelming support and encouragement from
other Christians as well.

In typical "signs of the times" fashion, the city ordered diversity
training for Blaine Adamson. After two years of litigation, Lexington's
Human Rights Commission issued its ruling in October 2014, finding
the t-shirt business guilty of the town's "fairness ordinance," so they
ordered Adamson to undergo reeducation. Even more disturbing,
in a statement that would make Hitler proud, Raymond Sexton, the
Commission's Executive Director, said it's time for Christians in the
marketplace to "leave their religion at home."[36]

PRECEDENTS SET FOR DISCRIMINATING
AGAINST CHRISTIANS

Charles Patrick, pastor of Sunago Christian Fellowship in Compton,

---

36   Tony Perkins' Washington Update, "Intolerance Fits Liberals to a T (Shirt)," 10/9/2014,
     http://www.frc.org/washingtonupdate/intolerance-fits-liberals-to-a-t-shirt.

California, was denied the opportunity to start a charter school in the Los Angeles area in 2012. Compton Unified School District rejected the two applications for a charter school allegedly because Patrick was a church leader. He insisted the applications had nothing to do with the church and would not be affiliated with the church but instead would be run under the secular guidelines of the state of California.

Yes, even a pastor is entitled by law to receive funding when the money is to be used for secular purposes including education. Frontier Legal Foundation filed a lawsuit against those involved with the denials on the grounds his First Amendment rights were violated. It makes you wonder if a Muslim imam's application would have been denied as well.

In another very recent case involving the removal of a Bible verse and some apparent confusion at the U.S. Air Force, a cadet wrote the following on his dorm whiteboard:

> *I have been crucified with Christ and I no longer live, but Christ lives in me. The life I now live in the body, I live by faith in the Son of God, who loved me and gave Himself for me* (Galatians 2:20 NIV).

For one, Lt. Gen. Jerry Boykin (USA-Ret.) couldn't believe this was a controversy and confirmed the academy had allowed the personal use of whiteboards by cadets. He said "censorship of religious commentary is unacceptable." Regardless, just two hours after Mikey Weinstein, director of Military Religious Freedom Foundation (MRFF), heard about the Bible verse, he led the opposition, and the offending Scripture was removed. He insisted the cadet be punished for misconduct. Weinstein said posting a Bible verse created a hostile environment and the academy was already a "hyper-fundamentalist Christian institution." He stated:

> It massively poured fundamentalist Christian gasoline on an already raging out-of-control conflagration of fundamentalist Christian tyranny, exceptionalism and supremacy at USAFA.[37]

According to Breitbart News, Mike Berry, the attorney and Director of military affairs with Liberty Institute, flew to Colorado Springs for some answers. He called it "a stunning development" as he found out

---

37   Air Force Academy removes Bible verse from cadet's whiteboard; Todd
      Starnes, Fox News, 3/11/2014, http://www.foxnews.com/opinion/2014/03/11/
      air-force-academy-removes-bible-verse-from-cadet-whiteboard/.

the Air Force interprets federal law and military regulations a bit backwards. While speaking with Col. Paul Barzler, the Air Force Academy Staff Judge Advocate, Berry mentioned that under the Constitution and federal law, cadets have the right to the free exercise of religion. Imagine his shock when the Colonel informed him that in the Air Force policy (from the Pentagon) the words *religious exercise* do not include written or verbal speech.

Cadets apparently disagreed with the decision, and Bible verses started appearing on dry erase boards in dorm hallways as an act of religious expression as well as a little rebellion. The cadets provided a teachable moment as they stood up to the bullies and spoke by exercising their constitutionally protected freedoms. Naturally, this outraged the Military Religious Freedom Foundation (MRFF). Reacting to the actions of the cadets, Weinstein belittled Academy Superintendent Lt. Gen. Michelle Johnson, called her spineless, and ended his tirade with "see you in court." This is another example of tolerance being preached but not practiced. The controversy led the Pentagon to issue a new directive and agree that religious expression of service members should be protected.

Reports are increasing about discrimination in the sports world and at colleges across America. A conservative group at Stanford University was blocked by the Graduate Student Council in a 10-2 vote from hosting a conference called "Communicating Values: Marriage, Family & the Media." Stanford claimed it was "hate speech" even though the Anscombe Society tried to find common ground with Stanford LGBT groups. A compromise could not be reached because same-sex proponents wanted to cancel speakers they considered to be "hatemongers." Sadly, the majority of students favored censoring the conservative group's beliefs "in the name of tolerance." This is the new age of discrimination in America's secular university system.

MOST AMERICANS STILL SAY "CHRISTMAS"

This chapter would not be complete without mentioning the persistent, annual attacks on Christmas and the celebration of the birth of Jesus. In 2013, Pew Research conducted a poll revealing 92% of Americans celebrate Christmas in some way. A Rasmussen poll came in a bit lower showing 87% of Americans celebrate Christmas in their family, 68% of these primarily as a religious holiday as opposed to commercial.

In a telling 2012 poll, Rasmussen reported 82% of American adults voted in favor of celebrating Christmas on public school campuses. In other words, parents have no issues with kids celebrating the birth of Jesus Christ during school hours. These are some very high numbers to keep in mind.

As you and I both know, opposition to Christmas isn't directly about the presents, the songs, the decorations or traditions. This is about the person of Jesus Christ. Every year the efforts to squelch Christmas in public continue, and last year they started in early October. Parents from one Wisconsin school district were outraged when annual Christmas concerts were cancelled in fifteen public schools apparently to avoid offending people. Phil Buch, choral director at Wausau West High School since 1981, said he was given the following ultimatum (and remember, this was for a Christmas concert):

> Choose five secular or non-religious songs for each religious (Christmas) song performed; hold a concert and have no holiday music whatsoever; or postpone any concerts in December.

Wausau School Board President Michelle Schaefer said they wanted more balance in "holiday" music out of respect for other faiths and noted concern over "the amount of religious music performed in the schools." A meeting was held and some parents called for Schaefer to be fired. Hundreds of concerned parents, taxpayers, students, and alumni voiced their strong opposition to the new policy. Wausau East High School auditorium buzzed for nearly four and a half hours, and only one person spoke in favor of cancelling Christmas concerts.

The Alliance Defense Fund and Wisconsin Family Counsel got involved, and the Wausau School Board reversed their controversial decision to limit religious music, passing a resolution to leave the concerts up to the music teachers at individual schools. They also passed a resolution that returns the music selection for concerts policy to what it had been prior to the sudden change. An additional resolution was also passed to form a committee to study this issue and make recommendations to the board for policy changes and refinements.

I will not mention too many more cases, but here are a few more reminders that enemies of God and of Jesus Christ will not stop using any means necessary to minimize Christianity in America.

- A North Carolina first grader was not allowed to recite a poem in an assembly because it mentioned God.

- Rhode Island Governor Lincoln Chafee replaced the state's Christmas tree with a "holiday tree."

- In Alsip, Illinois, a forty-year Christmas tradition of displaying a cross on the water tower was stopped.

- In Santa Monica, California, a sixty-year tradition of displaying a Nativity scene in a public park was discontinued due to atheist demands.

- In Moanalua, Hawaii, the high school orchestra cancelled its Christmas concert.

- In Warren, Michigan, the town was forced to remove their Nativity scene (displayed since 1945) due to an atheist lawsuit.

- A Florida elementary school replaced a Nativity scene with Frosty the Snowman.

- A billboard in Chicago was put up by atheists saying, "Are you good without God? Millions are." This is true by the way, but they don't tell the whole story. There are approximately 3.6 million atheists in America, just a fraction of a population close to 314 million people.

- In Cincinnati, a billboard read, "Don't believe in God? You're not alone."

- In Seattle, the Freedom From Religion Foundation put this billboard up during Christmas: "YES, VIRGINIA… THERE IS NO GOD."

- And finally, in New York City's Times Square, one billboard declared, "Who needs Christ during Christmas?" The name of Christ was crossed through, and the question was answered: "Nobody."

Their expression is also protected as free speech under the constitution, but it's important we remember they are vastly outnumbered. The problem is the majority of us have been either inactive or silent for too long.

UNCHECKED POWER OF A DEMOCRAT EXECUTIVE BRANCH

It should not be surprising the majority of courts, justices, government agencies, and the Democrat Party leadership in this country now lean to the extreme Left. This administration has an elitist mentality, and they show more of a quest for power than a concern for the people being governed.

> When a President can pick and choose which laws to follow and which to ignore, he is no longer a President.
> —Senator Ted Cruz

Where the Executive Branch is concerned, the president and his right hand man, Eric Holder of the Department of Justice, often act as if they are above the law – and perhaps there is some truth to that. Those of us who have been informed know what they have done and how little scrutiny they receive. Some critics agree President Obama feels emboldened, knowing the media will not hold him accountable for much of anything. In his 2014 State of the Union Address, one of the things Obama vowed was to take action where his agenda is concerned:

> America does not stand still – and neither will I. So wherever and whenever I can take steps without legislation to expand opportunity for more American families, that's what I'm going to do.[38]

This president has rarely reached across the political aisle, and he could not care less about those who oppose his agenda. When he said he plans to expand opportunity for families, he told a partial truth because he's been doing this all along for gay and lesbian families, pro-abortion families (including Planned Parenthood employees), families that have become dependent on welfare, families of liberal public sector unions, and families of government employees. He's right – he has no intention of standing still, and Obama will bypass Congress to force more of his agenda through whether the rest of us like it or not.

---

38   CBS News, Obama's 2014 State of the Union Address, Full Text, January 28, CBSnews. com http://www.cbsnews.com/news/obamas-2014-state-of-the-union-address-full-text/.

Trampling on states' rights, Obama directed Eric Holder to disregard the will of voters in states that defined marriage as only between one man and one woman. Holder flippantly decreed that homosexual couples across the country will receive federal benefits (lawfully) reserved for natural marriage status. Host of *Sandy Rios in the Morning* on American Family Radio commented on the brazen move saying "money and privilege for homosexuals trumps life and liberty for other Americans" as far as Obama and Holder are concerned. Rios added:

> In no phrase or article of the Constitution is there a clause
> that grants the president or his attorney general the right to
> ignore laws passed by Congress while granting rights that
> do not exist.

Witnessing our government's blatant displays of hubris is alarming, but if you think the Obama administration is out of control, they are not. They know exactly what they are doing. Worried about the next few elections at the time, Obama decided to play politics with his signature legislation by delaying ObamaCare's employer mandate. He announced the law won't be enforced as it was passed in order that employers with fifty or more employees wouldn't have to provide mandated health coverage for at least another year. As most of us know, the president is not authorized to change a date or amend parts of any law without going through Congress.

According to the Heritage Foundation, the president also decided to give Congress and their staffs special taxpayer-funded subsidies for ObamaCare after finding out they were not originally covered when the law was passed. Then, when Americans began receiving cancellation notices from their insurance companies, the administration had to act quickly because the 2012 election was approaching. In another executive action that has no basis in law, Obama announced insurance companies were to go back to original health care plans – just for one year.

The president also found out large companies were preparing to lay off employees in Fall 2012 due to the unstable economy. Since there is a "60-day notice" rule that large employers are required to give prior to mass layoffs, all this bad news would have hit mailboxes days or weeks before the presidential election. The Obama administration prevented massive layoff notices from being mailed out by telling large companies not to issue the notices. What's more, the administration offered to reimburse any employers – at taxpayer expense – if challenged for failure to give the 60-day notice.[39]

> The biggest problems that we're facing right now have to do with George Bush trying to bring more and more power into the executive branch and not go through Congress at all. And that's what I intend to reverse when I'm President of the United States of America.
> —Senator (presidential candidate) Barack Obama, 2008

Since it's the sworn duty of every member of Congress to uphold the Constitution of the United States, and the Obama administration has established a pattern of failing to do so, what action can be taken? In November 2013, the House of Representatives introduced a bill setting forth articles of impeachment against Attorney General Eric Holder.

H.Res.411.IH charges Holder with engaging in "a pattern of conduct incompatible with the trust and confidence placed in him in that position." In H.Res.411.IH, "Impeaching Eric H. Holder Jr., Attorney General of the United States, for high crimes and misdemeanors,"[40]

Holder was charged with:

1. Refusal to comply with a subpoena issued by the House Committee on Oversight and Government Reform regarding Operation Fast and Furious.

2. Failure to enforce multiple laws, including the Defense of Marriage Act, the Controlled Substances Act, and the Anti-Drug Abuse Act of 1986.

3. Refusal to prosecute the IRS officials involved in the targeting and disclosure of tax records belonging to political donors.

4. Lying under oath before Congress about the Justice Department investigation of journalist James Rosen.

39   Heritage Foundation, Elizabeth Slattery, Andrew Kloster; "An Executive Unbound: The Obama Administration's Unilateral Actions," Legal Memorandum #108, Feb. 12, 2014, http://www.heritage.org/research/reports/2014/02/an-executive-unbound-the-obama-administrations-unilateral-actions.

40   Library of Congress, Thomas; Bill Text, 113th Congress (2013-2014), H.RES.411.IH, Impeaching Eric H. Holder Jr. Attorney General of the United States, http://thomas.loc.gov/cgi-bin/query/z?c113:H.RES.411.

The bill passed the House, but stopped there because the Harry Reid Democrats controlled the Senate. Let's give credit to those in Congress trying to uphold the law and ensure *some* level of accountability on behalf of the people.

Enemies of the Lord Jesus Christ have been gaining ground, and more citizens are being forced to choose God or government, to obey their consciences and the Bible or give in to an employer, union, bureaucrat, or judge on a power trip. In a 2004 speech in Dallas, Texas, entitled "The Final Moments of Crisis," Ambassador Alan Keyes declared:

> I don't believe for one instant that America ends up as some mediocrity in history. We are either going to be a commanding power for great good, as we have been, or a commanding power for great evil, as we must become if we do not succeed in mobilizing those communities who mean to stand for truth, and against those who have declared war upon God in our public life.[41]

May God help us in these last days to wake up and speak out. Contact your local and state representatives. When unelected judges get out of control, our elected representatives should be intervening to protect our rights and freedoms; if not, we must vote for others who will intervene and hold the judiciary accountable.

Has the conflict for the soul of America reached a turning point? Souls, truth, godliness, and righteousness are on the line, and our children are watching. Our freedoms will not last if the majority of Christians remain casual observers and spectators. Let's encourage each other in Christ to be active, effective citizens and servants of God.

> *To whom then will you liken God? Or what likeness will you compare with Him? He it is who reduces rulers to nothing, Who makes the judges of the earth meaningless* (Isaiah 40:18, 23). *They do not know the way of peace, And there is no justice in their tracks; They have made their paths crooked, Whoever treads on them does not know peace. Therefore justice is far from us, And righteousness does not overtake us; We hope for light, but behold, darkness, For brightness, but we walk in gloom* (Isaiah 59:8-9).

---

41   Mark I. Sutherland, *Judicial TYRANNY- the new kings of America?* (St. Louis, MO, AmeriSearch, 2005) p. 180.

CHAPTER 7

FROM ROE V. WADE TO KERMIT GOSNELL

"Christ died that we might live. Abortion kills so that someone might live differently."
—Author and Pastor John Piper

HOW ONE COURT CASE LED TO AMERICA'S HOLOCAUST

The billion-dollar abortion industry is one of the least regulated in America, and the shocking practices at Kermit Gosnell's Philadelphia clinic were one more example of disturbing operating procedures that are regularly overlooked. This chapter should stir up some righteous anger that will hopefully motivate us to pray and take action. Then in the next chapter, we'll focus on the personal anguish and the need for greater understanding and compassion toward women who have had abortions.

Kermit Gosnell is a depraved soul who performed close to 1,000 abortions per year during his forty-year killing spree. The reason *some* of us now know who Kermit Gosnell is might surprise you. He was not caught because of his complete lack of respect for human life, the fact he stored babies in freezers, or the multiple abortion-related reports and complaints filed about him. He was caught because he was illegally selling 200 prescriptions a day for narcotics! The Drug Enforcement Administration (DEA) received reports on his activity and raided the clinic.

What the DEA found was finally exposed. According to the grand-jury report, to say Gosnell's Philadelphia "clinic" was unsanitary would be an understatement. The place stunk of urine, flea-ridden cats defecated freely, and untrained staff wouldn't bother to wipe down bloody tables or clean rusty equipment. To reach quotas and make as much money as possible, many abortion clinics rush women in and out. One might ask 'how is this about women's health?'

Here are a few of the disturbing facts about Kermit Gosnell's killing clinic:

- The remains of 45 babies were found by authorities at the Philly clinic.

- Gosnell preyed mostly on poor and minority women.

- At least one fetus over 16 weeks old was found in a freezer.

- The bigger the baby, the more Gosnell charged.

- One forty-one-year-old victim of a botched abortion, Karnamaya Mongar, died because the clinic was so crammed with junk, it took paramedics twenty minutes to find their way out.

- Gosnell collected baby feet in jars.[42]

The truth about this alarming story, one of the most horrific killing sprees in recent history, was covered up, minimized, or omitted altogether by the media. Are you surprised? The 2013 murder trial of abortionist Kermit Gosnell has cemented forever the fact the pro-abortion media has chosen ideology over journalism. Some liberals in the media even admitted they didn't want to report on the Gosnell story because they felt it would hinder progress for abortion rights.

Gosnell's clinic didn't earn the label "House of Horrors" for nothing. During the trial, Steven Massof, a former Gosnell assistant, who did not even have a medical license, described how he jabbed scissors into the backs of babies' necks or snipped their spinal cords to kill them. Calling it a "beheading," Massof stated, "It is separating the brain from the body."

One young woman who worked at the Gosnell clinic as a teenager testified she saw a baby's chest continue to move even after the gruesome snipping procedure Gosnell used to end the baby's life. Convicted

---

42   Jonah Goldberg, "Kermit Gosnell and Abortion's Darkest Side",
      4/17/2013 http://www.nationalreview.com/article/345722/
      kermit-gosnell-and-abortion%E2%80%99s-darkest-side.

of three counts of first degree murder and sentenced to life in prison, Kermit Gosnell is America's most unknown serial killer.

I have not yet heard an acceptable answer to this question: What is the moral difference between killing a living, newborn baby and killing a baby inside a mother's womb ninety seconds from being born? The fact that one is legal in America and the other act is illegal does not answer the question. Are both babies human or not?

For the record, according to the grand jury report, the reason Pennsylvania's Department of Health failed to inspect any of the state's twenty-two abortion facilities in seventeen years was because officials thought inspections would put "a barrier up to women" seeking abortions.[43]

Tragic, yes, but let's acknowledge the good that has resulted from the Gosnell case. Because *some* of the truth has been exposed about abortion atrocities in the last several years, over seventy pro-life policies have now become law in many American states. Several polls show fewer and fewer voters are calling themselves pro-choice. In addition, an overwhelming majority of Americans not only favor abortion restrictions, but people support restrictions much earlier during pregnancy. In June 2013, the U.S. House of Representatives passed the Pain-Capable Unborn Child Protection Act.

Digging deeper in search of more truth, Family Research Council's Marriage and Religion Institute (MARRI) analyzed abortion data from a recent five-year period in which nearly 90% of women having had one or more abortions have also had three or more male sexual partners. Not surprisingly, the report also found women are more likely to have abortions the more sexual partners they have, as well as the younger a girl is when she starts having sex.

Cohabitation is also closely related to abortion, but one of the more eye-opening statistics from the survey is 99% of women who have aborted have used contraceptives. Translation: contrary to liberal talking points, birth control often fails miserably in preventing pregnancy and abortions.

---

43 Arina Grossu, "Gosnell's depravity brings pro-life awakening," Washington Times, 2/17/2014, http://www.washingtontimes.com/news/2014/feb/17/ grossu-gosnells-depravity-and-the-pro-life-awakeni/?page=1#ixzz31315BIqR.

HOW IT HAPPENED: THE SUPREME COURT'S WORST DECISION

Though sexual promiscuity, feminism, and abortions were increasing prior to the case, *Roe v. Wade* truly was a catalyst of epic proportions. The Supreme Court's controversial 1973 decision still astounds some of us. Taking a different angle on this issue, I'd like to provide some pertinent excerpts from the dozens of pages of actual case transcripts, arguments, and the reasoning the Supreme Court gave to justify their ruling. Some of this dialogue will amaze you.

Sarah Weddington represented Norma McCorvey (Jane Roe) and Robert Flowers represented Henry Wade and the State of Texas. We'll look at statements from multiple Justices as well. In opening arguments for *Roe v. Wade*, Weddington stated:

> A pregnancy to a woman is perhaps one of the most determinative aspects of her life. It disrupts her body. It disrupts her education. It disrupts her employment. And it often disrupts her entire family life.

Calling the precious gift of human life a disruption reminds me of the worldview of President Obama, especially when he stated if one of his daughters got pregnant, "I don't want them punished with a baby."

During arguments in *Roe v. Wade*, Associate Justice Potter Stewart asked how the question of abortion be decided.

> Is it a legal question? A constitutional question? A medical question? A philosophical question? Or, a religious question? Or what is it?

To reach the ruling they did, the Court obviously chose not to decide this case based on the Bible and God's Law. Moreover, today's science and biology has proven the fetus in a mother's womb is human, a human baby. Personhood has been clearly established.

As you read the following case discussions, keep in mind back in 1973 they did not have ultrasound, sonograms, and other technology:

JUSTICE BLACKMUN: Let me ask another question, then. Last June 29th this Court decided the capital punishment cases.

MRS. WEDDINGTON: Yes, sir.

JUSTICE BLACKMUN: Do you feel that there is any inconsistency in the Court's decision in those cases outlawing the
death penalty, with respect to convicted murderers and rap-
ists at one end of life's span; and your position in this case,
at the [beginning] other end of life's span?

MRS. WEDDINGTON: I think **had it been established that
the fetus was a person**, under the Fourteenth Amendment,
or under constitutional protection, then there might be a dif-
ferentiation. In this case, it has never been established that
the fetus is a person, or that it's entitled to the Fourteenth
Amendment rights, or the protection of the Constitution. It
would be inconsistent to decide that, after birth, various classifications of persons would be subject to the death penalty
or not but here we have a person—the woman—entitled to
fundamental constitutional rights, as opposed to the fetus
prior to birth, where there is no establishment of any kind of
Federal constitutional rights.

JUSTICE BLACKMUN: Well, do I get from this, then, that
your case depends primarily on the proposition that the fetus
has no constitutional rights?

MRS. WEDDINGTON: It depends on saying that the woman
has a fundamental constitutional right; and that the State has
not proved any compelling interest for regulation in the area.
Even if the Court, at some point, determined the fetus to be
entitled to constitutional protection, you would still get back
into the weighing of one life against another.

JUSTICE STEWART: **That's what's involved in this case?
Weighing one life against another?**

MRS. WEDDINGTON: No, Your Honor. I say that would be
what would be involved, if the facts were different and the
State could prove that there was a "person" for the constitutional right.

JUSTICE STEWART: **Well, if – if it were established that**

an unborn fetus is a person, with the protection of the Fourteenth Amendment, you would have almost an impossible case here, would you not?

MRS. WEDDINGTON: I would have a very difficult case.

JUSTICE STEWART: I'm sure you would. So, if you had the same kind of thing, you'd have to say that this would be the equivalent – after the child was born, if the mother thought it bothered her health any having the child around, she could have it killed. Isn't that correct?

… CHIEF JUSTICE BURGER: Could Texas constitutionally, in your view, declare that – by statute, that the fetus is a person, for all constitutional purposes, after the third month of gestation?[44]

… JUSTICE BLACKMUN: Well, I think – I'm just wondering if there isn't basic inconsistency there. And let me go back to something else that you said. Is it not true – or is it true, that the medical profession itself is not in agreement as to when life begins?

MR. FLOWERS: I think that's true, sir. But, from a layman's standpoint, medically speaking, we would say that at the moment of conception from the chromosomes, every potential that anybody in this room has is present – from the moment of conception.

… JUSTICE WHITE: Well, if you're correct that the fetus is a person, then … the State would have great trouble permitting an abortion, would it [not]?

MR. FLOWERS: Yes, sir.

JUSTICE WHITE: In any circumstances?

MR. FLOWERS: It would, yes, sir.

---

44   TRANSCRIPT: Roe v. Wade Re-Argument October 11, 1972 pp. 9-10, http://www.scribd.com/doc/68497271/Transcript-Roe-v-Wade-Re-Argument-Oct-1972.

JUSTICE WHITE: To save the life of a mother, or her health, or anything else?

MR. FLOWERS: Well, there would be the balancing of the two lives, and I think that –

JUSTICE WHITE: Well, what would you choose? **Would you choose to kill the innocent one**, or what?

MR. FLOWERS: Well, in our statute, the State did choose that way, Your Honor.

JUSTICE MARSHALL: Well –

MR. FLOWERS: The protection of the mother.

JUSTICE MARSHALL: Well, did the State of Texas say that if it is for the benefit of the health of the wife to kill the husband?

MR. FLOWERS: I'm sorry; I didn't understand your question.

JUSTICE MARSHALL: Could Texas say, if it confronts the situation, for the benefit of the health of the wife, that the husband has to die? Could they kill him?

MR. FLOWERS: I wouldn't think so, sir.

… JUSTICE MARSHALL: Well, if a doctor performs a brain operation and does it improperly, he could be guilty of manslaughter, couldn't he?

MR. FLOWERS: I would think so, if he was negligent.

JUSTICE MARSHALL: Well, why wouldn't you charge him with manslaughter if he commits an abortion?

… MR. FLOWERS: Well, … Here's what [Texas state] 1195 says – provides: "Whoever shall, during the parturition of the mother, destroy the vitality or life in a child in a state of being born, before actual birth … and before actual birth – which child would have otherwise been born alive, shall be confined to the penitentiary for life, or not less than five years."

JUSTICE MARSHALL: What does it mean?

MR. FLOWERS: I would think that –

JUSTICE STEWART: **That it is an offense to kill a child in the process of childbirth?**

MR. FLOWERS: Yes, sir. It would be immediately before childbirth, or right in the proximity of the child being born.

JUSTICE MARSHALL: Which is not an abortion.

MR. FLOWERS: Which is not – would not be an abortion, yes, sir. You're correct, sir.

JUSTICE MARSHALL: **It would be homicide.**

MR. FLOWERS: **Gentlemen, we feel that the concept of a fetus being within the concept of a person, within the framework of the United States Constitution and the Texas Constitution, is an extremely fundamental thing.**[45]

... I believe that the Court must take these – the medical research – and apply it to our Constitution the best they can. I said I'm without envy of the burden that the Court has. I think that possibly we have an opportunity to make one of the worst mistakes here that we've ever made, from the – I'm sorry.

... JUSTICE MARSHALL: Is there any medical testimony of any kind that says that a fetus is a person at the time of inception?

... MR. FLOWERS: ... Perhaps it would be better left to that legislature. There they have the facilities to have some type of medical testimony brought before them, and the opinion of the people who are being governed by it.

... JUSTICE STEWART: Well, if you're right that an unborn fetus is a person, then you can't leave it to the legislature to play fast and loose dealing with that person. In other words,

---

45 TRANSCRIPT: Roe v. Wade Re-Argument October 11, 1972 pp. 12-14, http://www. scribd.com/doc/68497271/Transcript-Roe-v-Wade-Re-Argument-Oct-1972.

if you're correct, in your basic submission that an unborn fetus is a person, then [permissive] **abortion laws such as that which New York has are grossly unconstitutional, isn't it?**

MR. FLOWERS: That's right, yes.

JUSTICE STEWART: Allowing the killing of people.

MR. FLOWERS: Yes, sir.

… MRS. WEDDINGTON: Your Honor. I think Mr. Flowers well made the point when he said that no one can say "here is the dividing line; here is where life begins; life is here; and life is not over here." In a situation where no one can prove where life begins, where no one can show that the Constitution was adopted – that it was meant to protect fetal life, in those situations where it is shown that that kind of decision is so fundamentally a part of individual life of the family…

JUSTICE WHITE: Well, I gather **your argument is that a state may not protect the life of the fetus or prevent an abortion even at any time during pregnancy? Right up until the moment of birth?**

MRS. WEDDINGTON: At this time my point is that this particular statute is unconstitutional …We are here to advocate that the decision as to whether or not a particular woman will continue to carry or will terminate a pregnancy is a decision that should be made by that individual; that, in fact, she has a constitutional right to make that decision for herself; and that the State has shown no interest in interfering with that decision.

… JUSTICE BLACKMUN: To be sure that I get your argument in focus, if from your recent remarks that you are urging upon us abortion on demand of the woman alone, not in conjunction with her physician?

MRS. WEDDINGTON: I am urging that, in this particular context, this statute is unconstitutional. That in the *Baird versus Eisenstadt* case this Court said, "If the right of privacy is to mean anything, it is the right of the individual, whether married or single, to make determinations for themselves." It seems to me that you cannot say this is a woman of this particular doctor, and this particular woman.

… CHIEF JUSTICE BURGER: Thank you, Mrs. Weddington. Thank you, Mr. Flowers. The case is submitted.[46] (Bold emphasis mine)

There is obviously much more that could have been included here. However, for purposes of time, space, and having already understood the Bible teaches abortion is immoral, these were some of the more revealing arguments from *Roe v. Wade*.

Finally, let's take a close look at the Opinion of the Court, presented by Justice Blackmun.

We forthwith acknowledge our awareness of the sensitive and emotional nature of the abortion controversy, of the vigorous opposing views, even among physicians, and of the deep and seemingly absolute convictions that the subject inspires. One's philosophy, one's experiences, one's exposure to the raw edges of human existence, one's religious training, one's attitudes toward life and family and their values, and the moral standards one establishes and seeks to observe, are all likely to influence and to color one's thinking and conclusions about abortion.

In addition, population growth, pollution, poverty, and racial overtones tend to complicate and not to simplify the problem.

The problem is man justifying murder and playing God regardless of the "emotional nature" of the controversy. Also, I don't know what "racial overtones" he is referring to because Jane Roe was a white woman.

[Jane Roe] claimed that the Texas statutes were unconstitutionally vague and that they abridged her right of personal privacy, protected by the First, Fourth, Fifth, Ninth, and

---

46   TRANSCRIPTS, entire Roe v. Wade case, 1971-1972, http://www.aul.org/roe-v-wade-transcripts/.

Fourteenth Amendments. By an amendment to her complaint, Roe purported to sue "on behalf of herself and all other women" similarly situated.

Side note: By her own admission, Norma McCorvey was coerced into filing the suit under false pretenses, but this was not known by the court at the time.

[Dr.] James Hubert Hallford … alleged that … [the Texas abortion statutes] were vague and uncertain, in violation of the Fourteenth Amendment, and that they violated his own and his patients' rights to privacy in the doctor-patient relationship and his own right to practice medicine, rights he claimed were guaranteed by the First, Fourth, Fifth, Ninth, and Fourteenth Amendments.

Do you recall the specific mention of a right to privacy or even a "right to practice medicine" guaranteed by the Constitution? I don't recall either. Individual states have full authority over all individual licensing, including the medical profession.

Despite the use of the pseudonym, no suggestion is made that Roe is a fictitious person. For purposes of her case, we accept as true, and as established, her existence; her pregnant state, as of the inception of her suit in March 1970 and as late as May 21 of that year when she filed an alias affidavit with the District Court; and her inability to obtain a legal abortion in Texas.

…We feel it desirable briefly to survey, in several aspects, the history of abortion, for such insight as that history may afford us, and then to examine the state purposes and interests behind the criminal abortion laws.

We are told that, at the time of the Persian Empire, abortifacients were known, and that criminal abortions were severely punished. We are also told, however, that abortion was practiced in Greek times as well as in the Roman Era, and that "it was resorted to without scruple." The Ephesian, Soranos, often described as the greatest of the ancient gynecologists, appears to have been generally opposed to Rome's prevailing free-abortion practices.

So, they "feel it desirable" to go back thousands of years when – for purposes of this 1973 American court case – the decision to legalize abortion was supposed to have been based primarily on whether abortion was a protected right under the U.S. Constitution, ratified in 1789? What does the Persian Empire or Soranos have to do with this case?

But the most ridiculous diatribe is when Blackmum mentioned the first criminal abortion statute in England.

> Recently, [1967] Parliament enacted a new abortion law …
> The Act permits a licensed physician to perform an abortion.

Again, we're going back in world history to justify a court ruling in America? Didn't we fight the British Empire in the American Revolution and make a complete break from England, its government, and their laws? I thought so.

> An AMA [American Medical Association] Committee on Criminal Abortion was appointed in May, 1857 … It deplored abortion and its frequency and it listed three causes of "this general demoralization": The first of these causes is a widespread popular ignorance of the true character of the crime.

> **The Constitution does not explicitly mention any right of privacy.**

(Wait. What? There's a period at the end of the sentence; no "ifs, ands, or buts." However …)

> This right of privacy, whether it be founded in the Fourteenth Amendment's **concept of personal liberty** and restrictions upon state action, **as we feel it is**, or, as the District Court determined, in the Ninth Amendment's reservation of rights to the people, is broad enough to encompass a woman's decision whether or not to terminate her pregnancy.

> … On the basis of elements such as these, appellant and some might argue that the woman's right [to personal privacy] is absolute and that she is entitled to terminate her pregnancy

at whatever time, in whatever way, and for whatever reason she alone chooses.

There you have it. Now let's look at some opposing thoughts from Justice Rehnquist, who specifically mentioned paying a physician for a medical procedure is hardly "private," but a commercial transaction that normally falls under the regulatory power of the state. His response is self-explanatory:

REHNQUIST, J., Dissenting Opinion

The Court's opinion brings to the decision of this troubling question both extensive historical fact and a wealth of legal scholarship. While the opinion thus commands my respect, I find myself nonetheless in fundamental disagreement with those parts of it that invalidate the Texas statute in question, and therefore dissent.

…[T]he Court uses her complaint against the Texas statute as a fulcrum for deciding that States may [p172] impose virtually no restrictions on medical abortions performed during the first trimester of pregnancy. In deciding such a hypothetical lawsuit, the Court departs from the longstanding admonition that it should never "formulate a rule of constitutional law broader than is required by the precise facts to which it is to be applied."

I have difficulty in concluding, as the Court does, that the right of "privacy" is involved in this case. Texas, by the statute here challenged, bars the performance of a medical abortion by a licensed physician on a plaintiff such as Roe. A transaction resulting in an operation such as this is not "private" in the ordinary usage of that word. Nor is the "privacy" that the Court finds here even a distant relative of the freedom from searches and seizures protected by the Fourth Amendment to the Constitution, which the Court has referred to as embodying a right to privacy.

The decision here to break pregnancy into three distinct

terms and to outline the permissible restrictions the State may impose in each one, for example, partakes more of judicial legislation than it does of a determination of the intent of the drafters of the Fourteenth Amendment.

The fact that a majority of the States reflecting, after all, the majority sentiment in those States, have had restrictions on abortions for at least a century is a strong indication, it seems to me, that the asserted right to an abortion is not "so rooted in the traditions and conscience of our people as to be ranked as fundamental," Snyder v. Massachusetts, 291 U.S. 97, 105 (1934).

... To reach its result, the Court necessarily has had to find within the scope of the Fourteenth Amendment a right that was apparently completely unknown to the drafters of the Amendment.

... The Texas statute is struck down in toto, even though the Court apparently concedes that, at later periods of pregnancy Texas might impose these self-same statutory limitations on abortion. My understanding of past practice is that a statute found [p178] to be invalid as applied to a particular plaintiff, but not unconstitutional as a whole, is not simply "struck down" but is, instead, declared unconstitutional as applied to the fact situation before the Court.[47]

In other words, though Justice Rehnquist disagreed with the Court ruling, he believed the decision should have been applied only to the *Roe v. Wade* case. It should not have been used to ban all abortion laws in Texas and every other state in America! Sadly, we continue to live with the tragic consequences and the evil which has resulted from a flawed ruling.

That was over forty years ago; why has there been so little political and spiritual resistance from Christians against the immorality of ripping apart a baby in the womb? Why are most of us still silent? We

47   Roe v. Wade, 410 U.S. 113 (No. 70-18) Decided: January 22, 1973, http://www.law.cornell.edu/supremecourt/text/410/113#writing-USSC_CR_0410_0113_ZD.

can trust God with the outcome and we can pray until we're blue in the face. The Bible teaches faith without corresponding action is useless, and our faith is perfected when combined with our deeds (James 2:22, 26).

Not everyone can pray on a sidewalk in front of an abortion clinic or attend pro-life rallies, but every one of us can speak up, register to vote, and cast our ballot for God-fearing political candidates who respect and value all life.

If we don't do what is within our power to do, are we not being complicit to evil? When we choose *not* to decide or to ride the fence, we still have made a choice: indifference. With all the studies, facts, and technology available, it is indisputable abortion is a violent act and horrible evil – and according to God, a sin.

We examined key portions of the transcript from the *Roe v. Wade* decision, and the staggering loss of human life continues in America as an abortion occurs every twenty-six seconds. Millions of young girls and women suffer from the aftereffects of abortion in our "civilized" society. After reading this and the next chapter, further understanding the pain women face plus how damaging abortions are to women, you may ask in bewilderment how we can remain silent.

CHAPTER 8

THE ANGUISH OF ABORTION

Listen to Me, O islands, and pay attention, you peoples from afar. The LORD called Me from the womb; From the body of My mother He named Me.
Isaiah 49:1

"If you are considering an abortion, please understand that it will affect you for the rest of your life. It will not bring an end to your problems or your difficult situation. It will leave you feeling empty, guilty, and full of shame."
—Barbara G. *testimony*

EXPOSING THE PAINFUL TRUTH

Depending on how you look at it, Americans have come a long way. Fifty years ago, abortion was taboo and people were embarrassed to even say the word, let alone consider the act. Today, abortion is so common one out of every three women in America will have at least one abortion in her life. Abortion has gone from being prohibited to being a private matter to being an openly promoted money-making procedure. Millions, including large numbers of Christian women, have had abortions, so let's lay out some painful but neglected facts.

If you've had an abortion, do not give in to self-hatred; you are not alone and you can still be forgiven. Please turn back to God immediately. To every man and young boy, if you got someone pregnant outside marriage and have been an accomplice to abortion, you can also be forgiven if you repent. Abortion doctors and clinic workers can be forgiven, and every politician that has supported the life-destroying act of abortion can also be forgiven. Confess your sins, lay them at the foot of the cross, and walk away!

I pray you take this chapter to heart. God loves you and can use your testimony, but the consequences of your choices may not easily be forgotten or removed from your life. We're going to examine abortion from medical, moral, psychological, scientific, and spiritual aspects. My goal is to encourage healing and inform those who have carried a precious human life in their womb, but have no child to show for it due to their choice.

Taking responsibility for your actions is important, but don't be too hard on yourself. Long before the normalization of homosexuality in America; feminism, promiscuity, and rebellion helped lead to the sexual revolution, increased adultery, and the devaluing of human life. It started in the early 1900s and kicked into hyper-drive in the 1960s. On top of this, kids have to deal with many influences: pressure from peers, teachers, Hollywood, Planned Parenthood marketing campaigns, pop culture idiocy, and immoral role models.

With everything that is against young women today, it's that much more important for parents to be involved and aware of what's going on in their lives; this includes what they are being taught in school under the guise of "health" or sex education.

Looking at some current trends, a 2014 study by the Guttmacher Institute shows the abortion rate to be at its lowest point since 1973. Though it is good the rate has dropped to 16.9 abortions per 1,000 women, millions of lives are still being destroyed.

THERE IS PLENTY OF GOOD NEWS!

The number of Americans with pro-life views is increasing. Education, technology, and pro-life campaigns are exposing the dangers, health risks, and the immorality of a society that kills their offspring for convenience sake.

More young people today are growing up with a respect for life many of us did not have decades ago. Medical advances and ultrasound technology are responsible for much of this. Research proves more women who see sonogram pictures of their babies or hear the heartbeat prior to birth change their minds about having an abortion.

Today, any informed or remotely educated individual would admit the question about whether a child in the womb is human is settled science. (It is tragic we didn't take God's word for it from the beginning.) But we're still left with the problem of rampant sexual activity and fornication throughout our culture and even among many sitting in the pews every Sunday. Sex has been flaunted and promoted for decades in TV commercials and programming, in movies, video games, magazines, billboards, and now on the Internet.

Regardless of this ongoing challenge, we must pray more Christians and church leaders speak up about what the Bible teaches about marriage, sex, and the value of each life. We must work to educate, inform, and promote life-saving legislation by supporting pro-life candidates. Abortion is a fiscal, medical, moral, political, psychological, social, *and* spiritual issue.

The truth is the pro-life movement is growing, and more pro-life legislation has been passed in the last several years, helping limit the number of abortions. Great strides have been made in this fight for life in America. Since 1990, the number of abortion clinics has fallen by 73%. Even more revealing, a January 2014 Marist poll found that 84% of Americans think abortion should be restricted!

Dr. Janice Shaw Crouse, Executive Director and Senior Fellow of Concerned Women for America's Beverly LaHaye Institute (BLI), affirmed that concrete data shows the success of abstinence education, which not only limits the murder of babies, but also improves the future for many of our nation's teenagers. When Planned Parenthood's agenda is exposed, young girls win. Dr. Crouse added,

> ...[C]ommon sense legislation is exposing the profit-centered motivation of the abortion industry. Our young women are benefiting as fewer are engaging in too-early sex, fewer are choosing abortion, fewer doctors are willing to do abortions, and more clinics are closing.[48]

The U.S. Department of Education, Planned Parenthood, and the Democratic Party would deny or hide the fact abortion continues to decrease and public support for abortion is steadily declining. According

---

48   New Guttmacher Study Shows Abortion Rate at Lowest Point Since 1973; Concerned Women for America, Feb. 3, 2014, http://www.cwfa.org/new-guttmacher-study-shows-abortion-rate-at-lowest-point-since-1973/#sthash.RbCmNXmP.JIJNodLY.dpuf.

to Life Site News, Breitbart News, and others, eighty-seven abortion clinics either closed their doors or discontinued surgical abortions in 2013 alone.

Be encouraged – those on the side of God's Word, life, and women's health are winning far more battles in the war on the unborn. Let it be known, the pro-abortion movement would face serious defeats if it were not for the Obama administration digging their heels in to continue supporting Planned Parenthood with taxpayer dollars.

Just as encouraging is the recent increase of pro-life bills signed into law on the state level. In the last three years, the total number of abortion restrictions was more than the previous decade combined. A Guttmacher State Policy Review for the last four years reveals the total number of pro-life bills that were passed: It started slowly with 23 bills in 2010, then a whopping 92 bills in 24 states (2011), 43 bills in 19 states (2012), and 70 bills in 22 states (2013).[49]

That's 205 pro-life bills passed in three years! Clearly, hearts must change on the issue of life and, hopefully, on biblical values as well so keep praying. The best way to save more lives, affect culture, protect young girls, and increase awareness is through laws and policy.

If you don't think legislation and the political process is an important part of this battle, please consider a few possible reasons for such a jump in pro-life activity. In 2010, many Americans felt blindsided by the passage of ObamaCare, aka the Affordable Care Act, which did not receive one single Republican vote. In the midterm elections that November, Republicans were voted in to a record number of state legislatures which allowed them to pass bills that were not possible when pro-abortion Democrats held the majority.

Before the healthcare law was forced through Congress, expanding the role and control of government, many battles were fought over abortion policy. One debate about ObamaCare was over whether federal funds, our tax dollars, would help pay for abortions as part of the insurance requirements. The president vehemently denied this was the case.

Of course, we found out the truth *after* the bill was passed when

49   Gosnell's Depravity Brings Pro-Life Awakening, Washington Times, Feb. 17, 2014, http://www.washingtontimes.com/news/2014/feb/17/grossu-gosnells-depravity-and-the-pro-life-awakeni/.

people realized what was in the law. The actions and deception of a power-grabbing administration resulted in a landslide of epic proportions against them in those 2010 midterms and more recently in the 2014 midterm elections. Democrats lost a record number of seats leading to a Republican landslide and the passage of pro-life bills, some of which restricted insurance coverage of abortion under the new law. Don't tell me elections do not matter anymore.

FRAMING THE ABORTION ARGUMENT

The tragedy of abortion haunts women from all walks of life. Abortion advocates are spending millions to package their tired rhetoric and half-truths in cutting-edge advertising campaigns targeted to young women … Life is short. My mother died when I was 12. There's no guarantee that we're going to be here tomorrow … as a Christian, it will not be Barbra Streisand I'm standing in front of when I have to make an accounting for my life.

The early feminists were pro-life. And really, abortion is a huge disservice to women, but it hasn't been presented that way. I think pro-choice is a ridiculous name … I find it impossible to subscribe to a philosophy that believes the destruction of human life is a legitimate solution … In reality, most women "choose" abortion because they believe they have no other choice.

—Actress, author, and proud Mom, Patricia Heaton

The word *choice* has been used by the Left to imply freedom, when in fact it has been used to deny the right to life of an unborn child and shackle a woman psychologically. This redefinition has led to a disregard for life in general. Once the use of this term was allowed to become part of the political lexicon, our ability to defend babies was weakened. If our enemies can get us to define a battle using *their* terms and meanings, the conflict becomes more difficult.

Would you like coffee or tea, premium or unleaded, paper or plastic;

small, medium, or large? These are choices. A baby, once conceived in the womb, is not a choice.

Though many good nonprofit groups have been in the trenches fighting, the church generally has not been very active or outspoken about abortion. Many Christians refuse to touch the subject in public and on social media. Some of us would rather not acknowledge how gruesome an act ripping a baby apart in the womb happens to be – so we look the other way.

By our silence as well as avoiding the public debate over abortion, we let the other side win, and we all pay for it in one way or another. Activists and lobbyists for the abortion business will never stop pushing this culture of death.

Again, social issues and financial issues and political issues are *all moral* issues!

While we've been deciding if we should speak up and stand for life, Planned Parenthood and its president, Cecile Richards, are conducting business as usual. In just over three years, they have eliminated over one million lives in the womb, averaging 330,000 abortions every year. Although the group insists our tax dollars go to programs that improve women's health, Planned Parenthood does admit 93.8% of its "pregnancy services" involve abortion! Here are a few facts to remember when discussing this issue with friends and opponents.

- During fiscal year 2012-2013, Planned Parenthood reported receiving $540.6 million in taxpayer funding, or nearly $1.5 million per day.

- Planned Parenthood reported $58.2 million in excess revenue and more than $1.3 billion in net assets.

- In 2012, Planned Parenthood performed 327,166 abortions, a 2% drop from 2011, *but* 100,000 more abortions than they did 10 years ago!

- In 2012, prenatal care and adoption referrals accounted for only 5.6% (19,506) and 0.6% (2,197), respectively. An important ratio you can confidently cite is for every one adoption referral, Planned Parenthood performed 149 abortions.[50]

A worldview that can justify these numbers must out of necessity be opposed to the Bible because to support mass killing for the sake of money or convenience, a person and country must believe man is god, and there are no moral absolutes. This mindset is becoming more common among American elites, among the wealthy, and those in positions of power. Sadly, large percentages of youth have bought into this evil, godless philosophy.

How do some on the Left define life? In a 2014 interview, Planned Parenthood Action Fund President Cecile Richards said the lives of her three children began when she delivered them.[51] Really – life begins at delivery? Let's analyze this worldview.

She also said people hold different views on when life begins. So what?

It doesn't matter how many views there are! What matters are the biological facts and scriptural truth about when life begins and Who creates life. Either believe the Bible, or make up the rules on right and wrong. Life begins at conception according to the one true God – end of debate.

Let's dissect Richard's interview with Jorge Ramos on *Fusion*, a cable channel owned by ABC News and Univision. Show host Jorge Ramos asked Cecile Richards several times, "When does life start? When does a human being become a human being?"

She tried dodging the subject by arguing the question of when life begins is not relevant to the issue of abortion. (Huh?!) Richards also deflected by saying the question "will be debated through the centuries" and said when life begins is not part of the conversation about whether abortion should be legal or not.

"But for you, when is that point?" Ramos pressed.

Richards suggested every woman needs to make her own decision

50   Planned Parenthood Report: $540 Million in Tax Dollars, 327,000 Abortions, LifeNews.com, 12/11/13, http://www.lifenews.com/2013/12/11/planned-parenthood-report-540-million-in-tax-dollars-327000-abortions/.
51   Life Begins at Delivery, Planned Parenthood President Says, Feb. 28, 2014, http://www.christianpost.com/news/life-begins-at-delivery-planned-parenthood-president-says-video-115443/.

and Planned Parenthood wants all women to have "all their options for health care."

Ramos then asked a third time: "Why would it be so controversial for you to say when you think life starts?"

She finally explained,

> For me, *I'm the mother of three children. For me, life began when I delivered them.* They've been probably the most important thing in my life ever since. But that was my own personal decision (Emphasis mine).

SHOW ME THE MONEY

Ray Comfort is a well-known author and evangelist, founder of Living Waters Ministry, Way of the Master television program, and producer of documentaries such as *180 Movie*. Comfort explains how lucrative the big abortion business is and how money fuels their passion for death. He makes a shocking comparison when he says, "it's all legal, efficient, and done behind closed doors, just like the Holocaust." How's that for some perspective? Comfort states:

> With the efficiency of a drive-through, they will expedite the killing of your baby for just $765 for up to a 16-week-old child, but the price increases if the baby is over 19 weeks; you will be shelling out three times the amount, and paying a whopping $2,165. That's pretty good income for a few minutes of ripping off the arms, the legs, and head of a baby onto a table; checking the body parts to make sure they're all out, and then putting them in the trash.[52]

Sadly, it takes less than thirty minutes for an abortion doctor to complete the task. How on earth did human beings with hearts, souls, and consciences – in America – allow this slaughter to reach the level it's at today? More importantly, why do we allow it to continue unchecked? We must have fallen away from God. If only our side were as committed to the cause of life as they are to death.

The greatest destroyer of love and peace is abortion, which is

---

52   Ray Comfort, 2011 LivingWaters.com, http://store.livingwaters.com/
      index.php?option=com_k2&view=item&id=2789:hitler%E2%80%
      99s-best-kept-secret?&Itemid=353&lang=en.

war against the child. The mother doesn't learn to love, but kills to solve her own problems. Any country that accepts abortion is not teaching its people to love, but to use any violence to get what they want.
—Mother Theresa

Your hands made me and formed me. Give me understanding, that I may learn Your commandments (Psalm 119:73).

More children from the fit, less from the unfit – that is the chief aim of birth control . . . The undeniably feeble-minded should, indeed, not only be discouraged but prevented from propagating their kind.[53]
—Margaret Sanger

Many people forget Planned Parenthood's founder, Margaret Sanger, set out to use birth control "to create a race of thoroughbreds," as she put it, and to control the population in America. She had been writing about and promoting eugenics before the early 1920s. Sanger openly commissioned Adolf Hitler's top eugenicist, Dr. Ernst Rudin, to not only write for her *Birth Control Review* publication but to serve as an advisor to her organization! She supported Nazi Germany's infanticide program in the 1930s as well as Hitler's goal of Aryan white supremacy. Margaret Sanger believed it necessary to sterilize "genetically inferior races" and exterminate those considered "human weeds."

Abortion rates, particularly those from many of America's inner cities, should cause us to wonder if the original vision and work of Margaret Sanger to reduce minorities is becoming a reality right before our eyes. Sanger's *American Birth Control League* laid the groundwork for her first clinic in Harlem in 1929, an area of New York City heavily populated by blacks. Not many people have heard the truth about the dark history of Planned Parenthood.

Margaret Sanger's mission is not only being accomplished today, but continues to be promoted. Shocking new statistics show black and Hispanic populations taking the biggest hit. Is this not racism? Where are Al Sharpton and Jesse Jackson? Where's Oprah?

---

53   Margaret Sanger, Birth Control Review, May 1919, page 12.

Center for Disease Control and Prevention (CDC) numbers indicate the horrific fact that nearly 72% of black babies are aborted in Mississippi.[54] In February of 2014, CNS News also reported more heart-wrenching news. There are now more black babies aborted than born in New York City according to the NYC Department of Health and Mental Hygiene, Office of Vital Statistics. The number of black abortions in NYC is over 42% while Hispanics are not far behind at 31%.

The abortion figures are more staggering when you consider 82% of New York City abortions were done on black or Hispanic babies. In Georgia it was 73% and even in Texas, 64% of abortions are done on minorities.[55]

This begs the question: If the media, Hollywood, and Democrats are truly concerned about protecting women, why is there no outcry over this? Since wombs are dangerous places for black babies, isn't there a story on racism here? The media reports practically any other story remotely resembling a race issue, so why the silence on the one thing that should matter the most – life? Margaret Sanger sure would be proud of America today.

> Woe to those who call evil good, and good evil; Who substitute darkness for light and light for darkness; Who substitute bitter for sweet and sweet for bitter! Woe to those who are wise in their own eyes And clever in their own sight! Who justify the wicked for a bribe, And take away the rights of the ones who are in the right! (Isaiah 5:20-21, 23)

DECEIVING WOMEN: COVERING UP ABORTION TRAGEDIES

In early 2014, the liberal media ignored a major court case resulting in Planned Parenthood being ordered to pay two million dollars in a wrongful death settlement. Tonya Reaves, a twenty-four-year-old black woman, died at Northwestern Memorial Hospital after suffering

---

54   Michael W. Chapman, In Mississippi, 72% of the Babies Aborted Are Black, CNS News, 2/25/2014, http://www.cnsnews.com/news/article/michael-w-chapman/mississippi-72-babies-aborted-are-black.

55   Steven Ertelt, 82 Percent of Abortions in NYC, 64% in Texas Were on Black or Hispanic Babies, 12/4/13, http://www.lifenews.com/2013/12/04/82-percent-of-abortions-in-nyc-64-in-texas-were-on-black-or-hispanic-babies/.

an incomplete abortion. Cook County Circuit Court in Illinois ruled wrongful death because she did not receive proper treatment. Reaves died at Northwestern Memorial Hospital July 20, 2012, from uncontrolled bleeding at Planned Parenthood's Loop Health Center. She did not receive proper medical treatment, and the autopsy showed Reaves suffered from an incomplete, late-term abortion and perforated uterus.

There was a delay of over five hours in getting her to the hospital, followed by more delays in getting treated at Northwestern. Reaves' living son is now three years old and will receive $1,479,571.39 after attorneys get their cut. Payments begin when the boy turns eighteen. There was no proper media exposure of this tragedy and no consequences for Planned Parenthood after quietly paying out "hush money" to the victim's family.[56]

Other issues have been cited in the case, including the condition of the facility and the inexperience of the "surgical" staff performing abortions. Some reports reveal Reaves lay on the table, writhing and bleeding for hours before staff arranged to have her transported by ambulance to the hospital. They did *not* call 911! Tanya Reaves should be another face in the real "war on women." The media cover-up is not surprising when we understand their worldview and support of progressive politics. Abortion to them is some sort of sacrament.

They would like to believe the tragedy never happened. In any other situation in which there is a two-million-dollar court settlement, the story would surely make the news. I wonder what the Reaves family and others who have lost daughters due to botched abortions thought when President Obama asked for God's blessing on Planned Parenthood and the abortion industry? In the transcript of his two-page speech last year in Washington D.C., the president never once mentioned the word *abortion*. He used euphemisms, such as choice, contraceptive care, health care, and a right to privacy. He's just towing the ideological line.

The president praised Planned Parenthood for "the lives you've saved, women you've empowered, families that you've strengthened." Wait – saved lives? Families strengthened by *not* having children? In an article

---

56   Ben Johnson, Planned Parenthood to pay $2 million in 'wrong-
      ful death' of Tonya Reaves, 2/7/14, http://www.lifesitenews.com/news/
      breaking-planned-parenthood-to-pay-2-million-in-wrongful-death-of-tonya-rea.

on RedState.com, the last paragraph contained a warning to Obama and Richards that God's judgment will not be held back for much longer.

> Mr. Obama closed his speech by asking God's blessing upon Planned Parenthood and the work they do. I will close by asking God to forgive our nation for electing a man who calls evil good and good evil – a man whose whole agenda is a repudiation of the Judeo-Christian worldview and Scripture. "I tremble for my country when I reflect that God is just; that His justice cannot sleep forever." (Thomas Jefferson) Barack Obama and Cecile Richards should remember that as well.[57]

Another tragic abortion-related death took place after a counselor advised eighteen-year-old Marla Cardamone to abort her baby. Marla died at a Pennsylvania hospital from complications. Her mother, Deborah Cardamone, vowed to expose the truth and continues to fight for pro-life causes today. At Marla's viewing prior to the funeral, her parents requested an open casket even though Marla's face was still bruised and swollen. She hopes to raise awareness about the ongoing abortion industry cover-up and wants people to understand abortions may be legal, but they are not always safe. Mr. and Mrs. Cardamone even provided some graphic, heart-wrenching autopsy photos of Marla for pro-life websites.

You may be surprised to find out hundreds of women have died from abortions; they just don't get reported (See SafeandLegal.com). Deborah Cardomone approached Life Dynamics President, Mark Crutcher, to ask for help with getting the truth out. The pro-life movement hasn't had images such as Marla's to show the horrors and brutality of women being killed in America's abortion clinics. Crutcher and other pro-life leaders have vowed to let people see "what it looks like when women climb onto a [clinic] table in one of these places and end up on an autopsy table a few hours later."

In another case, eighteen-year-old, Holly Patterson from Livermore, California, entered a Planned Parenthood clinic in Hayward, California,

---

57 Kipling, President Obama asks for God's Blessing upon Planned Parenthood and the Abortion Industry: The Audacity of Evil and a Facade of Lies, 4/26/2013, http://www. redstate.com/diary/kipling/2013/04/26/president-obama-asks-for-gods-blessing-upon-planned-parenthood-and-the-abortion-industry/.

seeking a chemical abortion. The day after visiting Planned Parenthood, Holly experienced bleeding and pain and went to a local hospital where she was given painkillers. Three days later, she was admitted to the hospital but it was too late. She had taken abortion drug RU-486 and died seven days later as a result of an incomplete abortion causing a severe bacterial infection. According to the coroner, the cause of death was septic shock resulting from inflammation of the uterus from a drug-induced abortion.[58]

A state investigation found that Holly's death wasn't reported to the Food and Drug Administration (FDA) by either the hospital where she died or by Planned Parenthood. At the abortion clinic, Holly was given mifepristone, an abortion inducing drug. Mifepristone blocks progesterone, the hormone needed to carry a pregnancy to term. After Holly's death, the FDA changed mifepristone's black box warning label to add new information about the risk of serious bacterial infection, sepsis, bleeding, and death.

RU-486 is generally viewed as a safe alternative to surgical abortion, but Holly died tragically of a massive infection after taking the drug protocol. Monty Patterson, Holly's father, said she suffered in silence, and "I want to make sure no other women go through the same experience."

The figures are available; they're just not acknowledged or reported by the media. According to the FDA, there have been at least fifteen deaths and thousands of adverse events after women used the RU-486 regimen. This includes over 612 hospitalizations, 339 blood transfusions, and 256 infections including 48 "severe infections" as of a few years ago.

GRIEF, PAIN, DEPRESSION, REGRET

Also largely unreported is the fact abortion often causes women years of emotional pain, torment, and guilt. Many young women try to act normal and hide the fact that they are in pain, often experiencing severe trauma soon after receiving an abortion. Moreover, countless women have experienced increased alcohol or drug use and eating disorders. They suffer from depression and nightmares. They agonize

---

58   Teen Death Steers RU-486 Bill to Congress, Women's enews, 11/15/04, http://womense-news.org/story/reproductive-health/041115/teen-death-steers-ru-486-bill-congress#.U15Y_vldXEz.

with self-destructive behavior and suicidal thoughts or attempts. God help us help them!

There are two battles on this front and we should be engaged in both. We must raise awareness about biblical truth that God is the Author and Creator of *all* life. He values every single human being. Life begins at conception, and destroying innocent life is an immoral act against His law. Second, we must love, support, and care for women and young girls who have had abortions, pointing them to the forgiveness of Jesus Christ and loving arms of the Father. We also need to embrace and support struggling single moms, praying and caring for them however we can.

If you have had an abortion, here are some questions to consider: Would you now advise your best friend or sister *not* to have an abortion if she were considering it? If you were a Christian before having an abortion, has your relationship with God or with those in the church changed?

A young woman who gets pregnant is often confused and intimidated into aborting her baby through emotional, financial, or relational threats. According to a 2004 study on post-abortive women reported by the Medical Science Monitor, 64% of the women felt pressured to have an abortion. Sadly, an often-neglected subject is how women are affected *afterwards*. As many as 91% of all abortions cause severe psychological problems, both immediate and long-term, according to reports of the Department of Education and Alan Guttmacher Institute.

Approximately 40% of minors who've had an abortion don't tell their parents, and 51% of women having abortions are under twenty-five years old. This is another important reason to have open communication with your daughters. Conversely, in cases where young women do tell others about their abortion, they often try to act normal and hide the fact that they are unhappy or in any kind of pain. Many experience severe trauma soon after receiving an abortion. The following are post-abortion symptoms that may be experienced:

- Alcohol or drug use to distract from the pain; anger, anxiety (probably non-specific or in forms of a panic attack), abusive relationships (believing she doesn't deserve better).

- Denial or repression (the "pushing down" of intolerable emotions), depression, deterioration of self-worth/self-image, disruption in relationships (increasing inability to be intimate or social with friends and family), anger, violent behavior.

- Eating disorders, feelings of helplessness or powerlessness, flashbacks, grief, guilt, purposely having unprotected sex or increased sexual activity as self-punishment.

- Nightmares about a baby or babies crying, the same nightmare over and over; preoccupation with the abortion procedure or thoughts of babies.

- Regret, remorse, sadness to the point of inability to handle basic responsibilities, self-destructive behavior and suicidal thoughts or attempts; death.

In a study of post-abortion patients eight weeks after their abortion, researchers found 44% complained of nervous disorders, 36% had experienced sleep disturbances, 31% had regrets about their decision, and 11% had been prescribed psychotropic medicine by their family doctor.[59] A New Zealand study that tracked women for more than three decades discovered 42% of women who aborted experienced major depression.

According to Priscilla Coleman of Bowling Green State University,

> Women who have had an abortion have an 81% higher risk of subsequent mental health problems compared to women who have not had an abortion. Also, women who aborted have a 138% (another study showed 160%) higher risk of mental health problems compared to women who have given birth.

Tragically, many so-called "counselors" at abortion clinics downplay mental and physical health risks the majority of the time in order to sell customers abortions, not to mention the fact the procedure will violently end their child's life. My heart goes out to those who believe the godless lie that this "procedure" can be justified in any way.

---

59 Abortion Risks: A list of major psychological complications related to abortion, Elliot Institute, Afterabortion.org http://afterabortion.org/2011/abortion-risks-a-list-of-major-psychological-complications-related-to-abortion/.

BUILDING ON THE PRO-LIFE FOUNDATION

I came across a familiar Bible verse from the story of Mary that you and I have probably read dozens of times through the years during Christmas. But something jumped out at me this time when I read Luke 1:43-44:

> But why am I so favored, that the mother of my Lord should come to me? As soon as the sound of your greeting reached my ears, the baby in my womb leaped for joy (NIV).

Notice babies in the womb are able to sense such feelings as "joy."

It is also indisputable and documented that babies in the womb have a developed nervous system and feel pain. How irrational to think a baby senses or feels nothing until the very moment they are delivered, and then all of a sudden upon seeing daylight or when the umbilical cord is cut, pain receptors kick in. Abortion mills such as Planned Parenthood do not give a baby in the womb pain medication before they are destroyed.

Here is some eye-opening information about newly *conceived* babies:

- Her DNA, everything she will grow into, was fully present at the moment of conception.

- Her heart began to beat eighteen days after conception.

- Her brainwaves were detectable forty days (six weeks) after conception.

- Your baby could move at six weeks.

- She could suck her thumb (and hiccup!) at seven weeks.

- Eight weeks after conception, all of her major organs had developed.

- Your baby's respiratory system began to function, and she began to breathe amniotic fluid at nine weeks.[60]

PERSPECTIVE OF AN ABORTION SURVIVOR

I was blessed to interview Kim Pearson, living proof that God has a plan for every human life. Through an abortionist's mistake, Kim survived.

---

60   http://www.selfevidenttruth.org/pregnant.html.

Originally from the Detroit, Michigan, area, Kim's mother became pregnant during her senior year in high school. She was ashamed and quit school. Being pregnant and unmarried was frowned upon at that time. Her mother kept Kim even though their home environment was not ideal.

Kim was sexually abused by her stepfather when she was only four years old, so she went to live with her grandmother, a strong Christian woman, who took her to prayer meetings at a Pentecostal church. Being at church gave Kim some comfort and would later give her some understanding about God that she would desperately need. Her parents divorced when she was thirteen years old, and because of constant physical and mental abuse by her stepfather, Kim resorted to drugs, which he gladly introduced her to.

Kim sank into depression. About four years later when Kim was seventeen, she learned she was an abortion survivor. Heartbroken after finding out her Mom intended to abort her, Kim remembers:

> That's when I started hearing the lies of the enemy such as "nobody wants you." Rejection is an ugly tool of the devil, and I battled depression for years because of this.

She became pregnant by a boyfriend, had her first child, and considered giving him up for adoption to her mom and new dad. Then Kim found out Josh, her newborn son, had jaundice, and Kim decided to keep the baby. She and her boyfriend planned a wedding but cancelled it six days before the ceremony, because, as Kim explains, she was messed up at the time and very confused.

She got pregnant again less than two years later, made an appointment for an abortion, and went to a Fourth of July parade in town to try to forget her troubles. Partying with friends and watching the parade, she saw a float approach with a sign that said, **"Abortion: Thou Shalt Not Murder."**

The second she read the sign, Kim thought, "I couldn't go through with it," so she cancelled the appointment for the abortion. Here she was, a single mom with a very young son, wondering how she was going to make it, but somehow she thought God would come through for her. Kim confessed:

I know myself well enough that if I had gone through with
the abortion, I would have been suicidal. I really don't think
I could have lived with myself.

Today, her daughter is a beautiful, intelligent, talented young
Christian woman. If you're curious about Kim's mother – she is also
a Christian now, and they have a strong relationship today. They pray
together and can talk openly about the past without dwelling on it.
Kim has had a third child, Michael, and considers herself blessed by
the gifts God has given her.

God used my children to save my life; they are my jewels and
joy; I can't imagine what I would do without them.

I asked her what she would tell a confused young woman today who
has already gone through an abortion:

Don't look back except to heal and to help someone else out,
but keep your thoughts and your heart fixed on Jesus. He is
our only source of help and healing. He alone can deliver
you from the pain or bondage of an ugly past. To walk in the
fruits of the Holy Spirit, we must keep our eyes fixed on Jesus
and not on our past.

We ended the interview with Kim sharing one of her four favorite
Scripture passages in the Bible, Psalm 139:14-16.

*I will give thanks to You, for I am fearfully and wonderfully
made; Wonderful are Your works, And my soul knows it very
well. My frame was not hidden from You, When I was made in
secret, And skillfully wrought in the depths of the earth; Your
eyes have seen my unformed substance; And in Your book were
all written, The days that were ordained for me, When as yet
there was not one of them.*

PRO-LIFE EXCEPT IN CASES OF RAPE?

Next, meet Rebecca Kiessling. She was adopted shortly after her birth
and grew up with a deep longing to know the truth about her biological mother. When she was eighteen, she learned that she was conceived
out of a brutal rape at knifepoint by a serial rapist. Until then, Rebecca

never fathomed abortion or rape would ever be issues she would be concerned about, but suddenly she could almost hear the echoes of people who claim to be pro-life: "Well, except in cases of rape." Sadly, some are adamant, saying "*especially* in cases of rape."

She felt as if people who didn't even know her were standing in judgment of her life, "so quick to dismiss it just because of how I was conceived." No one should have to justify their existence or prove whether they are worthy of living or not. Moreover, no one should decide who is allowed to live or who doesn't get to live. We saw this in Hitler's Germany and nearly experienced the same in America thanks to the eugenics efforts of Margaret Sanger and others. This became very personal to Rebecca:

> Please understand that whenever you identify yourself as being "pro-choice," or whenever you make that exception for rape, what that really translates into is you being able to stand before me, look me in the eye, and say to me, "I think your mother should have been able to abort you." That's a pretty powerful statement. I would never say anything like that to someone. I would never say to someone, "If I had my way, you'd be dead right now." But that is the reality with which I live.

To anyone who might say Rebecca was "lucky" to be born, let it be known the fact she is alive and well is because abortion was illegal in Michigan at the time her mother became pregnant. Similar to the sign Kim Pearson saw at that Fourth of July parade, Rebecca is grateful to people who fight the public pro-life battles in our society and to those who vote against abortion – even in cases of rape – in elections. "I wasn't lucky, I was protected," she declares.

What's one of the most significant things Rebecca has learned? God the Father in heaven is her Creator; a rapist did not create her. The Bible teaches that God is a father to the fatherless (Psalm 68:5) and *Though my father and mother forsake me, the Lord will receive me* (Psalm 27:10 NIV). Rebecca explains:

> We are told in the New Testament it is in the spirit of adoption that we are called to be God's children through Christ

our Lord ... The truth is that you don't have to prove your worth to anyone, and if you really want to know what your value is, all you have to do is look to the Cross because that's the price that was paid for your life! That's the infinite value God placed on your life! He thinks you are pretty valuable and so do I. Won't you join me in affirming others' value as well, in word and in action?[61]

TWO MORE HEARTBREAKING STORIES

Tana (last name withheld) was a nineteen-year-old woman from Wisconsin. She thought that the man she was dating at the time would marry her, support her through pregnancy, and help raise their child. Instead, he offered to pay for an abortion. She "felt incredibly angry with him, but went ahead with the abortion." This is how strongly she feels about her experience:

> I have never been the same. For years I hated myself, and I cried myself to sleep many nights. Sometimes I woke up to the sound of a baby crying. But there was no baby ... only a sad, sad dream. I thought I was going crazy. I suffered for seven years before getting to the point where I was ready to get help. I found hope and healing through an abortion recovery group. There I shared with others who had many of the same problems I did. Together, we grieved the loss of our children and I worked toward healing. Although I still feel regret over my decision, I have been able to forgive my former boyfriend and recover from the pain of the abortion. I hope you will read this ... and reach out for help.

Finally, Marianne Anderson is a nurse who worked at Indiana's largest abortion facility because she once thought she could help keep women safe. A former employee of Planned Parenthood, in early 2014 she went public with the horrors she witnessed at the successful abortion business during her time there. Anderson now admits, over two years after leaving, she is still haunted by the suction machines the doctors

---

61   Rebecca Kiessling, testimony, http://www.rebeccakiessling.com/index.html.

used – especially when they had trouble locating all of the baby's body parts: "It just made me sick to my stomach."

Anderson explained how much pressure was on young women to go through with an abortion because workers were told by headquarters they had to reach a certain quota of abortions per month to keep the business open. Employees were also threatened to be sent home early or have their hours cut if they didn't sell enough abortions. Some doctors would become impatient when "some girls would start crying on the table" during the procedures. They would be told to sit still and one doctor even scolded confused young women, saying, "You chose to be here."

Marianne Anderson said the overall experience of working for Planned Parenthood was "absolutely miserable."

> It was a money-grubbing, evil, very sad, sad place to work .
> . . I was always getting in trouble for talking too long to the
> girls, asking if they were sure they wanted to do this.[62]

Anderson was fired by Planned Parenthood and immediately hired as a nurse by Community North Hospital in Indianapolis. She now loves her job and gets to work with "wonderful Christian people." However, the real war on women lives on in Planned Parenthoods across America and in other abortion mills, funded by our confiscated tax dollars, supported by a corrupt government, and protected by a complicit media.

CONCLUSION: PLEASE CHOOSE LIFE

Abortion in America has created a culture that disregards the dignity and value of human life, endangers women, and demeans motherhood. Our sexually permissive and progressive culture encourages young women and teenage girls and boys to be sexually active. Those who have had abortions need our prayers, not our judgment. Being a product of America's secular culture, post-abortive women, especially religious women, suffer enough for their sin. They first need God's forgiveness; they then need to learn how to forgive themselves.

Christians can and should promote healing and hope for women

---

62   Kirsten Anderson, Former Planned Parenthood Worker: 'It was a money-grubbing, very evil, sad place to work,' Life Site News, 2/14/2014, https://www.lifesitenews.com/news/former-planned-parenthood-worker-it-was-a-money-grubbing-evil-very-sad-sad.

who have had abortions. We can also raise more awareness about this awful act which should be illegal. However, restricting the murder of the unborn is not enough because the heart of mankind is bent toward evil and the promotion of promiscuity will continue.

We hear little talk of purity and self-restraint. The teaching of biblical principles and abstinence education in churches, schools, and society is vital to effect positive change. Stop messing around, yes. Limit abortions, yes. Vote for pro-life candidates, yes. Stop funding Planned Parenthood with our tax dollars, yes! But we also need to remember the power of prayer and true, caring Christianity. People may not respond to debates, laws, or rules, but many will – eventually – respond to genuine love and truth.

Saving young people from drowning is one thing; finding out *why* so many are drowning and working to prevent them from reaching the point where they are thrashing around in the water in a desperate panic is just as important. Churches and parents need to get back to the basics: Model Christian morality and help young people counteract culture by teaching them the Word of God. This will require discipline. We were all young once and know the evil, worldly lures of peer pressure, public schools, and pop culture.

Are we willing to confront abortion defenders and speak about some of these facts? Will we do a better job promoting the truth that every baby is a gift from God, created in His image and has value? We need to reach people with the message "every single life matters." The root of this culture of death and of every problem is sin, and the only solution is Jesus Christ.

From this point forward, we can no longer say we did not know.

> Now the word of the LORD came to me saying; "Before I formed you in the womb I knew you, And before you were born I consecrated you (Jeremiah 1:4-5).

> Can a woman forget her nursing child, and have no compassion on the son of her womb? Even these may forget, but I will not forget you (Isaiah 49:15).

> [God] set me apart, even from my mother's womb, and called me through His grace (Galatians 1:15).

CHAPTER 9

THE CULT OF LIBERALISM

*For no man can lay a foundation other than the one which is
laid, which is Jesus Christ.*
1 Corinthians 3:11

*For this reason we also constantly thank God that when you
received the word of God which you heard from us, you accepted
it not as the word of men, but for what it really is, the word of
God, which also performs its work in you who believe.*
1 Thessalonians 2:13

A THREAT WITHIN THE CHURCH

Americans are divided over moral issues, but our greater concern
is that the church is divided as well. Some Christians have bought
into the progressive politics of Planned Parenthood and now support
abortion. There is confusion about marriage as well. Many in our society live as if the Ten Commandments are ten suggestions. Shouldn't
the faith and morality of those within church walls be vastly different
from those in culture?

Barna Research recently revealed that 34% of American adults believe
moral truth is absolute, with the lowest percentage of believers being
between eighteen and twenty-five years old. The number of Christians
who believe in moral absolutes is also decreasing – including those who
believe abortion, adultery, homosexuality, and idolatry are sins. We are
not so separate from the world after all.

Earlier we began answering the question "how did the diluting of
Scripture, progressivism, and liberalism find its way into the church?" For
our purposes, we may define liberalism as "a philosophy or movement
toward humanism, science, and socialism and away from traditional

religion; emphasis on freedom *from* authority and fundamentalism, esp. individual freedom; believing the goodness of human beings rather than acknowledging God."

Not much difference exists between someone who is liberal and someone who is progressive, and often the words are interchangeable. A liberal generally favors less moral restraint and higher taxes; a progressive supports government power. Progressive Christianity leans toward economic Marxism and allows for political activism and government endorsed social justice, placing emphasis on global efforts to manage the earth. Many progressive Christians support Universalism or collective salvation. This departure from biblical truth minimizes scriptural authority and the reality of hell, teaching that entire cultures and societies will be saved – regardless of individual repentance and faith.

We should not be surprised at the sharp divide in many churches and denominations over the Bible, sound doctrine, Sola Scriptura, and moral absolutes because Liberalism has officially invaded Christianity. We can call it a revival of post modernism, modern theology, liberation theology, social theology, or even neo-orthodoxy; but disciples of these teachings can be found in most churches. The apostle Paul warned about them because some appear to be believers, *holding to a form of godliness, although they have denied its power; Avoid such men as these* (2 Timothy 3:5).

Why refer to Liberalism as a cult?

Political liberalism is one thing; we know exactly where anti-Christian, anti-American folks stand by the politics they endorse, and they make no claim to have the same God or morality you and I have. But religious liberals are dangerous because they generally believe the same thing as leftists and yet claim to be Christian. They often use the same terminology, but have very different meanings from what traditional Bible-believing Christians hold to be true.

Furthermore, where theology is concerned, most of us know the difference between a Mormon, Muslim, Wiccan, Jehovah's Witness, Unitarian Universalist, or a New Age mystic, and a true Christian. We can see them coming so to speak. Many religious liberals, however, have assimilated into American Christianity. Some may not even realize the error of their ways while others are emergent leaders having set out to divide and deceive believers.

We can define a cult in three ways. (1) A particular system of religious worship or spiritual beliefs, especially an informal or nontraditional belief system regarded by others as false, misguided, extremist, or unorthodox. (2) A group or sect bound together by veneration or worship of the same thing, person, or ideal. (3) Idolization of somebody or something; an extreme or excessive admiration for a person, philosophy of life, or activity.

Cults often add beliefs, requirements, or teachings that are not found in God's Word, or they remove beliefs, requirements, or teachings. The Bible contains strict warnings against doing so. A cult usually has a charismatic, popular, or authoritarian leader or structure. In order to achieve salvation, acceptance, or good standing with God, cults tend to emphasize and require good works or practices based on man's efforts.

Specific to our context, a cult is simply a religious individual or group believing or defending doctrines other than the central or essential teachings of Christianity clearly defined in the Bible. Many liberal Christians deny the authority of God's Word, suggesting the Bible is fallible, but they try to retain or profess many of the values found within Christianity. Some downplay, ignore, or flat out deny many foundational doctrines of historical, traditional Christianity. Their attack on truth is most concerning as they reject the reliability and historical accuracy of the Bible.

Evangelical Christian theologian, pastor, and author, Francis A. Schaeffer wrote:

> Any denomination or parachurch group that forsakes inerrancy will end up shipwrecked. It is impossible to prevent the surrender of other important doctrinal teachings of the Word of God when inerrancy is gone.

In the case of liberal church leaders, the New Testament refers to them as wolves in sheep's clothing. With the departure from sound doctrine, we've seen the stage set for many professing believers to accept false teachings and fall away. The good news is that this apostasy is prophetic and must occur to usher in the end times. The bad news is it happened so gradually many Christians never saw it coming, so they went along with the modern ideas and teachings.

Over the last two centuries some have tried to sound the alarm and warn believers in America to repent, return to Christ, and stay true to the faith. Others have been concerned about the poisoning of the church. While Jesus said *whoever has ears to hear, let them hear* (Mark 4:9 NIV), we have to wonder why these warnings have mostly fallen on deaf ears.

In a 1987 sermon, Apologist Dr. Walter Martin, founder of the Christian Research Institute and author of *The Kingdom of the Cults*, said:

> What is the great danger in the Christian church today? Is it from the psychologists … psychiatrists … sociologists? No. The danger to the church today, whatever the denomination, is the person who wears the cloth of Christ; the person who wears the white collar or the cross and who stands behind the sacred desk [pulpit] and who is unfaithful to the Word of God… The corrupt and apostate shepherds who infest our theological seminaries and our colleges, and fill our pulpits across the United States and Canada; who know not God, do not believe the gospel of Jesus Christ, and will stand in the way of anybody that wants to preach it. That is the ultimate danger to the church because it is inside the church. The cancer is within, it eats away and we don't recognize it. Or, when we do recognize it, we don't do anything about it because we're afraid that people will be offended."[63]

Martin has helped equip believers through his ministry and writings. When he refers to liberal Christians as dangerous and insidious, we need to take his warning seriously. Emerging churches have merged with secular culture and politics, and have submerged from the solid foundation of biblical teaching.

Immediately after Jesus told His followers the way to life was a narrow one, He cautioned them to *Beware of false prophets* and also said, *you will recognize them by their fruits* (Matthew 7:13-20 ESV). He instructs believers to observe what they produce. The result of what we see from today's emergent church teachings is a church becoming

---

63   Dr. Walter Martin, "The Cult of Liberal Theology," 1987, http://www.youtube.com/watch?v=qduSN8G7-Xw.

more like the world. A little yeast can work through an entire batch of dough. Nearly three decades ago, Dr. Martin declared the liberal church movement an "all-pervading cult that's loose in the United States right at this moment."

Your church or denomination is not entirely safe and has probably been compromised to some degree. Be on guard in your local church because no organization made up of imperfect people is immune from false believers and teachings. Liberals have infected many church groups and nonprofits. They have been deceived and need the truth to be saved.

Since the early 1900s, a perfect storm had been brewing in America, paving the way for emergent teachings and liberal leaders. Then along came the hippie counter-culture and the flower-power days of the 1960s, a movement based on rebellion against authority that promoted drugs, peace ("Make love, not War"), and free love (sex without consequences). Absolute truth was discounted and biblical standards were questioned and labeled as too rigid.

As an outreach to lost, unsaved people, some churches responded with the "come as you are" movement in the 1970s which welcomed many hippies into church. This was not a bad idea, but many churches were not ready for the numbers of potential new converts. As a result, little follow-up and practically no equipping of new Christians took place – a problem we still deal with today. Thinking they were saved, many went right back into the world without being convicted to change their habits and pursue holiness. Therefore, their lives were not built upon the rock of Scripture and its application, and many fell away.

Jesus Christ would probably agree with the idea of inviting lost people to "come just as you are" to church; the difference is He loves us too much to leave us that way. The process of discipling is crucial to build strong Christians and families. Growing and maturing in Christ along with sanctification – a purposeful and decisive shift away from the world's ways – must be part of every believer's life at some point.

ENTERTAINING GOATS OR FEEDING THE SHEEP?

Within those two decades came the development of the Christian music industry. Most of the early industry pioneers were sincere, God-fearing, and ministry-minded, but I wonder if they would approve of Christian music as a whole today? The industry has changed and often operates as a business first. The song lyrics they write and sing often tell us little of what some musicians believe. In too many cases, bands place more emphasis on entertainment than on saving lives for eternity or building up the body of Christ with His eternal Word.

The attempt to make church more appealing to unbelievers while entertaining young Christians caused biblical truth within the music to become irrelevant to millions of young music fans. Too few pastors checked the doctrines of the bands being invited into our churches to perform. It was a perfect set-up for "Christianity Lite."

Dan Haseltine, Jars of Clay front man, is an example of a recent high-profile casualty of the cult of liberalism. The band has been around for about twenty years, but Haseltine, their lead spokesman, questions biblical inerrancy and the conservative Christian view on marriage. He shared his opinion on Twitter, saying he supported homosexual marriage and rejected the inerrancy of Scripture. About his Christian upbringing, he stated, "I'm not that way now." Of course, once traditional Christian news outlets and bloggers got wind of his apostasy, a firestorm erupted. Naturally, he attempted a vague apology of sorts, but not a clear retraction of his statements.

We don't know Haseltine's heart or anyone else's. We also don't know what kind of foundation (there's that word again) of biblical truth his faith was built upon or how he was raised. Resisting the worship of fans and maintaining a healthy witness while on the road is tough for Christian bands, but they must stay true to God's Word. What kind of accountability and teaching are these musicians receiving, assuming they have a home church to go to when they are not travelling?

Music is entertainment; some Christian music may be edifying, but is it a pure form of worship? Some musicians are good, scripturally sound artists. But many bands are jumping around, performing rock, rap, or whatever, with lyrics that are hard to understand, let alone know if they are based on the Bible. Shouldn't the message in the music be clear?

A wide chasm exists between entertainment and worship. Entertainment is permissible, yes; but not all entertainment is beneficial. Many [Christian] songs on the radio today are not exactly anointed, Holy Spirit-filled, Scripture-based songs with lyrics glorifying to God.

> *Let the word of Christ richly dwell within you, with all wisdom teaching and admonishing one another with psalms and hymns and spiritual songs, singing with thankfulness in your hearts to God* (Colossians 3:16).

Notice the apostle Paul implies here that to have the wisdom of God and the ability to admonish others with psalms and songs, we must first allow the word of Christ to "richly dwell" within us. Believers become prone to fall for false teachings and susceptible to the cult of liberalism when we do not know the Word of God as well as we should. We can hardly expect less mature Christians to discern the error of subtle emerging doctrines.

Churches have incorporated music, creative arts, and drama presentations. They have provided videos, concerts, and seminars. Even the children's programs are used to grab people's attention or compliment the pastor's message during services. These things are not bad or wrong, but how much time is taken away from teaching the life-changing, living Word of God? The bigger question might be what did the apostles, disciples, and early churches do?

Pursuing Jesus wholeheartedly and seeking His kingdom first takes discipline and effort, including the study of His Word. It does not take much effort to be like the world, dilute sound doctrine, and tell people what they want to hear. The Emergent Church fits this latter description.

A CULT CALLING ITSELF "CHRISTIAN"

Holding the belief we're now in a "postmodern" society, the Emergent Church is a rapidly growing network of individual believers and churches who would prefer to be understood as a conversation, friendship, or movement. These folks don't like structure and they generally do not support traditional Christianity. Those involved mostly agree that their disdain and disillusionment with the organized and institutional church led them to seek something new.

In 2010, I researched and wrote about the Emergent Church after witnessing a few local churches and organizations develop a pattern of compromise on biblical issues. If we operate more like a business or corporation than a ministry, we have a problem. We are naïve if we say "liberalism could never affect my church."

> The Emergent Church favors the use of simple story and narrative rather than reading lots of Scripture ... The hallmark of the Emergent Church is the new age aspect including the practice of [emptying the mind as well as] contemplative monastic meditation and prayers. While some emphasize eternal salvation, many in the emerging church emphasize temporary issues such as environmentalism. Much of its doctrine rejects systematic Christian theology, the integrity of Scripture, and gospel exclusivity. They don't believe Christianity is the [one] true religion and they promote homosexuality. They call for diversity, tolerance, and camaraderie among all religions, and they modify and expand their teachings. It is clearly a war against the Truth.[64]

As American Christians became busier and invested less time studying the Bible and participating in the church's central mission of preaching the gospel, conforming to culture happened naturally, and liberalism crept into churches at an accelerated rate.

When we stop filling our hearts and minds with the things of God, the world will fill us with something else. You might be asking why church leaders didn't perceive this infiltration, let alone stop it. The acceptance of unbiblical teachings was gradual, and some did try sounding the alarm, but they were sadly outnumbered or ignored, resulting in the state of the American church that exists today.

Liberals also worked their way into the seminaries as instructors as the older, wiser theologians retired, opening the door for the potential grooming of young church leaders with watered down doctrines. The same process took place in the churches as mature pastors retired, and eager, young, indoctrinated rookies took over pulpits. Many emergents went on to make disciples of liberalism rather than disciples of the Word – Jesus Christ, *the way, the truth and the life.*

---

64 David Fiorazo; "Where Did the Emergent Church Emerge From?" Good Fight Ministries, July 2010, http://www.goodfight.org/a_t_emergent_church.html.

In a video presentation, author and speaker, Eric Barger, of Take A Stand Ministries explains:

> They gradually reeducated sincere believers into this new form of Christianity based upon feelings instead of sound doctrine. Social programs, community service, and good works have replaced salvation by grace. Once people's theology becomes corrupted, the gospel is emptied of its power. Liberals have continued to use "the shell of the church" to collect money from the congregants and to gain more power. Liberalism claiming to be Christianity is the most dangerous cult in the world today.[65]

Barger also discussed liberalism's origins, tracing them back to the so-called "German Enlightenment," notably through the philosophy of Immanuel Kant, who argued human reason is the source of all morality. Influenced by Plato as well as mystic and scientist Emmanuel Swedenborg, Kant has had a major influence on political philosophy and religious movements. Barger emphasized that he knows all about liberalism because he "lived like a pagan, but called myself a Christian for about a dozen years before I repented and dove back into the Word of God as my first love and final authority."

Some works that fall under emergent church liberalism include support for abortion, environmentalism (save the earth – don't worry about preaching the gospel), and social justice (partnering with government on national and global efforts). These churches proclaim class warfare, promote universalism (*everyone* will be reconciled to God), and encourage uniformity (sin is not the big issue, all religions should coexist). They advocate tolerance, push general diversity (many types of people, many pathways), and exalt specific diversity (homosexuality or racism). They prefer unregulated immigration (open borders equal more votes) and preach anti-war views such as "America is the world's bully." To top it off, liberal Christians generally criticize Christian conservatives, evangelicals, fundamentalists, traditionalists, and true (not RINO) Republicans.

---

65   Eric Barger, "The Most Dangerous Cult," January 2003, http://www.ericbarger.com/mdcult.htm.

THE [SPIRITUAL] CIVIL WAR WITHIN

Understanding how mainline denominations and theological seminaries in America split over doctrinal issues is helpful. We already discussed the debate in the Presbyterian Church over the inerrancy of Scripture during the 1890s, which eventually led to the famous five (fundamentals) points in the 1920s that fueled the conservative movement. Prior to this, the Azusa Street revival birthed the Pentecostal movement, and the outpouring of the Holy Spirit continued for nearly ten years. The World Conference of Christian Fundamentals took place in Philadelphia in 1919 with forty-two states represented.

A few years later, the International Church of the Foursquare Gospel was established in Los Angeles, California. I had the privilege of working at a radio station on Sunset Boulevard called KFSG, which was started by evangelist Aimee Semple McPherson. She founded Angelus Temple in 1923 and developed ministries to preach the gospel and serve those in need, feeding more than 1.5 million people during the Great Depression. Known as a pioneer of women in ministry, McPherson summarized her message into four points, which she called "the Foursquare Gospel": Jesus is the Savior, Jesus is the Healer, Jesus is the Baptizer with the Holy Spirit, and Jesus is the Soon-Coming King.[66]

The end of that decade brought a shift to modernism at Princeton Theological Seminary in New Jersey, one of the first seminaries for biblical instruction that began in 1812. Princeton's modern reorganization and openness to liberal ideas caused the formation of a conservative venue for instruction, Westminster Theological Seminary, founded in 1929 in Philadelphia. Westminster's motto is "The whole counsel of God."

Remember J. Gresham Machen and his stand for the Five Fundamentals from chapter two? In a public address he delivered in Pennsylvania in 1921, he said the chief modern rival of Christianity is liberalism, further stating:

> An examination of the teachings of liberalism will show that at every point the liberal movement is in opposition to the Christian message.

---

66   Aimee Semple McPherson, "Our Story: The History of the Foursquare Church" http://www.foursquare.org/about/aimee_semple_mcpherson.

Machen wrote what he called a "little book," *Christianity and Liberalism*, in 1923 declaring Modernism to be completely anti-biblical, explaining the many offshoots of liberalism that have tentacles in the church and showing the issue within the church "is not between two varieties of the same religion," but between two essentially different types of thought and life. Yes, there are similarities, but the two worldviews spring from very different roots.

Machen refers to liberal Christianity as "nondoctrinal religion" and to conservative, fundamental, biblical faith as "historic Christianity." Machen explains:

> Modern liberalism, it has been observed so far, has lost sight of the two great presuppositions of the Christian message – the living God and the fact of sin. The liberal doctrine of God and the liberal doctrine of man are both diametrically opposite to the Christian view. But the divergence concerns not only the presuppositions of the message, but also the message itself.[67]

The National Association of Evangelicals was formed in 1942. Until around 1950 in America, the terms *evangelical* and *fundamentalism* were interchangeable. In general, historical patterns have shown it takes about seventy-five years for Christian churches, denominations, or institutions to drift away from a commitment to believing in the inerrancy of the Bible.

In his outstanding book, *New Evangelicalism*, author and pastor, Paul Smith, identifies historical markers of liberalism invading the church. These included movements, battles for sound doctrine, the Emergent Church, and the influential Christian leaders who played key roles bringing us to where we are today. While explaining some of the momentum evangelicals experienced in the 1940s, Smith also highlights a battle between nonprofits and Christian organizations beginning with the American Council of Christian Churches (ACCC):

> The Council's purpose was to promote and defend biblical orthodoxy in contrast to the liberally infected Federal Council of Churches (FCC), which was the precursor to the current,

---

67 J. Gresham Machen, Christianity & Liberalism, 1923, WM. B. Eerdman's Publishing Co. Grand Rapids, MI page 69 http://www.reformed.org/books/chr_and_lib/index.html.

extremely liberal National Council of Churches (NCC), the American arm of the highly ecumenical and liberal World Council of Churches (WCC).[68]

April 1942 brought about the creation of the National Association of Evangelicals (NAE) in St. Louis, Missouri, birthed out of the conference called United Action Among Evangelicals. Pastor Harold Ockenga rallied believers with his keynote address:

> Evangelical Christianity has suffered nothing but a series of defeats for decades. In virtually every area of culture, evangelical Christianity has been placed on the defensive. The terrible octopus of liberalism, which spreads itself through our Protestant Church, has dominated innumerable organizations, pulpits, and publications, as well as seminaries and other schools.[69]

These evangelical Christians shared a strong degree of acknowledgement at the time about the evils of liberalism, but solutions on how to combat it most effectively would not be easily agreed upon. While Ockenga's speech electrified attendees, he also sought to reform fundamentalism, not doctrinally, but in regards to cultural, political, and social involvement where the gospel was concerned. These ideas led to the birth of "neo-evangelicalism."

Neo-evangelicalism was a term used to describe a movement within the evangelical (fundamentalist) Christian church of that day. It was a call to repudiate separatism and a summons to more social involvement. Neo-evangelicalism was to reform fundamentalism from what was perceived to be anti-cultural.

Some believe the neo-evangelicalism movement was one born of compromise, nurtured on pride of intellect, and in an effort to engage in conversation became inclusive of liberals, their politics, and unbiblical views.

The question remains: How do we avoid contamination by a world polluted by sin, while at the same time making disciples and preaching

---

68   Paul Smith, *New Evangelicalism,* 2011 Calvary Publishing, page 54.
69   Garth M. Rosell, *The Surprising Work of God* (Grand Rapids, MI: Baker Academic, 2008), p. 97.

the gospel? The biblical doctrine of separation (sanctification) is founded upon a teaching that appears in both the Old and New Testaments:

Depart, depart, go out from there, Touch nothing unclean; Go out of the midst of her, purify yourselves, You who carry the vessels of the LORD (Isaiah 52:11).

Do not be unequally yoked with unbelievers; for what partnership has righteousness and lawlessness, or what fellowship has light with darkness? … Therefore go out from their midst, and be separate from them, says the Lord, and touch no unclean thing; then I will welcome you (2 Corinthians 6:14, 17 ESV).

How do we resist the spiritual pollutants of this world and of liberalism as we share our faith in order to reach the lost? What is the best way to be salt and light in our society? The liberal movement was well funded and organized and has been highly influential in America. One way neo-evangelical leaders achieved their goal was by focusing on promoting new ideas and changing Christian attitudes and beliefs through books, colleges, sermonettes, and superstar personalities in mega churches as well as on Christian television.

One pastor said that from its inception, new evangelicalism has been determined to impress the world with its intellect. It has craved the respect of academia. Similar to the Fabian Socialists, intellectuals who came to America from Europe to spread socialism here, neo-evangelicals have been dispersed in churches and seminaries.

WHAT HAPPENED AT FULLER SEMINARY?

Dr. Charles Edward Fuller (1887-1968) was a fundamentalist preacher shaped by his education at BIOLA University in Los Angeles. A visionary, Fuller preached on an ABC Radio Network program he created, "The Old-Fashioned Revival Hour," from 1937 to 1968. His desire was also to train young men to go out and share the gospel. A group of fundamentalist scholars, including Harold Ockenga, supported the founding of Fuller Theological Seminary in Pasadena, California. The goal was to send out "Holy Spirit-empowered men" to reach the lost.

Evangelical author and scholar, Harold Lindsell, was pivotal in establishing Fuller on the doctrine of inerrancy and later worked at *Christianity Today* magazine and Wheaton College. The seminary's beginnings in 1947 were on the solid footing of biblical inerrancy, but it took just over a decade for infighting to occur. Denominationalism was becoming a problem, but the biggest issue that challenged Christian leaders in America continued to be the inerrancy of Scripture. Conservative evangelicals understood what happened in Germany when humanism, idolatry, and moral relativism helped bring a formerly vibrant Christian state crashing down.

Harold Lindsell would leave Fuller Seminary in 1962, penning a letter to Ockenga on Christmas Day stating it was "a tragic day" and instead of joy and peace, there was infighting. He wrote that in place of prayer and the filling of the Holy Spirit, "there is bickering, deception, and antagonism." Lindsell further wrote:

> The very Spirit of God seems to have departed from our midst. I ask myself the questions: Where did we go wrong? What did we fail to do? What did we do that we shouldn't have done? We need divine help for deliverance, yet my tongue cleaves to my mouth and the words do not form. God have mercy on us … even yet.[70]

What occurred at Princeton Seminary basically repeated itself at Fuller with debates over the statement of faith and departure from sound biblical roots. The process of decline took about forty-eight years at Princeton and around thirty-one years at Fuller. It's happening much quicker in today's church. The term "evangelical" now must be clearly defined in conversations because it has become discredited and vague as it relates to accurately describing Christianity.

Entering Fuller Seminary, the class of 1950 came in with a 75 percent belief that the Bible is inerrant. Upon graduation in 1952, approximately 48 percent remained firm in that view. Those were the early days. By 1982, it was reported that the commitment to inerrancy had dropped to 15 percent of graduates from Fuller Theological Seminary! Compromise

---

70   Billy Graham Center Archives, Wheaton, IL. Harold Lindsell Collection 192, Folder 7-27A, Item 5.

and accommodation produced tragic results which continue diluting Christianity in America today.[71]

After detailing the decay, author Paul Smith summarized the sad reality that Fuller Seminary no longer affirms belief in an inerrant Bible. Just as harmful, "humanistic sociology, psychology, and cultural studies are accommodatingly sown into the fabric of church growth methodologies." We no longer need to ask "whatever happened to the seminary originally envisioned by Charles Fuller?"

I mentioned separatism as one of the ideas dividing believers. We are in the world for God's purposes. If He were done with us, wouldn't we be taken home? It goes without saying our job has not yet been completed. Ken Silva of Apprising Ministries helps clarify our challenge:

> Separation is not a passive activity. In these perilous times, believers are called upon more than ever to be on guard against the seductions of heretical teachings and their teachers. It is a defensive posture that requires standing firm on the Word, and continually filtering every teaching through the lens of the whole counsel of Scripture. To avoid heresy requires active resistance on the part of the believer. Sometimes a believer must physically flee from temptation and its circumstances.
>
> At other times the Lord would have believers speak out in defense of the Truth of the Gospel. *And have no fellowship with the unfruitful works of darkness, but rather reprove them* (Ephesians 5:11 KJV). Here Paul says that believers should "reprove them," because all things that are reproved are made manifest by the light (Ephesians 5:13). Jude 3 tells believers to earnestly *contend for the faith which was once delivered unto the saints* (KJV). The new "tolerance" ethic blunts this directive, and many Christians remain silent.[72]

The notion many leaders have today is Christians must become postmodern in order to reach secular America, but as a result, they

71   George M. Marsden, *Reforming Fundamentalism: Fuller Seminary and the New Evangelicalism* (Grand Rapids, MI: Eerdmans, 1995), p. 302.

72   Ken Silva, "Postmodern Infiltration: The Neo-Evangelical Heretical Idea," Dec. 30, 2013, Apprising Ministries, http://apprising.org/2012/12/30/postmodern-infiltration-the-neo-evangelical-heretical-idea/.

have locked arms with liberals and conformed to the world. This new evangelical shift includes a definitive move away from belief in absolute truth. Think about it; do liberals ever compromise and become more holy, or do conservatives typically compromise and become more worldly?

As we find with most good things, even the things of God, we can become comfortable and allow a gradual departure from solid doctrinal foundations. By 1957, fundamentalism was fading, and many believers backed out of culture, flinging the door wide open for the 1960s cultural rebellion and sexual revolution.

THE GOAL OF HUMANISM: ERADICATE CHRISTIAN INFLUENCE

Humanism is any system or view in which human interests dominate; man is god. Humanism emphasizes reason, science, and human fulfillment while rejecting the existence of or the importance of God. It promotes moral relativism and denies there is a right and wrong, discounting the Bible completely; so this secular worldview directly conflicts with the biblical Christian worldview.

It bears repeating we are either advancing toward God and spiritual things or we are heading toward man's idea of order and natural things. For humanists, man is the center of all things. This philosophy is nothing new; it came from the Greeks some 2,000 years ago. It descended from Gnosticism that views the mind of man as the center of reality. Contrast this with the Christian belief that an eternal God created man in His image and He is sovereign over all creation.

The problem with humanism and liberalism is they both begin with man with no room for accountability to Christ. Man is either an animal or a biological machine with no higher calling. If our ancestors were monkeys, or life evolved from nothing, our existence is meaningless and mankind has no purpose. This kind of thinking dominates public education and can often lead to depression, despair, and even suicide.

But if God is Creator, if Jesus is the only Way, and if the Bible is true, humanists are in big trouble. Moreover, so is our country! Will we turn back to God and repent or will the church continue becoming more like secular culture? This deception slithered into the church practically unnoticed for half a century or more.

The flesh *sets its desire against the Spirit, and the Spirit against the flesh; for these are in opposition to one another* (Galatians 5:17). The fruit of man is greed, power, corruption, and control. Believers filled with the Holy Spirit see things from an eternal perspective and can easily discern depravity and duplicity.

> *Now the deeds of the flesh are evident, which are: immorality, impurity, sensuality, idolatry, sorcery, enmities, strife, jealousy, outbursts of anger, disputes, dissensions, factions, envying, drunkenness, carousing, and things like these, of which I fore-warn you, just as I have forewarned you, that those who practice such things will not inherit the kingdom of God. But the fruit of the Spirit is love, joy, peace, patience, kindness, goodness, faithfulness, gentleness, self-control; against such things there is no law. Now those who belong to Christ Jesus have cruci-fied the flesh with its passions and desires* (Galatians 5:19-24).

Similar to the fallout among many Protestant churches in Germany in the 1930s and 40s, we're seeing a doctrinal divide in many evangelical Christian churches in America today. The authority and integrity of Scripture is not a frequent teaching. In public schools, Humanism is the norm while Christianity has been sent packing.

Even in mainstream evangelical churches, these philosophies are becoming more accepted, and the Emergent Church has been progressing in their efforts to influence the body of Christ. The early church was warned by Jesus, the apostle Paul and others; we've been warned as well.

In this age of biblical illiteracy and historical ignorance, we must ensure our own foundation is established on the essential doctrines of Jesus and His atoning sacrifice. Far too much indifference toward spiritual things exists, so let's pray for a revival while we encourage believers to study and know the Word of God. In Paul's day, it was assumed Christians had a solid foundation and were growing in their faith!

> *Therefore leaving the elementary teaching about the Christ, let us press on to maturity, not laying again a foundation*

of repentance from dead works and of faith toward God, of instruction about washings and laying on of hands, and the resurrection of the dead and eternal judgment. And this we will do, if God permits (Hebrews 6:1-3).

Notice what doctrines are considered "elementary," and let's make sure we are secure in these teachings so we're building our house on Christ, not on what is popular. Messengers and methods may change, but the message of truth never changes. We must remember that when biblical truth is abandoned, it opens the door to bless what the Word of God condemns, and lessens our resistance to a pop culture morality.

I've had debates with liberal friends who identify with the "Christian Left," and we had to agree to part ways. I still love them, but they could not or would not answer questions regarding their accommodation of certain sins and apparent contradictions with what the Bible teaches. I have learned it is often easier to talk with a nonbeliever than with someone who justifies liberalism and secular humanism within Christianity.

Someone recently said political liberalism basically makes sin public policy. I had to think about that for a moment and realized it all comes back to "God or man." Whether you call it progressivism, secularism, atheism, leftism, or a combination of these, they lead to or incorporate Marxism and socialism by building on the worldview of man without God. The cult of liberalism supports a rebellion against His laws and His truth, having no perceived need for accountability while embracing chaos, disorder, and moral relativism.

They package and promote liberalism as something good, desirable, and even necessary, promising things the Bible does not support or prioritize. Liberalism has led to a host of cultural and societal problems. For example, if it were possible to combine the cities of Chicago, Detroit, New York, San Francisco, and Los Angeles, *that* is what the United States would look like as one nation under liberalism.

For Christians believing in one God and having faith in Jesus, the *King of Kings and Lord of Lords* (Revelation 19:16), opposing any secular philosophy in which man is king would seem natural because this philosophy threatens the unity of the church and leads young believers to conform to the lies, lusts, and lures of this world.

Dr. Walter Martin issued stern warnings about liberal theology and the Emergent Church:

> It is a cult because it follows every outlined structure of cultism; its own revelations; its own gurus, and its denial – systematically – of all sound systematic Christian theology. It is a cult because it passes its leadership on to the next group that takes over – either modifying, expanding or contracting – the same heresies; dressing them up in different language, and passing them on ... it denies the authority of Scripture, it ruins its own theology. And it ends in immorality; because the only way you could have gotten to this homosexual, morally relativistic, garbage – which is today in our denominational structures – is if the leadership of those denominations denied the authority of the Scriptures and Jesus Christ as Lord ... Test all things; make sure of what is true (see 1 Thessalonians 5:21). I'm not being harsh; I'm not being judgmental. I am being thoroughly, consistently, Christian; in the light of historic theology, and the holy Bible.[73]

We must stop playing church or pursuing our own comfort and get out on the front lines where the battles are being fought in order to let our voices be heard. Let us not give up trying to impact culture and weed out deceivers from within our ranks. I'd rather they be saved, but if not, they have no business influencing the church. May God give us the boldness to speak now as we pray for the healing of our church and our land.

The diagnosis: Liberalism is a malignant cancer that has metastasized, even within the evangelical Christian church.

The prognosis: This political and spiritual disease will cause the death of many if it remains untreated with the blood of the Lamb and the truth of God's inspired Word.

For the disciple: Since Jesus Christ is our Lord and our allegiance is to Him alone, we will know the truth *and the truth will set us free* (John 8:32). Be assured we are on the right side – His.

---

73   Dr. Walter Martin, lecture; http://apprising.org/2010/03/25/
      brian-mclaren-and-his-new-emerging-progressive-theology/.

Dear friends, although I was very eager to write to you about the salvation we share, I felt I had to write and urge you to contend for the faith that was once for all entrusted to the saints. For certain men whose condemnation was written about long ago have secretly slipped in among you. They are godless men, who change the grace of our God into a license for immorality and deny Jesus Christ our only Sovereign and Lord (Jude 1:3-4 NIV).

CHAPTER 10

THE REBELLION AGAINST GOD ORDAINED MARRIAGE

And He [Jesus] *answered and said, "Have you not read that He who created them from the beginning MADE THEM MALE AND FEMALE, and said, 'FOR THIS REASON A MAN SHALL LEAVE HIS FATHER AND MOTHER AND BE JOINED TO HIS WIFE, AND THE TWO SHALL BECOME ONE FLESH'?* [Genesis 2:24, Emphasis mine] *"So they are no longer two, but one flesh. What therefore God has joined together, let no man separate."*
Matthew 19:4-6

"The Bible is the Word of our Creator, and Genesis is literal history. Its science and history can be trusted. Therefore, we have an absolute authority that determines marriage. God made the first man and woman – the first marriage. Thus, marriage can only be a man and a woman because we are accountable to the One who made marriage in the first place. And don't forget – according to Scripture, one of the primary reasons for marriage is to produce godly offspring. Adam and Eve were told to be fruitful and multiply, but there's no way a gay marriage can fulfill this command!"
—Answers in Genesis President, Ken Ham

When Jesus was challenged, He listened to his opponents and often responded with a question. But He was always prepared because He always prayed. We should do no less when it comes to our interactions with people about biblical issues. In the introductory verses,

Jesus responded to the Pharisees who questioned him on the subject of divorce and pointed to the Word of God. He asked them if they had not read the account of creation and the first marriage. He spoke with authority to the most educated and religious leaders in the world at that time. He indirectly stated that any departure from the foundations established in the beginning was wrong.

Their aim was to set him up to contradict the Law of Moses, but Jesus shows us how to dialogue with people who disagree with us: Ask questions and invite your opponents to defend their position. It also helps to know God's Word.

Before we attempt to fight these cultural battles, we must get our own houses in order by strengthening and protecting our own marriages. God hates divorce, and marriage has been suffering for decades. The divorce rate among Christians is not much different from that of unbelievers, but marriage is still ordained by God and extremely important.

We cannot ignore the problems in our churches and families where marriage is concerned. If you are unequally yoked and your spouse is not a believer, keep praying and never give up hope. If your marriage is rocky right now, pray for God to soften both of your hearts; open communication could lead to forgiveness and a renewed commitment to love and serve each other. If you are separated, know God is a God of miracles, but He won't force His will on anyone. If you are divorced, there is healing, mercy, and hope in Christ. If you are in a same-sex relationship and wonder if God cares or if He will forgive you, yes to both! Turn to Him now.

Studies prove marriage provides a healthy spiritual, emotional, physical, and psychological environment for raising children. Procreation is a natural outcome of marriage resulting from the biblical standard of a man who leaves his father and mother, joins (has union with) his wife, and they become one flesh (Genesis 2:24).

We often forget our Creator's plan for marriage is woven through Scripture and has been implemented through history. Marriage predates kings, governments, and nations; so why do secular progressives and God-haters now feel compelled to attack the institution that once helped stabilize America? They hate most everything we stand for.

Christianity, the family, our God-given freedoms, and the Constitution have all contributed to our strength and prosperity as a nation. We were fine without same-sex marriage for over two hundred years.

By committing to a lifetime of building and investing in strong marriages, we set an example for people that the benefits far outweigh the sacrifices. Loving, stable marriages give others hope if their family was not ideal growing up. If the family unit is the bedrock of a healthy society, we must be more disciplined in our promotion and protection of marriage and natural families.

For Christians, once we say "I do," that marriage is God's will. He takes covenants seriously. A gay or lesbian couple may love each other, but a ceremony or union considered "marriage" by man will never be approved of or sanctioned by a holy God. So, why don't we let homosexuals do whatever they want and marry whomever they want? One reason is it will not stop there; the extremists aim to make others capitulate to every one of their demands for special rights.

MAN'S DEFINITIONS & CULTURAL CONFUSION

As of January 8, 2015, in thirty states where citizens were allowed to vote for natural marriage, over 41 million Americans have cast their votes to protect laws supporting marriage between one man and one woman. Ironically, thirty states now have legalized same-sex "marriage." Compare the 41 million to only 3 million voters in three states – Maine, Maryland, and Washington – who cast a ballot in favor of unnatural (same-sex) unions.[74]

Gay activists and judges are using the courts to gain ground and change the climate in America to favor gay marriage. Their marketing has been effective, but this is not a grass roots movement. Its expansion is manufactured and manipulated in part with millions of dollars in public advertising and years of propaganda in public schools.

Tragically, we are now paying for our silence. For more than half a century, Americans – and particularly too many Christians – have looked the other way, saying, "as long as it doesn't affect me." To compound

---

74   Family Research Council, "Godly Government; Despot Courts, 10/9/2014, http://www. frc.org/prayerteam/prayer-targets-godly-government-despot-courts-pastors-jerusalem-pentecost-walk-ipledge-sunday.

the problem, the average Christian does not know how to respond to the "in-your-face" gay movement and what many incorrectly perceive as inevitable or unstoppable.

By our silence, we indirectly support government policies such as same-sex benefits; we penalize married couples at a higher tax rate, and allow the discrimination of Christian business owners. The traditional family has been weakened in America. The normalizing of same-sex unions and the minimizing of natural marriage will continue to be a destructive force in our culture if the current trends continue without much resistance. If we listened only to the media and Hollywood, we might believe gays and lesbians are victims and hated by Christians; or we might believe they are inferior to us. Not true.

The media and Hollywood conveniently ignore that the Bible teaches we were all once in the same spiritual boat, sinners living in rebellion against God and the teachings of Jesus Christ. True believers have acknowledged our spiritual poverty and desperate condition. Healthy people don't need a hospital; sick people do. All Christians were once sinners separated from God and hostile toward Him, but since we've been saved, we can now have more compassion for those who haven't yet allowed Jesus to rescue them.

BORN THAT WAY?

Are some people born gay or is homosexuality a chosen lifestyle? If some are born with a gay gene, the Bible must be wrong referring to homosexual behavior as a sin. According to a gay magazine, *The Advocate*, 90% of gay men surveyed claimed to have been born gay. Is God a liar? Are men the final authority? Who is right?

The answers to these questions should have instant repercussions on our society – unless of course, the truth is buried, hidden, or covered up. If it were revealed that gays and lesbians' sexual orientations are *not* innate and they were not "born that way," the very foundations of their movement would crumble. This is one reason they have so much anger or hostility toward those who do not affirm their existence as natural, normal, and unchosen.

The debate is about sexual activity, behavior, preferences, and chosen lifestyle. Are any of these innate? Some go so far as to equate the plight of gays with the Civil Rights movement and discrimination based on skin color, regardless of the fact it has never been successfully proven that a person is born homosexual.

Aside from Scripture, plenty of anthropological, biological, historical, medical, and scientific information is available on this subject. Just as the arguments supporting evolution cannot be backed up with conclusive, factual data and historical evidence, the claim people are born gay is also a stretch based upon assumptions and people's modern attitudes toward sin over the years; it has nothing to do with facts and truth.

Many anthropologists and historians maintain that the innate sexual orientation of homosexuality didn't exist until about 150 years ago when it became a product of Western society. Even though there is some evidence of same-sex *behavior* and relationships throughout history, including pre-modern times, individuals or groups identifying as gay could not be found in any society prior to the 19th century.

Expert research backed by professors proves there is no "gay gene" accounting for sexual orientation from birth. By the end of this chapter, you may agree the information presented here is indisputable, but still hardly known and discussed. Though this is a very public debate; the facts and truth are not.

I could interview, quote, and cite many evangelical Christians, apologists, pastors, and church leaders on this subject as most of them stand on the truth of God's Word. However, let's look at some other sources such as homosexual writer, David Benkof, who admits nobody is "born that way":

> Journalists trumpet every biological study that even hints that gayness and straightness might be hard-wired, but they show little interest in the abundant social-science research showing that sexual orientation cannot be innate.[75]

Benkof openly states many in the LGBT community try to portray homosexuality as "a naturally arising subset of every human population." I reference David Benkof because he is not just some random

---

75   David Benkof, "Nobody is 'born that way' gay historians say," Daily Caller, 3/19/2014, http://dailycaller.com/2014/03/19/nobody-is-born-that-way-gay-historians-say/.

blogger; he is a Stanford-trained historian and also happens to be gay. To sum up his article, sexual orientations are specific to our culture and not basic human nature. Those who demand social or political change because they think some people are born gay just don't know much about history. In his own words, Benkof concluded, "the totality of the scholarly research on homosexuality indicates gayness is much more socio-cultural than biological."

One reason they are pushing so hard in the states to sway public opinion is because societal acceptance coincides with their effort to have the Constitution's equal protection clause applied to gays and lesbians. Experts and scholars, however, disagree; and they consider being gay a "recent social construction."

Surprisingly, those with the highest levels of education, knowledge, and respect in their professions, including many who identify as LGBT, are appalled by the media's mishandling of the facts on this important debate. From the University of Chicago, gay history professor, Dr. John D'Emilio, acknowledges the idea of the social construction, but also declared "the essentialist notion that gays constitute a distinct minority of people different in some inherent way has more credibility in American society than ever before."

In other words, the one nation uniquely established as "Under God, indivisible" has adapted to the idea of homosexuality. We've been conditioned by culture starting with public school propaganda, driven by a godless government, and influenced by a liberal media supported by a garbage-infested entertainment industry to promote immorality.

Increased sexual activity, especially homosexuality, seems to flourish in nations that have experienced an increase in materialism and standard of living without any comparable increase in moral convictions or spirituality. Every time the issue arose in the Old Testament, God addressed it and warned the people to turn from their wickedness.

Commenting on a study linking sexual orientation to biological traits, University of Michigan cultural anthropologist, Dr. Esther Newton, called it ludicrous and proclaimed, "Any anthropologist who has looked cross-culturally knows it's impossible." Further debunking the lie that people are born gay, even the founder of the Center for Lesbian and Gay

Studies, historian Dr. Martin Duberman, concluded "no good scientific work establishes that people are born gay or straight."[76]

In America, identifying gay/straight/bisexual/transgender people seems normal, obvious, and logical because we live within the system godlessness created. Until about 150 years ago, homosexuality was something one could do, not something one could be.

We could then ask why there were no classifications of "heterosexuals" in past societies. Evidently, historians believe there was no heterosexual orientation simply because it was not necessary! This obsession with sexual orientation is a consequence of our rebellion. Again, let's clarify that for thousands of years, people have been seeking new ways to gratify their sensual lusts, and same-sex attractions and expressions were part of that. However, no established, proven cases of life-long homosexual relationships are found, and, therefore, no need existed to identify mankind as heterosexual.

CONSIDER THE CONSEQUENCES

In my previous book, *ERADICATE*, I wrote a chapter called "Normalizing Homosexuality" which is exactly what the Left has accomplished in America over the last fifty years. I cited medical studies and documented sources revealing shocking health statistics as well as medical concerns for both gays and lesbians. According to the Centers for Disease Control (CDC), 94% of HIV cases among boys and young men up to age twenty-four were linked to homosexual sex. Tragically, this number includes boys as young as thirteen years old.[77]

In another example, similar to the abortion figures, we find that lesbians have a much higher rate of depression as well as emotional and psychological problems than married women.

Remember these facts when you hear someone say homosexuality doesn't hurt anyone, so let them do whatever they want. The CDC has also reported the 2% of the U.S. population that are gay account for 61% of HIV infections. Other studies have shown the average number of

76   Ibid.
77   Peter LaBarbera, "CDC: 94 to 95 Percent of HIV Cases among Boys and Young Men Linked to Homosexual Sex, 2011, Citizens for Community Values, http://www.ccv.org/issues/homosexuality/cdc-94-to-95-percent-of-hiv-casesg-men-linked-to-homosexual-sex/.

sexual partners in the lifespan of a homosexual male is in the hundreds; some have had over five hundred sexual encounters in their lifetime. Is it surprising people in traditional marriages live up to twenty-five years longer?

According to international and national sources, including The Family Research Institute, that studied the mortality rate for gays and lesbians vs. that of married men and women, gays and lesbians lived twenty years *less* than married heterosexuals.[78] Think of how difficult this survey is to calculate due to the fact some people become gay in their teen years while others make the switch as late as their forties or fifties. The most common age a person first identifies as gay or lesbian is the early twenties, but the cultural shift is moving this even younger due in part to the pro-gay curriculum in public schools.

You shall not lie with a male as one lies with a female; it is an abomination (Leviticus 18:22).

Scripture clearly condemns all forms of sin including any kind of sexual action or desire outside of marriage. In Leviticus 18:20-23, sins of adultery, abortion, homosexuality, and bestiality are each mentioned. Homosexuality is an abomination to God – something detestable, shameful, or hateful. The Bible does not directly mention gay orientation for the same reason we already discussed; the concept has been historically nonexistent.

When someone tries arguing "Jesus never specifically mentioned homosexuality," we can always respond with love and sprinkle in facts mixed with truth. It shows you've done some research. Some, however, will still try to accuse you of being hateful because you want homosexuals to be saved. This, they say, is bigoted and intolerant. To them, a good Christian is a silent, invisible Christian.

Let me go out on a limb here: The more awareness we can raise regarding the whole truth about homosexuality and the more facts we can share about the importance of marriage in our society, the more people will be encouraged to defend traditional marriage and fewer people will publicly support same-sex unions. We have the truth on our

78   Dr. Warren Throckmorton, "Danish Study sheds light on gay mortality" http://www. crosswalk.com/blogs/dr-warren-throckmorton/danish-study-sheds-light-on-gay-mor-tality-11595737.html.

side; they have moral relativism. Some may hate us for speaking up, but it is Truth (Jesus) alone that can set them free from the bondage of sin.

How can someone approve of the life-creating, life-giving process – the birth of a baby – as a result of male and female intercourse while simultaneously approving of a counterfeit "marriage" between two people that cannot naturally produce a life? Confusing? Christian friend, the approval of same-sex unions indirectly supports sin and death. Homosexuality puts more limits on life and can only result in a dead end for individuals and for a society as well.

HEAVEN AND NATURE: STUDIES DON'T LIE

Political pressure, social activism, and good marketing are the primary reasons many have been convinced (duped) to support homosexuality. In order for society to continue, however, people must produce offspring. America has thrived when families thrive; and the family thrives when biological, loving parents of the opposite sex consummate their marriage and have children. This is one of God's greatest blessings on earth.

Nature supports God-designed marriage because all species must reproduce in order to survive. Our physical bodies were created in such a way mankind could easily figure out how to coordinate a unique sexual act between a male and female leading to another human life – which happens to be either male or female. Gender differences are good and should be valued, and each parent has unique gifts and skills with which to train up a healthy boy or girl. Countless studies have proven that monogamous, biological, heterosexual parents are ideal and optimal for the healthiest development of children and society.

Author James M. Arlandson writes that Jesus would define marriage as "one man and one woman living in a covenant of peace and harmony before God." In an article defending traditional marriage, Arlandson refutes ten arguments revisionists (those seeking to redefine marriage) use to justify changing marriage laws in America. Here are two of them:

> But, revisionists ask, "Isn't committed love the essence of marriage?" In reply, love is strong, powerful, and beautiful, particularly when it's expressed in a commitment. However, this is not enough, either. Two best friends who have been

roommates for many years can have a deep (nonphysical) committed love. So can two or more siblings – maybe they enjoy a deeper (nonphysical) committed love than a married couple does. But they're not marriages.

Revisionists often ask, "How does gay marriage hurt my [your] marriage?" That misses the point. It could also be asked, "How would polygamy or even incestuous marriage hurt your marriage?" … Your individual marriage doesn't matter in the debate. The point is these nonconformist relationships muddy the essence of marriage with no end in sight.[79]

I'm sure you've heard the argument that gay couples are just as committed and faithful to each other as a man and a woman. Some even go so far as to suggest "we're just like you." So can it be true, is it possible same-sex couples are just like us? This may be one of the weaker arguments for homosexual relationships, but let's address it.

First, same-sex male couples are much more likely to be unfaithful than a man and a woman in marriage. Second, lesbian couples are more likely to break up than gay men *and* straight couples.

Studies show "higher dissolution rates among same-sex couples" in Scandinavia than married heterosexual couples. Why cite an example from Scandinavia? It is one of the most gay-friendly cultures in the world. This study published in *Demography,* "Demographics of Same-Sex Marriages in Norway and Sweden," found "even though same-sex couples enter their legal unions at older ages – a marker related to greater relation stability – male same-sex marriages break up at twice the rate of heterosexual marriages."[80]

For lesbians, the break-up rate is a stunning 77% higher than the same-sex male unions. When controlling for possible confounding factors, the "risk of divorce for female partnerships actually is more than twice that for male unions."

Let's look at three important, but separate studies. The first is a recent

---

79   James Arlandson, "Ten Non-Religious Reasons to Keep Marriage Traditional," 1/13/2014,http://www.americanthinker.com/2013/01/ten_non-religious_reasons_to_keep_marriage_traditional.html.

80   Glen Stanton, "Are Same-Sex Couples Just Like You?" 5/23/2014, http://www.canonand-culture.com/are-same-sex-couples-just-like-you/.

study conducted by lesbian scholars called the National Longitudinal Family Study (NLLFS). It revealed "notable instability in lesbian homes, even those with children." They also found a significant difference in family dissolution rates when compared to traditional families with a mother and father. The break-up/divorce rate for lesbians was 56% and for heterosexual couples, 36%.

In "the Couples Study" done by gay-affirming scholars, by the end of the first year of their relationship, nearly half (49%) of the men made an arrangement for outside sexual relationships. An investigation by the American Psychological Association (APA) found only one-third of gay couples had monogamous agreements that "truly honored them with no outside sex."[81]

When it comes to gay couples in open relationships, that same study found the frequency of sex outside the relationship averaged 41.5 incidents since the start of their relationship, and in the last twelve months, an average of eight incidences of sex with someone other than their partner. The high number in the study was 350 occurrences of outside sex within the last year.

Several categories of people accept, support, or promote gay "marriage." Progressives and liberal elites often favor anything that goes against traditional Christianity because they cannot have any God above them or any moral accountability. This goes back to the worldview of Margaret Sanger and the support of eugenics and population control in America.

Most, not all, homosexuals are in favor of changing marriage laws in America. Many in Hollywood, the media, and government accept or support gay marriage as well. Even in the church, those who have caved to propaganda and public pressure now support homosexual marriage. Others in society blindly support homosexuality because they assume a majority of Americans have "evolved" on the issue. Ignorance is no excuse, so we should be informed with the facts.

---

81 Extradyadic Sex and Gay Male Couples: Comparing Monogamous and Nonmonogamous Relationships. LaSala, Michael C. Families in Society, Vol. 85(3), Jul-Sep 2004, 405-412, http://psycnet.apa.org/psycinfo/2004-19629-019.

MARKETING EVIL

A Pew Forum survey on media coverage exposed the truth a few years ago. In their reporting, the media supported same-sex marriage 5 to 1, hoping the public would soon believe it to be inevitable. This is not accidental bias; this is purposeful promotion. Because of the exceptional PR campaign for same-sex marriage in America, people overestimate how many homosexuals there are in the country.

Gallup did a poll a few years ago asking people to guess the percent of gays and lesbians in the U.S. population. Young adults and women think the gay population is 30%, and a quarter of all Americans guessed more than 25% of the population is gay!

So, what is the truth?

Homosexuals make up approximately three percent (that's 3%) of the U.S. population. In two different Gallup surveys taken about ten years apart, how many Americans do you think were correct or close to being accurate in guessing the gay population? The average was six percent of those surveyed! What does this mean? It proves the clever gay marriage marketers have done damage to public perception because people are typically way off, overestimating the number of homosexuals in our culture.

What are the repercussions? In an article for *The Atlantic*, Garance Franke-Ruta wrote that this level of misunderstanding had profound implications for the acceptance of the entire gay-rights agenda. We're talking about basic demographics of sexual behavior and identity and the fact we are ignorant, uninformed, or apathetic. Franke-Ruta stated:

> On the one hand, people who overestimate the percent of gay Americans ... seem likely to also wildly overestimate the cultural impact of same-sex marriage. On the other hand, the extraordinary confusion over the percentage of gay people may reflect a triumph of the gay and lesbian movement's decades-long fight ... One thing's for sure: it's hard to imagine the fact that so many think the country is more than a quarter gay or lesbian has no impact on our public policy.[82]

---

82   Garance Franke-Ruta, "Americans Have No Idea How Few Gay People There Are," 5/31/2012, http://m.theatlantic.com/politics/archive/2012/05/americans-have-no-idea-how-few-gay-people-there-are/257753/.

With a population of over 317 million in America, fewer than 75,000 state-sanctioned same-sex marriages have taken place, according to an estimate by Marriage Equality USA. Truly, this debate is becoming a fault line in America politically and morally regardless of the fact such a low percentage of our population is actually gay or lesbian.

The will of the people doesn't seem to matter to those who have an ideological agenda, the loudest voices, and plenty of public influence. This is *the* battle on our doorstep, like it or not. We have the overwhelming majority. We must speak up and vote.

On Tuesday, May 14, 2014, U.S. Magistrate Judge Candy Dale issued a ruling in the case of four same-sex couples who challenged the constitutionality of Idaho's marriage laws. She ignored 63% of Idaho voters by overruling the same-sex marriage ban. Dale proudly declared,

> Plaintiffs suffer these injuries not because they are unqualified
> to marry, start a family, or grow old together, but because of
> who they are and whom they love.

We identify as human beings, not human doings. "Who they are" is human; choosing to love someone and have sexual relations with them has to do with a person's actions. This is yet another case of failure to differentiate behavior from unchangeable human DNA. Moreover, heaven and nature are what disqualify them from starting a family.

If you think 63% of voters are a strong majority, one week earlier on May 9 another radical, local judge overruled 75% of Arkansas voters who in 2004 ratified their state's Marriage Amendment to protect traditional heterosexual marriage. The Bible considers gay and lesbian sex dishonorable and *contrary to nature* (Romans 1:26-27). Ironically, Arkansas' state motto is "The Natural State." Seventy-five percent of voters against one judge.

The circus has evolved into tyranny and the "marriage-go-round" continues in America between a handful of progressive judges vs. millions of concerned citizens having taken the time to go to the polls and vote. Arkansas Circuit Court Judge Chris Piazza put his political agenda above the people he supposedly serves, as he jumped on this country's lawless bandwagon, ignoring the people in one of the most socially conservative states.

Deceptively, Piazza waited until after the county clerk's offices had closed on a Friday evening to unleash his decision causing chaos and confusion throughout the state that whole weekend. One month earlier, even a poll by the one-sided *New York Times* and the Kaiser Family Foundation revealed support for gay marriage lagging in southern states. In Arkansas, only 35% of the people support Judge Piazza's position.[83]

Many states continue to battle and sort things out legally.

The groundwork for the divisive times we're seeing was laid, and the seeds were sown decades ago. The key to their momentum has been consistent action. Imagine if Christians were as dedicated to the Bible. Understand, as long as the LGBT movement continues framing the debate about sexual identity and politics, Christians will be portrayed as hating people for "who they are."

They have promoted their agenda by playing on people's emotions for years. After all, if homosexuality is just an expression of love, what is so bad about that? Shouldn't love be celebrated? Apparently, one way they celebrate love is to pridefully parade nearly naked down public streets in front of children. Activists have influenced American universities and colleges. They continue to influence impressionable young minds in grade school and high school, tirelessly working to convince hundreds of thousands of children to accept immorality.

When Republicans such as Ted Cruz and Mike Lee introduced legislation (State Marriage Defense Act) to protect states from judges overruling the voters, Democrats in the Senate went so far as to call it a "disgusting bill." Apparently, one side of the aisle considers it offensive to prevent government from trampling the will of the people and insulting majorities that voted for natural marriage as a state issue. When government controls the people, there is tyranny.

THE GLOVES ARE OFF!

Americans are being forced to change our morality, our thinking, and our laws to accommodate the lifestyle of a small group of people. Who else could get away with this with the full support of the mainstream

---

83   Mario Trujillio, "Poll: Support for gay marriage lags in
      Southern states," 4/23/2014, http://thehill.com/blogs/
      ballot-box/204136-support-for-gay-marriage-lags-in-southern-states.

media? Can you see where this is going in our culture if common sense, factual evidence, and the truth of Jesus Christ are not allowed to be considered or discussed?

Activists are not hiding their motives. They're bold, they're out of the closet, the masks are off and so are their gloves. They know this is a battle for the survival of their agenda because if more people catch on to the truth and find out the facts, they know public support of the LGBT movement would be in jeopardy.

And if they can't win fair and square, they'll lobby to buy off more Democrats and activist judges. Here's a brief look at some recent history:

- 2003: The Massachusetts Supreme Court ruled the state constitution *does* give gay and lesbian couples the right to marry, making the Bay State the first in the nation to allow same-sex marriage. Weddings began the next year.

- 2004: In Oklahoma, an overwhelming 76% of voters saw to it that their state's constitution to define marriage as the union of a man and a woman was amended. On January 14, 2014, U.S. District Judge Terence Kern ruled the amendment unconstitutional. (I wonder what will happen in Alabama where 81% of voters stood for traditional marriage.)

- 2004: In Utah, 66% of the electorate voted to amend Utah's constitution to define marriage as between a man and a woman. On December 20, 2013, U.S. District Judge Robert J. Shelby ruled the amendment unconstitutional.

- 2004: In Kentucky, 75% of voters amended their state's constitution to define marriage as between a man and a woman. On February 12, 2014, U.S. District Judge John G. Heyburn II was able to strike down part of the state ban.

- 2006: In Virginia, 57% of voters amended their state's constitution to define marriage as the union of a man and a woman. In February, 2014, U.S. District Judge Arenda Wright Allen ruled the amendment unconstitutional.

- 2008: In California, despite public protests as well as

pressure from homosexual groups and Hollywood, 52% of registered voters still amended their state's constitution to define marriage as between a man and woman. Then on August 4, 2010, U.S. District Judge Vaughn Walker ruled that vote unconstitutional.

Courts/judges in Virginia, Texas, Michigan, Ohio, Idaho, Pennsylvania, Oregon, and Wisconsin have also struck down marriage laws. The ACLU and collaborators have targeted all states that are holding on to natural marriage. The voting majority could not stop Judge Walker from overruling the people as he reasoned, "Proposition 8 fails to advance any rational basis in singling out gay men and lesbians for denial of a marriage license." Is he implying for all of history there has never been a rational basis for defining traditional marriage?

Author, radio talk show host, and columnist, Dennis Prager, put it this way:

> Vaughn Walker is convinced that he thinks more rationally than every moral leader and thinker in history, not one of whom advocated same-sex marriage. Judaism, Christianity, Islam, Buddhism, Hinduism, the Enlightenment – all were irrational regarding same-sex marriage, according to Judge Walker.
>
> …Society may no longer define marriage in the only way marriage has ever been defined in the annals of recorded history. Many societies allowed polygamy, many allowed child marriages, some allowed marriage within families; but none in thousands of years defined marriage as the union of people of the same sex.[84]

If history proves no society in thousands of years has ever redefined marriage or allowed same-sex marriage, who are the real radicals and extremists? Proponents of same-sex marriage are really on the wrong side of history here. To them, history is irrelevant and it won't stop them from working to change public perception.

The momentum is typically on the side with the most passion.

---

84   Dennis Prager, "Judges, Hubris, and Same-Sex Marriage," 2/08/2014, http://www.dennisprager.com/judges-hubris-sex-marriage/#.

Culture has shifted to the point that some polls say around fifty percent of Americans now support same-sex marriage, when just ten years ago (2004) the number was closer to thirty percent. But this is key: Who did the polling, who was polled, and how were the questions worded? It's one thing to accept gay and lesbian people; it's another thing to approve of their lifestyles and support changing marriage laws.

Also ten years ago, over seventy percent of Americans said religion was "increasing its influence" on public life. In 2014 however, over seventy percent said religion is "losing its influence" on America. Is it perception, truth, or a little of both? Just because something is popular or trending does not mean it is good, right, or beneficial for the country. In fact, some of the changes being caused by public perception and pressure should concern those of us who believe in the Bible and religious freedom.

SILENCING (BULLYING) CHRISTIANS OVER MARRIAGE VIEWS

Due to a firestorm across the Internet initiated by leftists and liberals, Brendan Eich, a chief executive of Mozilla, was forced to resign after receiving harsh criticism for his stance on marriage. (Mozilla is the organization behind the Firefox Web browser.) What happened? Mozilla found out Eich made a $1,000 donation to support marriage via the Proposition 8 ballot initiative in California – nearly six years earlier! His firing is a sign of the times. Liberals say they want diversity and tolerance, but they only tolerate those who agree with them.

Even though Eich had been with Mozilla since its inception sixteen years ago, he capitulated and issued an apology. Saying you're sorry isn't enough for bullies who now want to punish free expression rather than merely oppose it. Today, the freedoms that made our nation great are the same freedoms that can cause you to be unemployed by exercising them – if activists and Nazi's get their way. How did GLAAD, alleged promoters of diversity and tolerance, respond to Eich's treatment? They were pleased with "Mozilla's strong statement in favor of equality" because it reflects corporate America's "inclusive, safe" environment.

President of Family Research Council, Tony Perkins, warns:

We all need to be clear: We are not merely contending with a different political or social point of view. The forces of political correctness intend to run over all freedom in America; freedom of religion, freedom of speech, of assembly, of press. They cannot achieve their goal without oppression.[85]

Not all liberals and LGBT advocates approve of these tactics and many refuse to go along with the activists. Much damage is being done due to decades of behind the scenes work to glorify homosexuality, setting the stage for what we're experiencing today. Add decades of Christian silence and here we are.

I don't want a country in which homosexuals get fired for their lifestyle any more than I want people to be fired for believing in Jesus Christ or the biblical definition of marriage. But it doesn't matter what I want. Will they soon require people to start listing their personal beliefs on a resume or job application in addition to experience and qualifications? I hope not.

Another example occurred when Craig James was fired by Fox Sports in 2013 after just a few days on the job. James, a former college football star and analyst, was fired for statements he made two years earlier opposing same-sex unions. On behalf of James and Liberty Institute, the Texas Workforce Commission filed a formal charge of religious discrimination against Fox Sports West, and the network was investigated.

James previously worked for ESPN and also made a run for the Texas Senate in 2012 during which he made statements favoring marriage between one man and one woman. The most "controversial" comment James made was gays would "have to answer to the Lord for their actions," which is what any Bible-believing Christian would affirm. Why is that offensive? *Every one of us* will have to answer to God for our actions!

Fox Sports executives defended their decision by saying he wasn't vetted properly; they were concerned how someone like James would fit at Fox, and they blamed the poor decision on the regional network. A spokesman declared James would not be allowed to speak openly at Fox. "We just asked ourselves how Craig's statements would play in our human resources department. He couldn't say those things here."

---

85   Tony Perkins, "What Does the Fired Fox Say?" 4/13/2014, http://www.frc.org/
washingtonupdate/what-does-the-fired-fox-say.

This type of discrimination should give us chills. He was clearly fired due to his personal beliefs, not because of his job performance. This is becoming the climate in America, and it appears Fox Sports Southwest dug in their heels when a spokesman stated:

> Craig James is a polarizing figure in the college sports community, and the decision not to use him in our college football coverage was based on the perception that he abused a previous on-air position to further a personal agenda.

The funny thing is James had never mentioned his faith or his marriage stance on the job anywhere he worked. Shocked when the network fired him, James told the Associated Press:

> That's like a sucker punch ... For someone to call you and offer you a job, praise your talents, your credentials, put you on the air the next day and fire you the following day: That's like some kind of mean joke.

To those who love Him, God works all things together for good (Romans 8:28) because in April 2014, James was hired as an assistant to Tony Perkins, president of the Family Research Council in Washington D.C. James stated:

> Now it is my turn to offer encouragement to others encountering the same kind of religious bigotry. While the challenges to our freedoms are great, I strongly believe the game is far from over.

Craig James was fired for admitting he agreed with the majority of Americans on marriage between one man and one woman. Thankfully, James is refusing to be silent and is now serving in a role to raise awareness about this growing discrimination affecting Christians.

In another case on May 7, 2014, GLAAD intimidated HGTV (The Home & Garden Television network) into cancelling a new reality show featuring two Christian brothers, David and Jason Benham, because they support natural marriage and are also pro-life. The program, "Flip it Forward," was a real estate show that was expected to debut in October, but pressure from gay rights activists caused HGTV to cave.

The brothers from North Carolina, graduates of Liberty University and sons of an evangelical pastor, wrote in a statement, "With all of the grotesque things that can be seen and heard on television, you would think there would be room for two twin brothers who are faithful to our families, committed to biblical principles, and dedicated professionals."[86]

David Benham was also harshly criticized by Right Wing Watch for supporting an amendment protecting natural marriage and for leading a prayer rally outside the Democratic National Convention in Charlotte in 2012. David also said, "If our faith costs us a television show then so be it." The radical side of the LGBT movement will continue bullying and silencing people who refuse to get on board with their agenda.

Activists have been emboldened, particularly in the last six years.

AN ALLY IN THE WHITE HOUSE

We cannot overestimate the influence President Obama is having on the gay rights movement. Federal judges seem to have their marching orders from the White House; as do Hollywood producers, the Democrat Party, and the U.S. Department of Education. For whatever else this administration may be remembered for years from now, Obama will likely be referred to as the most pro-homosexual occupant of the White House.

As he has done each year since he was elected, President Obama released another White House Proclamation declaring homosexuality as normal and defended its advancement and promotion. He said it's about celebrating diversity and eliminating prejudice, but we know the agenda goes much deeper. The older you are, the more disappointing it is to see the leader of all Americans issue official orders endorsing immorality in any form. The younger you are, the less affected you probably are by these words:

> I, BARACK OBAMA, President of the United States of America, by virtue of the authority vested in me by the Constitution and the laws of the United States, do hereby proclaim June 2014 as Lesbian, Gay, Bisexual, and Transgender Pride Month.

As unelected, unaccountable federal judges overturn the votes and

---

86   Todd Starnes, "Ex-HGTV Hosts: If Our Faith Cost Us a TV Show, So Be It," 5/8/14, http://townhall.com/columnists/toddstarnes/2014/05/08/ exhgtv-hosts-if-our-faith-costs-us-a-tv-show-so-be-it-n1835455/page/full.

will of millions of Americans state by state, the president considers it "justice." Obama began his proclamation;

> As progress spreads from State to State, as justice is delivered in the courtroom, and as more of our fellow Americans are treated with dignity and respect – our Nation becomes not only more accepting, but more equal as well. During Lesbian, Gay, Bisexual, and Transgender (LGBT) Pride Month, we celebrate victories that have affirmed freedom and fairness, and we recommit ourselves to completing the work that remains.[87]

Do we not have the religious freedom in America to accept people without endorsing their behavior? We could ask the same question of adulterers, pornographers, pedophiles, drug dealers, murderers, fornicators, liars, and thieves. Everyone needs forgiveness and salvation, but if the message about immorality coming from our leaders is that changing laws to accommodate sin makes our nation "more equal," we'll never be a fair or equal society. Why? In order to elevate one behavior, we must minimize or eliminate the opposing behavior, which in this case happens to be Christian morality and freedom of religious expression.

Understand when the president says "we recommit ourselves to completing the work that remains," he's giving marching orders to the radical Left, encouraging them to keep taking their fight to the next level. Obama continued:

> Last year, supporters of equality celebrated the Supreme Court's decision to strike down a key provision of the Defense of Marriage Act, a ruling which, at long last, gave loving, committed families the respect and legal protections they deserve. In keeping with this decision, my Administration is extending family and spousal benefits – from immigration benefits to military family benefits – to legally married same-sex couples. My Administration proudly stands alongside all those who fight for LGBT rights.

Scrutinizing the words used in this declaration and others that Obama has issued helps us clarify and understand the agenda behind

---

87   Amy Spreeman, "President Proclaims June 2014 LGBT Pride Month" 6/5/14, http://standupforthetruth.com/2014/06/president-proclaims-june-2014-lgbt-pride-month/.

this movement. It does not seem to be about fairness and equality for all citizens; it is about conquest.

The president has been on their side from the beginning; the media simply gave him cover before he was elected. In five years, Obama has used the word "gay" 272 times, and following his 2014 State of the Union address, the gay rights lobbying group, the Human Rights Campaign (HRC), complained he hasn't done enough to help impose their agenda! He has done more than all forty-three previous presidents combined with federal benefits, same-sex marriage, "Don't Ask, Don't Tell," State Department policy, personnel hires, education projects, legal strategy, judicial nominees, and military "pride."

As Tony Perkins put it, "that doesn't satisfy his insatiable base, which, after a half-decade of the President's pandering, should be the happiest voters in all of America." The appetite of the Left is not easily satisfied, nor their thirst for power quenched.

Attorney General Eric Holder spoke to the HRC on February 8, 2014, promising to push for gay rights nationwide, thanks to the Supreme Court striking down part of the Defense of Marriage Act in June the previous year. Holder declared, "As attorney general, I will not let this department be simply a bystander during this important moment in history." Since the 1996 federal law prevented the government from recognizing same-sex marriages and Holder now saw an opening, he promised gays and lesbians widespread changes within the U.S. Justice Department to benefit same-sex married couples.

He did not disappoint them. Not only did the Obama Justice Department conclude the entire federal ban on same-sex marriages was unconstitutional, but they also stopped enforcing it nationwide! Holder then took it one step further and told state attorneys general to do the same. The first to follow the administration's lead were Pennsylvania and Oregon.

The very next day, University of Missouri football player Michael Sam came out as gay and was drafted in the seventh round by the St. Louis Rams. President Obama called it "an important step forward" and congratulated Sam who, after receiving the call, kissed his boyfriend and collapsed in his arms. Cameras were there to capture the moment.

The president also found time to congratulate NBA player Jason Collins in 2013 for publicly announcing he is a homosexual.

Before the Veterans Administration hospital scandal broke, how much time do you think the Obama administration spent investigating the problems American Veterans were having trying to get health care compared to the time spent fighting for the LGBT agenda? Tragically, many vets that served our country died waiting for care in a broken, corrupt system where top officials received benefits and raises.

As more men and women were speaking out about their issues with the VA, the administration announced the National Park Service would begin installing "markers at significant locations that note the advancement of lesbian, gay, bisexual and transgender Americans." Rather than give veterans the honor they deserve, team Obama plans to recognize contributions to America made by LGBT citizens.

These are the priorities of an administration out of touch with average Americans. The U.S. Department of Health and Human Services decided to provide taxpayer funded "sex reassignment surgery," adding the cost to the already overburdened Medicare system.[88]

What does this have to do with marriage? If the public can be convinced homosexuals are a people group deserving special "civil" rights, recognizing their unions as legal marriages is a logical step. In order for them to discredit biblical marriage and advance unnatural marriage, the LGBT lifestyle must be promoted as normal. We have a gullible, culture conforming society today, one in which people buy into emotional appeals, celebrity, and talking points rather than pursuing facts, evidence, and truth.

A sampling of White House history from the last several years exposes the Obama administration's attack on marriage and agenda to revamp the moral structure of America:

- The president appointed an openly homosexual assistant attorney general for the Civil Division of the Department of Justice who was part of the team arguing that the Defense of Marriage Act was unconstitutional.

---

88   Katy Steinmetz, "Board Rules That Medicare Can Now Cover Gender Reassignment Surgery" 5/30/14 http://time.com/2800307/medicare-gender-reassignment/.

- President Obama repealed "Don't Ask Don't Tell," the policy of seventeen years that prohibited homosexuals serving in the military from openly announcing their sexual preferences.

- The White House has hosted six LGBT Conferences.[89]

- Obama appointed John Berry to be the "Director of the United States Office of Personnel Management (OPM)" making him the highest-ranking openly gay official at the time. Berry was responsible for recruiting, hiring, and setting benefits policies for 1.9 million federal employees. Berry was then appointed to serve as ambassador to Australia. At least four other homosexual ambassadors have also been appointed.

- In a controversial recess appointment, he nominated lesbian Chai Feldblum to the Equal Employment Opportunity Commission where she sits as chair. Feldblum has long advocated the view that when in conflict, the sexual rights of homosexuals should trump the First Amendment religious rights of conservative people of faith.

- Obama jumped on the opportunity to be interviewed by lesbian journalist Robin Roberts and discussed his support for same sex marriage.

- In a pre-Super Bowl interview with Bill O' Reilly, Obama opined the Boy Scouts of America should allow openly homosexual boys to become members of the Scouts (which, lest we forget, take an oath to honor God).

- The president hosted a "bullying prevention" conference at the White House to which he invited the vile, anti-Christian, homosexual sex columnist and bully, Dan Savage.

- He supports the "Employment Non-Discrimination Act," which, if passed, will prohibit Christian employers from refusing to hire gender-confused cross-dressers.

---

89   President Obama and the LGBT Community, "White House LGBT Conferences," http://www.whitehouse.gov/lgbt/white-house-conferences.

- Obama supports the ironically named "Respect for Marriage Act," which, if passed, would repeal the Defense of Marriage Act in its entirety. This would mean states prohibiting same-sex "marriage" would have to recognize same-sex marriages performed in other states.

  *Many of these items were documented by the Illinois Family Institute.[90]

For Christians who think much of this talk is just about politics, understand that every time the gay rights movement advances by gaining legal ground, it comes at the expense of our freedom and our taxes. This cultural battle is not over constitutional rights – it is about *special* rights; and theirs trump all others.

Are we only protected when we're sitting in a church pew? To the radical Left, if we dare step out into public, we should no longer speak. The problem is we are commanded in the Bible to do so! What does this mean for us? It means seeking the approval of God rather than man, and living our faith every single day, everywhere we go, and not just on Sunday mornings.

Religious liberty is what has set us apart from all other nations in the world, and it was the first right our founders protected in the Constitution. Bryan Fischer of the American Family Association believes the same-sex marriage issue is *the* number one battle and indicator in America that will determine our future as a nation. Fischer writes:

> Religious principle, tolerance, and rights of conscience mean nothing to pro-sodomy advocates. They will remorselessly crush anyone and anything that gets in their path, without mercy and without a second thought. In their quest for cultural domination, they will relentlessly extinguish the light of sexual normalcy and morality, as well as the light of Christianity. They have the will to crush biblical Christianity into broken pieces. They lack only the power.[91]

---

90   Laurie Higgins, "Obama Chooses Homosexuals Over Veterans," 5/30/14, http://illinois-family.org/federal/obama-chooses-homosexuals-over-veterans/.

91   Bryan Fischer, "The battle for gay rights is THE battle – there is no other," 3/6/2014, http://onenewsnow.com/perspectives/bryan-fischer/2014/03/06/the-battle-over-gay-rights-is-the-battle-there-is-no-other.

The president of the United States and the Justice Department are working to give activists more influence. Rich, powerful corporate men and women along with Hollywood executives pay millions of dollars to lobby for gay rights; so naturally, a corrupt government takes their money and supports their depravity. Normalizing sin simply opens the door for more devious ways to sin publicly.

AN AGENDA OF FALLEN MAN

A video from Good Fight Ministries, "X-Men and the Gay Agenda," includes a few former Hollywood child actors who admitted they were molested and raped often as young children. They said pedophilia is one of the biggest unspoken problems inside the entertainment industry. Of course, it is not isolated within Hollywood, and not all homosexuals are pedophiles, but an established link exists between homosexuality and pedophilia: 46% of homosexual men and 22% of homosexual women admitted to having been molested by a person of the same gender when they were minors.

For those who are reading information like this for the first time and find some of it hard to believe, we simply need to understand sin and evil to be able to see what's happening in the country. In the 1980s, an essay was written called, "The Overhauling of Straight America" in which the goal was the subversion of this nation. The article was one of the playbooks for the gay movement and advocated using the media and advertising strategies to normalize homosexuality. The first goal was to desensitize people concerning gays and lesbians.

- Step 1: Talk about gays and gayness as loudly and as often as possible.

- Step 2: Portray gays as victims, not as aggressive challengers.

- Step 3: Give protectors (heterosexuals) a just cause.

- Step 4: Make gays look good.

- Step 5: Make the victimizers look bad.[92]

This playbook for homosexual leaders and Hollywood elites led to

---

92   Pete Winn, "The Gay Playbook and How it's 'Overhauling' America," 9/21/2011, http://
cnsnews.com/blog/pete-winn/gay-playbook-and-how-its-overhauling-america.

gay authors, Marshall Kirk and Hunter Madsen, expanding the gay agenda and public-persuasion tactics in their 1989 book, *After the Ball: How America Will Conquer Its Fear and Hatred of Gays in the 90s*. One key to their success was to, "portray gays as victims of circumstance and oppression."

Think about all the television shows since the 1980s in which gay characters were portrayed as likeable, heroes, or victims; they also used movies, media, and the advertising industry. Today homosexuals are prevalent on reality TV shows and commercials.

Watching the media gleefully announce practically every occurrence of a judge overturning the people's vote to ban gay marriage was disappointing. They parrot LGBT talking points and give airtime to every supposed incident of "inequality," but they can't be bothered to do their jobs by reporting on actual victims of the Gay Reich: Bakers, florists, and business owners are forced into bankruptcy. Teachers, pastors, and students are pressured to be politically correct. Broadcasters are threatened and the military is dismantled.

In an effort to protect religious liberty and defend all citizens, Arizona Governor Jan Brewer attempted to amend an already existing state law, but the hate and misinformation spewed against her caused her to cave to the activists. Brewer wanted to protect business owners (particularly Christians) from being sued and forced to close for choosing not to do business with someone. Gay rights activists called it a "horrendous" bill. How sad when states can no longer defend or amend their own laws! This deceptive propaganda campaign by the Left trumped truth and freedom.

Twenty-eight states including Arizona currently have Religious Freedom Restoration Act (RFRA) protections. The bill liberals cried foul over, SB 1062, was simply an improvement to this law and the Arizona legislature gave it a green light. The legislation would have also given gays and lesbians more protection, but the Left used the media to lie about the language in the bill. Out of blind opposition, even Apple, Delta Airlines, PetSmart, AT&T, Marriott, and the NFL came out against Brewer. The HRC called the bill the "License to Discriminate" Bill.

We have a new one-way freeway running across America today; it's called "Tolerance."

If a gay or lesbian business owner of a graphics design company chose to deny someone's business because they wanted banner ads saying "Jesus is Lord" or "God made marriage," should they be forced to do business with them? No. Christians don't sue over such expressions of freedom, but the Left does. They claimed the Arizona bill was intolerant and against their civil rights. Alliance Defending Freedom responded by saying the RFRA was about "making sure people of faith aren't [treated as] second class citizens because government passes laws willy-nilly infringing on religious freedom."

Unfortunately, liberal activists and critics of SB 1062 had the loudest voices and won that battle even though law professors from various universities encouraged Governor Brewer not to waver in the face of "egregious misrepresentations." They all seemed to agree with the sentiment of one professor who stated, "We don't want to run religious people out of the public square, nor do we want to drive lesbians and gays out of society."

From all appearances, however, the former is what is happening in America today as God continues to be blotted out – a necessary part of their agenda. The good news is we've reached a pivotal turning point moving us closer to the end times.

THE BIBLE, THE BEGINNING, AND THE END

Plenty of factual information has been condensed in this chapter, adding to the already convincing argument for marriage between one man and one woman, but the strongest evidence and the ultimate authority is the Word of God. We know we're approaching judgment when certain churches and denominations are capitulating to the demands of the gay movement. Decades ago, we failed to take a strong enough stance on adultery, divorce, abortion, promiscuity, and idolatry. We were silent. Most recently, homosexuality has crept in as a destructive, divisive issue in Christianity.

As Dr. Albert Mohler Jr. put it, "no surrender on this issue would have been possible if the authority of Scripture had not already been undermined." Either homosexuality is a sin or it is not a sin. If we trust the Bible, why are so many Christians accommodating those involved in sinful lifestyles? Perhaps we're back to the core issue: Is all of Scripture reliable, true, inerrant, and inspired by God, or is doctrine moldable and open to the interpretation of man?

We must remember a remnant remains. These committed believers are warriors for the truth of Jesus Christ and include pastors taking solid stands on the Word while equipping their flocks. They understand we're living in dark days, and they know they have a part to play in reaching lost souls. These saints of God have the wisdom to know this marriage debate is not going to make or break us; our eternal destiny is already set. The ultimate battle is over the foundation of absolute truth and the person of Jesus Christ.

When a Christian defends same-sex marriage, simply ask them, "Don't you think your support of homosexuality and the redefinition of marriage is a departure from the teachings in God's Word? If it wasn't moral in the beginning, what makes it acceptable now? Is it wise to abandon biblical truth and give your blessing to what the Bible condemns?" Prepare yourself for a defensive or hostile reaction to your questioning.

Author and radio talk show host Steve Deace has been consistent in his defense of biblical principles and common sense in the ongoing marriage debate. He agrees we have come to the proverbial fork in the road in a nation once founded by those who came here to worship God freely without interference and persecution from ruling elites. Deace said the "tolerance" that society demands from Christians really is silent compliance. After the fallout from A&E's mishandling of Phil Robertson, Deace concluded:

> After years of attempting to balance traditional Americana with political correctness, those pushing the new "my way or the highway" definition of "tolerance" have decided accommodating our differences of opinion is defeat … One sign says "liberty." The other sign says "political correctness." Every individual American and every American institution will have to choose one or the other. We can no longer have both,

and the truth is we really never could. It was always going to end this way, we just didn't want to believe it.[93]

Christianity is the biggest obstacle to the advancement of sin in any form. Are we willing to take the heat and stand for biblical marriage? We should be able to handle the name calling and the backlash without taking it personally. In the end, it won't matter if people attack or reject us; it *will* matter if they reject Jesus Christ.

Though they know God's righteous decree that those who practice such things deserve to die, they not only do them but give approval to those who practice them (Romans 1:32 ESV).

For the wrath of God is revealed from heaven against all ungodliness and unrighteousness of men who suppress the truth in unrighteousness, because that which is known about God is evident within them; for God made it evident to them. For since the creation of the world His invisible attributes, His eternal power and divine nature, have been clearly seen, being understood through what has been made, so that they are without excuse (Romans 1:18-20).

---

93 Steve Deace, "A&E fowls up 'Duck' flap," 12/21/2013, http://www.usatoday.com/story/opinion/2013/12/19/duck-dynasty-bible-religion-palin-robertson-column/4124181/.

Chapter 11

WORLDVIEW WAR

By faith we understand that the worlds were prepared by the word of God, so that what is seen was not made out of things which are visible.
Hebrews 11:3

The heavens declare the glory of God, and the sky above proclaims his handiwork.
Psalm 19:1, ESV

In the beginning God created the heavens and the earth. The earth was formless and void, and darkness was over the surface of the deep, and the Spirit of God was moving over the surface of the waters. Then God said, "Let there be light"; and there was light. God saw that the light was good; and God separated the light from the darkness. God called the light day, and the darkness He called night. And there was evening and there was morning, one day.
Genesis 1:1-5

CREATION vs. EVOLUTION

Similar to natural marriage, another subject overwhelmingly supported by Scripture is intelligent design. The creation and evolution debate is not even fair once we understand the Bible and read the strong case for the earth's origins as described in Genesis, Psalms, and other books. One problem, however, is that Christians are generally not equipped to discuss this important topic. We have lost much ground due to our silence, and the enemy now has an advantage: confusion and misinformation.

Examining some key arguments regarding evolution and the origin of man is crucial. Understanding how historical and observational science compliment and support the creation account in Scripture is essential.

We need to comprehend and address some of the objections used by those who do not believe the Bible in regard to creation and those who teach and believe evolutionary theory. Faith is required to believe in *either* worldview. I completely trust the authority of the Bible and invite you to investigate with me.

Scripture contains plenty of evidence – archeological, historical, anthropological, *and* scientific – supporting creation by the hand of God. How did the earth come to be? Where did human beings come from and what is our purpose? Answers to these important questions can be traced back to God.

For Christians, we are fooling ourselves if we say we believe in parts of the Bible and at the same time believe parts of man's theories about creation. Since we are intelligent beings, can we not assume we must have been created and designed by a being more intelligent than us? Otherwise, our lives are accidental, random, and the result of chance. People must believe in one or the other: a world with God or a world without God.

Without God, is morality even relevant? How would we measure character and conduct? If we somehow evolved into human beings, does society then teach us what's good and what's bad? If so, who was the first person to determine right and wrong and how do we know he was right? Perhaps each individual should just decide for themselves.

The truth is not only are we built with a conscience, but at the very least we all know about God. We concluded the last chapter with verses in Romans explaining we are without excuse because God made His existence evident to us by creation. We also possess a basic knowledge of Him in our hearts because He placed in us a longing for heaven.

> *He has made everything beautiful in its time. He has also set eternity in the human heart; yet no one can fathom what God has done from beginning to end* (Eccl. 3:11 NIV).

The argument for evolution, however, begins with speculation and theory, not evidence and fact. Synonyms for *speculation* are opinion, hypothesis, conjecture, and guesswork. Since evolution has never been proven factual or true, shouldn't we look more closely at what the Word of God teaches about creation? The Bible has never ever been proved wrong.

In Romans 1:21-22 the apostle Paul writes that even though people knew God, *they did not honor Him as God or give thanks, but they became futile in their speculations, and their foolish heart was darkened. Professing to be wise, they became fools.*

Furthermore, the theory of evolution has been taught for decades in most American schools while unbiased, untainted instruction on creationism and intelligent design are rarely found since government took over public education.

We often hear people suggest the Bible and science contradict each other and that we must keep them separate. The Bible is full of history and knowledge. Most scientists don't believe the Bible and yet search for knowledge! Here's the problem: scientists study evidence and discoveries (knowledge) and look for understanding, but they disagree with the Bible. Understanding comes from opening up God's Word (Psalm 119:130).

According to the dictionary, the word *science* simply means "knowledge." It means "a branch of knowledge or study; systematic knowledge, facts or principles." The word *conscience* is derived from two words: *con* meaning "with" and *science* meaning "knowledge." So, *conscience* is defined as "the inner sense of what is right and wrong in one's conduct or motives; an inhibiting sense of what is prudent" regarding our thoughts and actions.

Human conscience may be influenced by society, but society does not give it to us. Every sane human being intuitively knows the basic difference between right and wrong regardless of what they were taught. Since we all have a conscience and the knowledge within ourselves regarding morality, how did it get there if God didn't write His laws on each of our hearts?

If God exists, how can anyone think He is not powerful enough to create all things when confirmations, manifestations, and declarations of His workmanship are all around us? All creation testifies to His existence. We must decide where we stand on the origin of man and know why we believe what we believe so we will no longer be silent.

Now faith is the substance of things hoped for, the evidence of things not seen (Hebrews 11:1 NKJ).

Where creation is concerned, how do we answer those who don't believe in God or claim the Bible is not true? Many respected professors and "experts" say religion and science are irreconcilable. How do they know that? Most of these scholars do not believe in God, and others say God does not even exist. Therefore, they conclude there cannot be any moral absolutes or fixed-in-concrete truth. If they are right, how can they say *anything* is true?

In other words, if there are no moral absolutes, how can we be absolutely sure that what man claims is "truth'" is indeed true? The Bible teaches Jesus is the Truth and He is God, but according to the intelligence and wisdom of man, the Bible is not true and Jesus is not God. They just cannot prove what they claim.

Author and apologist, Frank Turek, has a book, curriculum, and seminar presentations entitled "I Don't Have Enough Faith to be an Atheist." He suggests we use their own assumptions and logic to refute those who say "there is no truth." Respond by asking them "is that true?" If it is really true that there is no truth, their statement "there is no truth" can't be true, but they claim it is true.[94]

Since Jesus said He is the only way to the Father, and John tells us by believing in Him we can have everlasting life in His name (John 20:31), we better get this whole thing right about creation and decide whether Genesis is true or not. Our salvation depends on the integrity of Scripture. If Jesus is "the Word" and He was "with God in the beginning," if "the Word *was* God," and if no one has ever disproven His resurrection from the dead, then it must be actual history which means Jesus truly is eternal. Christianity is faith securely founded on fact.

Jesus Christ is both Creator and God. Colossians 1:16 tells us *by Him all things were created, both in the heavens and on earth*. And John 1:3 affirms this truth:

All things came into being through Him, and apart from Him nothing came into being that has come into being.

Defending our faith involves pre-evangelism, meaning we need to

---

94   Frank Turek, "Does Truth Exist?" http://crossexamined.org/.

be planting seeds of the gospel and be ready to answer anyone who challenges our faith in Christ. Defending the faith also involves post-evangelism (follow-up), building one's faith on a solid foundation through Bible study, application, accountability, prayer, and consistent efforts to strengthen our understanding through apologetics. Apologetics is simply a branch of theology concerned with the defense or proof of Christianity.

Why is it so important to establish that the universe was intelligently designed by a Creator? For one, think about young children for a moment; their behaviors, beliefs, and lives reflect what they are taught regarding how they came into existence. If they know they were uniquely created and designed inside their mother's womb by a God who loves them, they will live and treat others much differently. They would value life and have a different morality than if they think they are here because of some undirected, random process.

Random means "proceeding, made, or occurring without definite aim, reason, or pattern." Synonyms for *random* include accidental, odd, arbitrary, unplanned, aimless, and haphazard. The opposite of random is planned, essential, specific, definite, methodical, and systematic. One thought pattern builds faith and confidence; the other builds insecurity and hopelessness.

The Bible provides many descriptors of each individual life, such as, *For You formed my inward parts; You wove me in my mother's womb* (Psalm 139:13).

And in Ephesians 2:10:

> *For we are His workmanship, created in Christ Jesus for good works, which God prepared beforehand so that we would walk in them.*

Every life is a work of art and has purpose! Some people accuse Christians of being anti-science when just the opposite is true. How can Christians be against science when the Bible is full of knowledge? What many scientists disagree with is the spiritual aspect of the Bible. What they cannot deny is practically every time a new archeological discovery is excavated in the Middle East or neighboring continents, it supports some scriptural reference to a people, place, or time.

NEWTON AND SCIENCE REINFORCE
FAITH IN THE BIBLE

Many of our greatest scientific discoveries and advancements were made by Bible-believing Christians like Sir Isaac Newton, Blaise Pascal, Louis Pasteur, and others. The earliest scientists most likely set out to learn more about God through the study of His creation as well as their discoveries. In fact, Sir Isaac Newton, considered one of the greatest scientists and mathematicians the world has ever seen, wrote much more about faith and the Bible than he wrote about science.

Born on Christmas Day in 1642, Newton and other scientists believed the creation account in the Bible as well as the account of the worldwide flood during Noah's time. Most educated people believed this until the late 1800s. Regarding creation, Newton stated:

> God is one and the same God always and everywhere ... He endures always and is present everywhere, and by existing always and everywhere he constitutes duration and space; ... Tis inconceivable that inanimate brute matter should (without the mediation of something else which is not material) operate upon & affect other matter without mutual contact.[95]

By the time Newton was ten years old, he was studying the book of Daniel and would later write about Daniel and Revelation in *Observations Upon the Prophecies*. Considered by others a theologian during his lifetime, Isaac Newton was a Bible scholar, fluent in ancient languages with extensive knowledge of history. He believed the Bible to be literal, and throughout his life he tested biblical truth against the scientific methods common at the time, never finding a contradiction.

Though some claimed Newton was a deist influenced strongly by Christianity, he viewed his own work as a ministry to reinforce faith in the Word of God. He believed God was and is the Creator, and nature overwhelmingly proves His existence. He questioned others who had opposing opinions and theories about the earth's origins and warned against those who held man's knowledge too highly. In his 1687 book, *Philosophiæ Naturalis Principia Mathematica*, Newton stated:

This most beautiful system of the sun, planets, and comets,

---

95   Isaac Newton, Stanford Encyclopedia of Philosophy, "Newton's Philosophy," 10/13/2006, http://plato.stanford.edu/entries/newton-philosophy/.

could only proceed from the counsel and dominion of an intelligent Being. [...] This Being governs all things, not as the soul of the world, but as Lord over all.[96]

Isaac Newton wrote approximately 1.3 million words about biblical subjects. He studied at Cambridge and attended an Anglican church, but some claim Newton was a heretic, claiming he did not believe in the Trinity. Historians disagree on whether Newton held to a more eastern or western orthodox view of Christianity.

Though he read the Bible daily, helped pay for the distribution of Bibles among the poor, and served on a commission to build new churches in England, he is not known to have preached the gospel and seldom made public statements about his theology. Because of the Blasphemy Act of 1697, some say Newton would have been punished had he spoken publicly about his faith. Regardless, Isaac Newton is most known for his scientific achievements and influence.

Many modern scientists assume that because there is observable change in nature, evolution must be a fact. An important distinction is evident; we all acknowledge much of the change they refer to, but that doesn't prove "molecules to man" evolution. When a person places the intelligence of man over God's Word, they can blindly support what other scholars have taught them. Observational science cannot prove evolution; nobody was alive to witness creation.

Historical science is the study of events that occurred in the past that cannot be examined or tested in the present day. Herein lies the controversy: Scientists differ in opinion as to what happened prior to mankind. We weren't here so how can they know for sure? Their theories must necessarily be based on assumptions which are where the Big Bang theory comes from. Observing or testing the event of creation is impossible. Not only is the theory based on educated guesses of man, it is impossible to know how and when the bang happened. Isaac Newton was correct in his order of study: He began with the Bible and worked outward from there.

That your faith should not rest on the wisdom of men, but on the power of God (1 Corinthians 2:5).

---

96   Isaac Newton; Principia, Book III; cited in; Newton's Philosophy of Nature: Selections from his writings, p. 42, ed. H.S. Thayer, Hafner Library of Classics, NY, 1953.

NOAH, THE FLOOD, AND THE SCIENCE GUY

Ken Ham, President of Answers in Genesis, said creation is the only viable model of historical science confirmed by observational science in the modern era. In February 2014, millions of people tuned in online to watch the debate between Ham and Bill Nye (aka The Science Guy) who says he is an atheist. The age of the earth was a primary focus. The Bible and Christianity provide a basis for the rules of logic and the order of nature, both of which are necessary for science. Regarding modern dating methods, Ham declared:

> I claim there's only one infallible dating method – a witness who was there and who knows everything and who told us – that's the Word of God ... All these [other] dating methods actually give all sorts of different dates, even different dating methods on the same rock.[97]

Bill Nye, in an attempt to discredit the Bible, asked how millions of species could have fit on Noah's Ark, "a boat built by one man." Let's talk about this, specifically remembering the Bible describes in minute detail exactly how Noah was to build the vessel. (The instructions included the kind of wood to use as well as its exact dimensions.)

One of the arguments Nye and proponents of evolution use is how could Noah have built an ark by himself big enough to fit millions of species of living things? There are several faulty assumptions that need to be addressed in this one sentence. Let's refute these one at a time.

Regarding the underlying premise that Noah built the vessel all by himself, Noah had a wife, three sons, and his sons each had wives. It is reasonable to assume they helped him in the building process. Also, would it be possible Noah received help from friends or that he hired locals to work on the project? We don't know for sure, but we could surmise even though people thought Noah was crazy, who would turn down a paying job? There could have been dozens of people building the big wooden ship over the span of many years.

Also within this assumption is the suggestion Noah was an unskilled carpenter. How long would it take for a man to learn carpentry? About

---

97   Tyler O'Neil, "Science vs. Bible? 5 Arguments for and Against Creationism From the Ken Ham, Bill Nye Debate," 2/5/2014, http://www.christianpost.com/news/science-vs-bible-the-5-best-arguments-for-and-against-creationism-from-the-ken-ham-bill-nye-debate-114005/.

three months perhaps? Now put God back in the mix; it doesn't matter how much Noah knew or how much experience he had building things if God enabled him to carry out His plans.

Third, forgetting the average lifespan of people at that time, we often overlook the fact Noah was 600 years old when the flood waters came and he lived to be 950. At that time, his son, Shem, was ninety-eight years old, and he lived to be 600. Ham and Japeth were around the same age, so they might have invested more than seventy-five years each helping their father.

In less than one hundred years, Noah and his sons and their wives – and whoever else helped them build the ark – became proficient at trimming and chopping down trees, measuring and cutting them to the sizes God specified, connecting pieces of wood into sections, and mixing the tar-like pitch before covering all the wood with it. (Pitch, bitumen in a soft state, is extracted by distilling or heating wood and was the substance used to waterproof the ark.)

Fourth, does anyone remember the pyramids? No one knows how those uniquely engineered, massive structures were built. It's true that possibly thousands of slaves built the ancient pyramids, but the point is these mysteries were a work of man. Evidence exists proving ancient man was quite capable of engineering achievements man cannot reproduce today. If there is a God and if He is all-knowing, how could we not believe He would have the wisdom to instruct and enable Noah to build a massive ship?

Finally, did Noah really have to fit millions of species on the ark? Impossible, right? Remember, every fish and every sea creature (numbering in the thousands) would not have been inside the Ark; they would have remained in the water. Moreover, not all the modern species we have today were on the Ark because many were not even around at that time. We also must recognize the common use of synonyms to describe the same animal in many cases. There is an ongoing debate over the definition of the word *kind* as it relates to the biblical account of the flood. Many suggest *kind* means "family" when used in this context.

Of the birds after their kind, and of the animals after their kind, of every creeping thing of the ground after its kind, two of every kind will come to you to keep them alive (Genesis 6:20).

> *On the very same day Noah and Shem and Ham and Japheth,
> the sons of Noah, and Noah's wife and the three wives of his sons
> with them, entered the ark, they and every beast after its kind,
> and all the cattle after their kind, and every creeping thing that
> creeps on the earth after its kind, and every bird after its kind,
> all sorts of birds. So they went into the ark to Noah, by twos
> of all flesh in which was the breath of life. Those that entered,
> male and female of all flesh, entered as God had commanded
> him; and the Lord closed it behind him* (Genesis 7:13-16).

The use of the word *kind* suggests there would have been one male and one female representative of the dog kind, the cat kind, the horse kind, the snake kind, the elephant kind, etc., all equipped with the genetic capability to produce future species within their kind. The word *species* is not found in the Bible. Noah did not need more than one pair of horses; in other words, he did not also need a pair of Clydesdales, zebras, and Shetland ponies. (Today, there are hundreds of species of horses and ponies.)

The same goes for dogs: one pair of dogs would later produce various sizes, shapes, and species of coyotes, foxes, wolves, domestic dogs, etc. Climate, food, genetics, geographical region, and terrain all help determine the breed of animal, length of fur, color, size, and more.

Dr. Jeff Miller of Apologetics Press wrote an extensive review of the Ham vs. Nye debate covering many points in depth. Miller reiterated our faith in the existence of God is based on plenty of evidence:

> [T]hat the Universe could not have created itself; that objective morality must come from God; that complex, functional design always, without exception, demands a Designer; that the religious inclination humans have could not have arisen from rocks and dirt. Our belief in the inspiration of the Bible is based on evidence: the scientific foreknowledge of the Bible; the unity of the Bible; the historical accuracy of the Bible; the predictive prophecies of the Bible; the lack of sustainable contradictions within the Bible. Once the Bible is accepted as inspired, the blueprint for the Creation model

can be uncovered, which shapes the creationist's perspective on science.[98]

We only addressed a few of the faulty talking points, but there are plenty more when it comes to their argument for evolution.

FOOLING WITH FOSSILS & FUDGING THE NUMBERS

Shouldn't those in the evolution theory camp be embarrassed by the fossil record? We can't possibly delve into every aspect of this subject to do it justice, but a few points can be made from a layperson's perspective. First, why would people put so much stock in the fossils being evidence for evolution? How many people do continued research or in-depth studying of evolution including the fossils *after* they become adults? Hundreds? And how many children were taught about evolution in public schools since it was first introduced? Millions?

In school, students are shown a representation of the fossil record displayed as a vertical column with small marine creatures on the bottom layer followed by fish, amphibians, reptiles, mammals, and then man on top. We've all seen it, haven't we? The textbook picture appears to show a process of time, from bottom to top, suggesting evolution from past to present. Most often, either this fossil column or a similar figure is presented as if it were real, indisputable data. Why would children think it wasn't true?

Columns such as those and other similar efforts used to visually display fossils are examples of assumed evolutionary thinking. Even I can understand the fossils do not occur from a simple to complex order in every case because some of the invertebrate creatures (without a backbone) are still around today; they never evolved. That's a pretty big leap of faith there. The earliest fossils are practically the same as their modern counterparts, proving the examples at the bottom of the textbook column are equal in complexity.[99]

What exactly does the record prove then? Many believe they complement the biblical model of creation and at the same time deny

98   Jeff Miller, Ph.D, "Bill Nye/Ken Ham Debate Review: Tying Up Really Loose Ends" Apologetics Press, Feb/2014, http://www.apologeticspress.org/APContent. aspx?category=9&article=4819.

99   Dr. John D. Morris, "Don't the Fossil Records Prove Evolution?" Institute for Creation Research, http://www.icr.org/article/dont-fossils-prove-evolution/.

204 | THE COST OF OUR SILENCE

the evolutionary hypothesis. Do fossils support the flood? There is a transition at every level from the dominant marine fossils to more and more earthbound fossils on typical charts. Approximately 95 percent of fossils discovered were seagoing creatures, so why are there more marine fossils than land fossils? Could the Bible be true regarding a past catastrophic event such as a worldwide flood because of which all living earthbound creatures, including human beings, were wiped out by deep, intense flood waters?

There may well be human fossils or more land fossils that have not been discovered yet. All we can do is use the evidence and knowledge we have available and make an educated, informed decision about the origin of man. If we take Scripture at face value and add the science that supports the evidence, like Isaac Newton did, it becomes clear a global flood occurred in which people were destroyed along with animals.

By contrast, if evolution were true, why all the hoaxes? Why would some atheists and evolutionists feel compelled to make up a creature and a story to go along with its fake discovery? We need to acknowledge some of these lies because I don't believe Christians have tried to manufacture physical evidence supporting the book of Genesis in the hopes of winning more converts to the intelligent design worldview. We do that by sharing the gospel.

Even the senior paleontologist at the British Museum of Natural History, Colin Patterson, admitted he would have included any evolutionary transitions from one species to another in his book had he known of any. The museum houses sixty million specimens which is the world's largest collection of fossils. Most of the general public, however, don't seem to realize that no verifiable transitions from one species to another have ever been found.

Tragically, a children's book, *The Wonderful Egg*, recommended by the American Council on Education and the Association for Childhood Education International, promotes the theory of quantum leaps in evolution. In the book, a mother dinosaur lays an egg, and it hatches into the world's very first bird; a fantasy insulting to genetic science.[100]

The reason this stuff has to be suggested is the absence of vertical

100 Henry M. Morris and Gary E. Parker, *What is Creation Science?* Rev. ed. (El Cajon, CA: Master Books, 1987), 148.

transitional forms in the fossil record. Because the theory of evolution by gradualism could not be proved, someone had to suggest a "jumping gene" theory.

In his book, *Christianity in Crisis*, author Hank Hanegraaff states the fossil record is an embarrassment to evolutionists, and the field of paleoanthropology "is fraught with ape-men fiction, frauds, and fantasies." The idea that the complexity of our universe came about through chance (happening without cause) is a statistical impossibility, and "has no chance in an age of scientific enlightenment." Hanegraaff continues:

> In the category of fiction is *Pithecanthropus erectus* (Java Man). Nineteen doctrinaire evolutionists who participated in the Selenka expedition – a trek bent on demonstrating that the evolutionary conjectures concerning Java Man were true – produced a 342-page scientific report demonstrating beyond the peradventure of a doubt that *Pithecanthropus erectus* played no part whatsoever in human evolution.
>
> Piltdown Man may be factually described as a fraud. While the fraud may have been cleverly conceived, it was crudely carried out. The jaw of an ape was stained to make it appear as though it would match a human skull. Peking Man might best be described as a pure fantasy conceived by physician Davison Black as he was about to run out of funds for his evolutionary explorations in 1927.[101]

Regarding Java Man (fossils discovered on the islands of Java) and Pekin Man (fossils discovered near Beijing), several "experts" classified both as human fossils in 1944. Well before this, a doctor named Charles Dawson announced he had found a jawbone and a cranial fragment in Piltdown, England, in 1912, supposedly 500,000 years old. The headline read, "Darwin Theory Proved True." Further proving how gullible people are, they were put on display in several museums, and for decades, scientific articles were written about Piltdown Man as well as hundreds of doctoral theses.

Of course, many drawings, interpretations, and sketches were put

101   Hank Hanegraaff, *Christianity in Crisis : 21st Century*, (Thomas Nelson, Nashville, TN, 2009), p. 306.

forth, and evolutionists were thrilled about the alleged breakthrough evidence for human evolution. Eventually, however, technology, truth, and science got in the way of their important discovery. In 1949, years after pictures of ape men had already saturated science books and people's minds, a new testing method became available for determining the date of fossils. Kenneth Oakley from the British Museum of Paleontology Department used "fluorine testing" on the Piltdown Man fossil. A trial testing was done, and he realized the jawbone did not contain any fluorine.

The skull revealed it was not older than a few thousand years at most. Naturally, the hoax was exposed. The teeth in the jawbone belonged to an orangutan, but someone filed them down to make them appear like a man's teeth. Teeth were arranged and added to the (monkey's) jawbone, and all the fossils were dyed with potassium dichromate so they would appear much older than they actually were. Evidence of "artificial abrasion" or in layman's terms "faking the fossil" was noticeable.

The forgery was revealed to the public in 1953 by Joseph Weiner. Molar surfaces had been filled, and the skull fragments belonged to a very old man. Of course, with much less pomp, Piltdown man was removed from the British Museum where it had been on display for over forty years. The damage, however, was done.

One of the biggest hoaxes may have been "Nebraska Man," allegedly discovered in 1922 by Henry Osborn, the director of the American Museum of Natural History. He found a tooth in western Nebraska that had characteristics of both an ape and a man. A debate arose about its true history, but many "experts" gave their approval and supported Osborn.

Are you ready for perhaps an even crazier stretch of truth? From one single tooth (that's all they had to go on), scientists and artists attempted to reconstruct Nebraska Man's entire head. But they did not stop there! They came up with his body and kept going, creating a wife and family for the poor old lonely fossil. Soon drawings of the ape family appeared in outdoor settings, and schools added the supposed find to their science instruction. Yup – it all started with one tooth.

But the atheist's and evolutionist's party came to a screeching halt in 1927 when other parts of the skeleton were found. The new fossil discoveries revealed Nebraska Man wasn't a man at all, nor was he an ape. In fact, it may be the reason atheists secretly don't like bacon to this day: The tooth came from an extinct species of wild American pig, *Prosthennops*. Mysteriously, drawings and paintings of Nebraska Man vanished from sight, scientists retreated, and Osborn supporters said "never mind." The "missing link" was removed from evolutionary literature, and they went back to the drawing board – literally.

Nearly every one of us has seen the ape-man image, supposedly still possible; they just haven't found that lost transitional link between man and beast. Regardless of the fact that no convincing fossil evidence exists backing up the evolution of man, it remains a popular theory in academic circles, not to mention public schools and classrooms. Why? Because they cannot possibly allow themselves to believe we are created beings in God's image. Man's creation via imaginary sketches was all they had to go on, and that was enough to start a movement.

At the time of the infamous Scopes monkey trial in 1925, Nebraska Man was presented as evidence to prove evolution was a fact. It created just enough doubt for some folks to buy the idea, but just two years later it would be proved wrong.

PLANTING SEEDS OF DOUBT: "DID GOD REALLY SAY?"

God created man in His own image, in the image of God He created him; male and female He created them (Genesis 1:27).

Over 150 years after Darwin and *The Origin of Species* and almost ninety years after the Scopes trial, why is evolution still being taught in schools and universities as a primary scientific model? In a nation where the overwhelming majority believed the biblical account of creation just a hundred years ago, the ground had to be prepared for seeds of doubt to be planted. In fact, for many people a major paradigm shift had to take place in thinking.

First, I submit to you the religious leaders in America were probably not often preaching from the book of Genesis, nor were they establishing God's Word as final authority and encouraging people's faith in the creation account. Giving religious leaders the benefit of the doubt, however, perhaps it was taken for granted. The church is responsible for allowing or influencing cultural shifts, whether in belief or in action.

When children attended Sunday school, many of them were taught (and some still are) "Bible stories" – as they are referred to – in a fun, cartoonish way to help them learn about God. This is not right or wrong in itself, but most Christians today would probably admit what they remember from those Sunday school lessons includes goofy images of Adam and Eve, Noah's Ark, David and Goliath, etc.

In other words, many kids grow up thinking of Old Testament history as a bunch of fairy tales like Saturday morning cartoons. Picture an ark looking more like a bathtub stuffed with animal's whose heads were sticking out from all sides because they can't fit properly inside. It's easy because it was drawn for us years ago. (Incidentally, not only was the actual ark bigger than a professional football field, but some evidence suggests the ark Noah built could have been larger than what was needed.) The definition of the word *story* is "a narrative, either true or fictitious, in prose or verse, designed to interest, amuse, or instruct the hearer; a fictitious tale."

When young children learn about a "Bible story" at church, they might be told to open up their coloring books, but in school during a science or history class, they learn about evolution (whether or not teachers use the word *theory* is insignificant for this point) and their teacher tells them to open up their textbooks. Do you see a small part of the problem here? Presentation and perception matter. Of course, this is not the case in every school or church, but the norm is to refer to "stories" in the Bible when in fact its contents are actual history.

Amazingly, in most public schools today, the teaching of evolution is mandated and teaching intelligent design has been rejected for the most part. Many states have even rejected the use of disclaimers that evolution is a theory, not factual, absolute truth. Even when the word *theory* is thrown in for good measure, in most cases no opposing or alternative teaching is allowed or provided to the students. One judge in Pennsylvania ruled intelligent design is "a religious view, a mere re-labeling of creationism, and not a scientific theory." Even though intelligent design is true, most government-run schools have banned it because it allegedly brings God and *religion* (read: Christianity) into the classroom.

Despite all this, a majority of Americans still reject evolution as an explanation for the origins of life and the universe. However, that didn't stop public schools from welcoming the theory and kicking creationism to the curb. I have a feeling the ACLU may have had something to do with it. Was there a turning point we can investigate?

THE BIBLE ON TRIAL

In 1925, worldviews collided in the courtroom during the case *The State of Tennessee v. John Thomas Scopes,* a trial that made headlines across the country. Several events led up to this court case, including the 1914 book *A Civic Biology* by George William Hunter which described a belief in evolution and was used by school teachers in Dayton, Tennessee.

Former Nebraska congressman and Secretary of State William Jennings Bryan was known for his speeches against evolution. Two of his speeches were titled "The Bible and Its Enemies" and "The Menace of Darwinism." Copies of one of Bryan's lectures, "Is the Bible True?" were delivered to the Tennessee legislature, and John W. Butler was inspired by the content, leading him to introduce legislation calling for a ban on the teaching of evolution in public schools. The bill would prevent the teaching that "man has descended from a lower order of animals."

The bill, known as the "Butler Act," passed by an overwhelming majority and became state law in Tennessee. The House approved it by a 71-5 vote; the Senate by 24-6. By the way, Butler had no objection to the teaching of evolution in schools that were *not* taxpayer funded. Less than two months later, the ACLU used a Chattanooga newspaper to announce their search for teachers willing to challenge the new law and test it in court. Town leaders got involved, hoping publicity for the trial would help the local economy. They found a substitute teacher and football coach, John Scopes, to agree to be indicted in order to bring the case to trial.

William Bryan agreed to the case as did criminal lawyer Clarence Darrow, and a battle between a Christian fundamentalist and self-proclaimed agnostic ensued. Darrow objected to the opening prayer in the courtroom and declared the Butler Act to be "as brazen and as bold an attempt to destroy learning as was ever made in the Middle Ages." The defense questioned zoologist Maynard Metcalf, who testified evolution was a "widely embraced" theory in the scientific community. But does that make *anything* true, just because some folks embrace it?

Judge John Raulston ruled against the defense's motion to have the Butler Act declared unconstitutional, saying public schools "were designed, instituted, and are maintained for the purpose of mental *and* moral development and discipline."

On July 20, 1925, one day before the verdict and close of the trial, the case took a surprising and unusual turn when the defense called prosecutor for the state, Bryan, to testify as a biblical expert. The move revealed an underlying agenda by the ACLU to put Christianity on trial. Darrow asked him a series of questions, including whether the Bible should be interpreted literally, mocking him and saying Bryan supported "ideas that no intelligent Christian on earth believes."

The proceedings were broadcast live on the radio nationwide, the first of its kind; and even though Scopes was found guilty, following just a nine-minute deliberation by the jury, the media portrayed the trial as a defeat for Christians. Scopes was fined one hundred dollars for violating state law by teaching evolution, and Bryan even offered to pay his fine for him. William Jennings Bryan planned a national speaking tour on the issue, but he died in his sleep five days after the trial.

Boston journalist H.L. Mencken used the trial to ridicule conservative Christians for their traditional interpretation of the Bible. From what I've read in several accounts of that time, many religious leaders and average Christians were either embarrassed or intimidated into retreating from the public square. The victory was short lived when an appeal was made two years later, and the Scopes decision was overturned on a technicality.

The Scopes trial rejuvenated liberal Christians and nonbelievers to fight harder for control in national politics and culture as a whole. Laws against the teaching of evolution were discredited due in part to the media portrayal of the Bible, and many such laws were eventually repealed. A few examples of the one-sided, ongoing battle of worldviews include:

- In 1968, the Supreme Court ruled laws preventing the teaching of evolution were unconstitutional (*Epperson v. Arkansas*).

- In 1975, Tennessee's "equal time" law was declared unconstitutional by a federal appeals court. The law required public schools to give equal emphasis to intelligent design ("The Genesis account") and other theories about man's origins. Liberals most likely could not tolerate one stipulation of the bill requiring a disclaimer be used when evolution was taught; the disclaimer was that it be discussed as theory, not as fact.

- In 1982, a U.S. district judge struck down an Arkansas law requiring public schools to give "balanced treatment" to evolution and creationism whenever either was taught (*McLean v. Arkansas Board of Education*).

- In 1987, the Supreme Court ruled a Louisiana law requiring schools to give equal time, "balanced treatment," to both creation and evolution is unconstitutional.

Do you see a recurring problem here? These are not examples of compromise; it again shows liberal intolerance, judicial tyranny, and the unrelenting agenda to indoctrinate American youth to one worldview – anything opposed to Christianity. They just can't leave a door open for God and the Bible or kids might actually use critical thinking and give consideration to both sides of the debate.

Atheists, progressives, and skeptics claim Christianity contradicts science; they would rather "suppress the truth in unrighteousness" (Romans 1:18) than allow the truth to be told. Calling a theory a fact is a lie, and for most on the side of human evolution, the object is to discredit the Bible and attempt to explain a world without God.

COMPROMISE ON THE AGE OF THE EARTH?

The science of dating is one more subject we cannot fully do justice to here, but it is important enough to mention so we can consider a few facts. Remember the truth that God is not bound by time. The question is not whether God *could have* created the world in six minutes or six million years; the question is what did God say He did?

There was evening and morning, one day (Genesis 1:5).

In parts of the Bible, when a number is linked to the word "day," it means 24 hours. When no number is associated with the word, it can mean a longer period of time such as the "Day" of the Lord. Therefore, the conclusion is reached that the earth is thousands of years old rather than millions.

In Exodus 20:8, God instructed the Israelites to keep the Sabbath "day" holy as one of the Ten Commandments. In verse nine and ten, God instructs them to rest on the Sabbath day and do all their work in six days. A few verses later, He mentions creation plainly and declares:

> *For in six days the Lord made the heavens and the earth, the sea and all that is in them, and rested on the seventh day; therefore the Lord blessed the sabbath day and made it holy* (Exodus 20:11).

Man's dating methods require assumptions. For example, radiometric dating seems to indicate rocks are millions of years old, but assumptions must be made about the content of the rocks and the decay rate in the past. How can we trust radiometric "clocks" if no one knows where the clock was set in the beginning? Also, has the clock been ticking at the same exact rate? Evidence suggests decay rates were actually sped up, which could be more proof of a global catastrophic flood as the Bible describes.

Andrew Snelling from Answers in Genesis stated that God the Creator told us how old the universe is when He created all things.

> God's Word unmistakably teaches a young earth and universe ("the heavens"). God has ensured the accurate recording and preservation of His eyewitness account of the earth's history, which Jesus Christ endorsed repeatedly during His earthly ministry. God took great care to include the necessary chronological details of the universe's creation in six literal days, as well as the unbroken genealogies of mankind from Adam to

Jesus. So we have absolutely no doubt that the earth is only around six thousand years old.[102]

For 1,500 years after creation, men lived such long lives that most were either contemporaries of the first man, Adam, or personally knew someone who was. The ten patriarchs (excluding Enoch) who preceded the great flood lived an average of 912 years. During the 1,000 years *following* the flood, however, the Bible records a progressive decline in the life span of the patriarchs from Noah until Abraham, who lived 175 years, to Moses (120 years).[103]

Most of the earth appears to have had a tropical type of environment, but after the flood, fossil records reveal a clear environmental change resulting in an ice age that covered nearly thirty percent of the earth with ice (primarily in the northern latitudes). This, together with other changes after the flood, could have adversely affected life spans.

Finally, let's examine "Theistic evolution," which accepts the central theory of evolution science, but modifies the Christian faith so it does not conflict with basic scientific arguments. You can imagine how confusing this could get and sadly, this is now one of the debates within the walls of Christianity. I agree with Dr. Albert Mohler Jr. who said many believers want to compromise by suggesting Christianity and evolution are generally compatible. He calls it "theological surrender."

A huge difference remains between science and the unproven *theory* of human evolution. Theistic evolution is an attempt to accommodate two opposing worldviews. Well-meaning evangelicals try finding middle ground, but there is none. Mohler stated:

> In my view, any Christian form of theistic evolution is a contradiction in terms. At the end of the day, the theological modifications required by the acceptance of evolution are vast and utterly disastrous for biblical Christianity ... Oddly enough, it is those who hold to the classically opposed

---

102   Andrew Snelling, "Does radiometric dating prove the earth is millions of years old?" 3/12/2014, http://dailyevidence.wordpress.com/2014/03/12/does-radiometric-dating-prove-the-earth-is-millions-of-years-old/.

103   Dr. Georgia Purdom, "Did People Like Adam and Noah Really Live Over 900 Years of Age?" 5/27/2010, https://answersingenesis.org/bible-timeline/genealogy/did-adam-and-noah-really-live-over-900-years/.

positions who agree that theistic evolution is both unsatisfactory and untenable.[104]

We cannot be silent about this key subject in the Bible, and we should arm ourselves with a basic understanding of the debate so we can discuss it confidently. Why is it we have such a hard time taking God at His Word?

Of old You laid the foundation of the earth, And the heavens are the work of Your hands (Psalm 102:25 ESV).

The authority of God's inspired Word is our foundation and that foundation begins in Genesis. Let's get back to the basics and stop leaning on our own understanding (Proverbs 3:5) in attempts to figure God out with our finite human brains. Creation is an extremely viable model of origins. What else could be more viable than truth?

The meaning of life is to glorify God. Our purpose is to believe, know, love, and worship Jesus Christ and to obey His commands as we make Him known to others. God sees the end from the beginning. In terms of eternity, we happen to be somewhere near the final days of His timeline. All we are required to do is live for Him today and trust Him for tomorrow. The truth will prevail in the end.

God saw all that he had made, and it was very good. And there was evening, and there was morning—the sixth day. Thus the heavens and the earth were completed, and all their hosts. By the seventh day God completed His work which He had done, and He rested on the seventh day from all His work which He had done. Then God blessed the seventh day and sanctified it, because in it He rested from all His work which God had created and made. This is the account of the heavens and the earth when they were created, in the day that the Lord God made earth and heaven (Genesis 1:31-2:4).

---

104 R. Albert Mohler Jr. "Science and Religion aren't Friends?" 10/13/2010, http://www.christianpost.com/news/science-and-religion-arent-friends-47178/.

CHAPTER 12

COMMON CORE AND ERODING EDUCATION

The person without the [Holy] Spirit does not accept the things that come from the Spirit of God but considers them foolishness, and cannot understand them because they are discerned only through the Spirit.
1 Corinthians 2:14 (NIV)

Where is the wise man? Where is the scholar? Where is the philosopher of this age? Has not God made foolish the wisdom of the world? For the foolishness of God is wiser than human wisdom, and the weakness of God is stronger than human strength.
1 Corinthians 1:20, 25 (NIV)

MORE GOVERNMENT, LESS GOD

From American patriots to world dictators to the average citizen, people have understood education is crucial to society. Through the years, many have warned against teaching children more worldly things and less from the Word of God. The government system and curriculum we have today is quite the opposite of what our founders believed best for the health, morality, and youth of this nation. For over a century, individuals have been seeking to capture the minds of children through public schools.

To begin, let's look at some recent history. In the mid-1990s during the Clinton administration, an effort was underway to push through national education standards, starting with the subject of history. The standards contained such anti-American and politically correct material, the agenda failed miserably. This led to Senate Resolution 66

(S.RES.66), "A resolution to prevent the adoption of certain national history standards,"[105] and on January 20, 1995, the United States Senate voted against the proposed history standards, 99 to 1.

From their failed attempt, national curriculum advocates and the Left learned several things, including: Do not refer to the curriculum standards as "national" or "federal;" implement the standards quickly and quietly before parents, legislators, taxpayers, and teachers have a chance to review them; do not begin by trying to change a controversial subject such as history; and start with less threatening subjects such as English and math.

We should have seen obvious red flags regarding the government's implementation of Common Core State Standards in public schools. It was a recipe for confusion and corruption when (1) Most American parents had never heard of Common Core, (2) Many teachers didn't even know how to explain the standards, and (3) The Left vehemently attacked anyone who opposed Common Core. The entire project was funded by a power-hungry government, special interest groups, and wealthy elites – not necessarily in that order.

Recent Christian movies such as *God's Not Dead* are not making stuff up for a storyline. The fact is many teachers at the high school and college level are opposed to God and the Bible. Sometimes in classrooms, new students have been asked how many are Christians, and after seeing hands raised by those who are brave enough, teachers have declared, "You won't be by the end of this semester." This is not a fictitious script, but real life in academia.

It should be alarming how far from God and Christianity America's public schools have strayed. After all, *The fear of the LORD is the beginning of knowledge; Fools despise wisdom and instruction* (Proverbs 1:7). The education exodus from Judeo-Christian principles has been by design and has now become the norm. Humanism and atheism have been welcomed while Christianity has been expelled.

Recent history has proven Jesus Christ will not be tolerated by the National Education Association (NEA). This is not to say there are no committed Christian teachers or administrators in public schools, but

---

105 The Library of Congress, Thomas, 104th Congress (1995-1996), http://thomas.loc.gov/cgi-bin/bdquery/D?d104:66:./list/bss/d104SE.lst:@@@L&summ2=m&.

at best they are missionaries with little influence in a pagan system. We need to pray for the small number of our brothers and sisters in Christ whose hands are tied, but are trying to do their job as educators while remaining faithful to the Lord at the same time – a daunting task.

Plenty of information is now available on Common Core, much of it extremely concerning, and yet people have little idea what the controversy is about. Americans generally give others the benefit of the doubt on most things – including changes in education. Parents tend to trust those in charge of enacting laws and making decisions regarding public schools. Most American parents would never have considered the possibility the government would force its way into the education system to influence, program, and teach children anything other than what would benefit them after high school. This is part of the problem because a naïve, blind trust breeds apathy and ignorance.

Though proponents of Common Core insist it is not "a curriculum" and that states will have the freedom to be in charge of their own curriculum, these claims are blatantly misleading because we know the whole point of standards is to drive curriculum. Standards are the road map and final say on what is to be taught in classrooms; the curriculum simply adds the details. Therefore, the Common Core tests will dictate what gets taught nationwide.

The U.S. Department of Education (ED) is run by progressives, and the liberal NEA is a far cry from the teacher's union of years ago. The NEA is a major progressive lobbying group for the Democratic Party, having supported every single Democratic presidential candidate from Jimmy Carter to Barack Obama. Stories and studies have emerged in the lopsided education system proving liberal values are encouraged and promoted while conservative values are discouraged and often attacked. Nonetheless, parents have been reluctant to discard the entire public school system.

Unfortunately, most people have little knowledge about the new Common Core State Standards which comprise a clear centralization of authority over America's K-12 education system. Some believe the Left does not *want* people to find out the details. Knowing government supports the antithesis of Christianity, if the ED is not allowing, endorsing, or teaching principles and standards from the Bible, whose standards do you suppose they are supporting – and at what cost?

Studies reveal more money is not the answer as per-student spending has tripled while test results remain stagnant. As cited in my previous book, federal spending on education is at record highs; student learning and test scores are low or mediocre at best, and polls show the public has lost confidence in the American schools. No wonder our scheming government and a leftist administration took this opportunity to jump in and "solve" the education dilemma.

According to University professor, Dr. Sandra Stotsky, despite the billions of dollars showered on our schools, American public education remains poor. For example, "only 7% of our grade 8 students reach the advanced level in mathematics" (on TIMSS tests), which seems to explain why little advanced coursework in mathematics and science can be taught in high schools. Contrast this with Asia where an average of 38% (27 to 49%) of grade 8 students in the five highest-achieving countries (all in East Asia) reached the advanced level.[106]

Can you recall news reports on Common Core in the mainstream media that reflected *negatively* on the standards and exposed valid concerns? I can't either. Local media often take their cues from national headlines, reports, and the biased Associated Press. One reason for people's ignorance of the subject is the awful lack of balance in media "coverage" of the controversial implementation of Common Core, not to mention its content. The press is happy to use interview clips of Common Core supporters, but they often fail to interview academic experts who can offer informed counterpoints. As a result, half of the story is not being told.

In Wisconsin for example, legislative hearings were held in a few locations in which academic experts were asked to validate the Common Core standards in English and math, but they refused to do so because the experts were concerned about the contents of the standards. By ignoring the testimonies of those who have experience creating successful standards, local media chose not to inform parents and the community. Few honest public debates about Common Core standards

---

106 Dr. Sandra Strotsky, Dept. of Edu Reform resources, http://www.uaedreform.org/sandra-stotsky/.

have been held, and this will have very real consequences, especially for our children.

Despite the participation of the National Governor's Association (NGA) and the Council of Chief State School Officers (NCSSO), the Common Core standards are not state-led initiatives as proponents would have us believe. This national project was created and signed off on, essentially in secret, without any input from qualified teachers or state legislatures.

For over a century, key individuals and groups have influenced education curricula to teach agenda-driven, politically correct, socialism-friendly lessons with important American history distorted or rewritten. Call it a "revision" if that sounds better, but wouldn't we all agree parents (and teachers) deserved to know what Common Core contained, and shouldn't they have had a voice about whether their state adopted the standards or not? After all, we are paying for the implementation of the new requirements to the tune of billions of dollars.

WHAT EXACTLY IS COMMON CORE?

Special thanks to Freedom Project Education (FPEUSA.org) for contributions to this chapter.[107]

Common Core is an abbreviated term used to refer to the Common Core State Standards Initiative, a set of national standards for English and mathematics (with science and history/social studies guidelines forthcoming) written and copyrighted by the National Governor's Association and the Council of Chief State School Officers. The standards were released to the states in June 2010; they are copyrighted, and therefore, unalterable. Most states were rushed into making a decision to sign off on the standards in order to receive federal money during the tough economic times in 2010.

Proponents may refer to Common Core as state standards, but they are not state led. The standards came about when Bill and Melinda Gates first began funding their vision for national educational standards through a $1.7 million grant to the James B. Hunt Institute. They also funded the Washington D.C. based nonprofit Achieve, Inc., which wrote the

---

107   Freedom Project Education, On-line, K-12 classical education; www.fpeusa.org.

standards (in conjunction with the U.S. Department of Education). In 2013, grants were awarded, including $3.2 million to the New Venture Fund to help support and promote Common Core to the public and a $2.5 million grant to the Rockefeller Philanthropy Advisors Fund.[108]

Because Common Core has been described and promoted with general but positive promises and assertions, the standards can be difficult to explain in depth. We do know it is an internationally influenced U.S. education initiative that seeks to bring diverse state curricula into alignment with each other by following the principles of standards-based education reform. On the Common Core website, the standards are described as being "robust" and "relevant to the real world," helping prepare students so "communities will be best positioned to compete successfully in the global economy." Investigative research has proven "robust" is hardly a word that can be used to describe the standards.

If the government succeeds, tomorrow's students will have neither the facts nor the freedom needed for independent thinking. The goals for education in America have changed to an outcome-based, social justice-infused environmental and global agenda rather than education based on actual American history, Western democracy, and the Judeo-Christian values that had once been taught. Our public schools no longer teach the kind of literacy, history, math, and morality we once considered essential to responsible citizenship. The new agenda infiltrating our schools is designed to train a new generation of postmodern "progressive" students to believe whatever might serve a predetermined "common good."[109]

The Bill and Melinda Gates Foundation has spent an estimated $200 million and counting toward the implementation of Common Core, a United Nations Educational, Scientific, and Cultural Organization (UNESCO) global education agenda. In the long run, with all the computers and technologies the new curriculum requires, the Gates Foundation and particularly companies such as Microsoft stand to make back the millions they've invested, and more. Because of Common Core

---

108   Valerie Strauss, "Gates Foundation Pours Millions into Common Core in 2013," 11/27/2013, http://www.washingtonpost.com/blogs/answer-sheet/wp/2013/11/27/gates-foundation-pours-millions-into-common-core-in-2013/.

109   Berit Kjos, A "Common Core" for a Global Community, 11/16/2013, Lighthouse Trails, http://www.lighthousetrailsresearch.com/blog/?p=13825.

testing requirements, states will incur massive costs in order to acquire and maintain necessary equipment and technology. (The government is very generous with taxpayer money.)

When Bill Gates partnered with UNESCO in 2005, they devised some basic goals for new standards in America that included making environmental education a priority. The Common Core standards are to line up with "sustainable development" as defined by the United Nations.

Because of this, the emphasis on the planet and efforts to "save the earth" will soon be integrated in every school subject. This is another way to teach children to idolize nature rather than worship the One who created all things.

Current Secretary of Education Arne Duncan is a strong supporter of UNESCO. In conjunction with the radical, progressive Tides Foundation of San Francisco, Bill Gates had the standards ready to be unleashed by the time Barack Obama was elected president.

Common Core was first introduced five years ago with the help of teacher's union "payback" funds courtesy of the 2009 Obama administration stimulus bill. Common Core funding was implemented without full knowledge and consent of Congress. This is why most U.S. representatives knew little or nothing about the standards when questioned by their constituents. About $4.35 billion in federal grant money was used to persuade states to adopt the administration-backed, nationalized K-12 English and math standards and tests.

States were bribed, I mean offered, cash if they switched over to Core education standards, plus other incentives were dangled before them such as exemptions from the failed No Child Left Behind (NCLB) program. Knowing what was in Common Core, however, was not one of the options. Former counsels general to the ED, Robert S. Eitel and Kent D. Talbert, explained, "By using their adoption as a condition for states to receive grants ... the U.S. Department of Education has accelerated the implementation of [Common Core]."

Let's clarify here; the states were not allowed to wait until the standards were available so they could see what was in them. (Reminds me of something Nancy Pelosi said about the ObamaCare bill.) States were basically coerced to sign on the dotted line quickly; otherwise they'd forfeit the chance for some federal cash. The result: Constituents were left in the dark.

Author and founder of Eagle Forum, Phyllis Schlafly, voiced her concerns a decade ago saying even though UNESCO was unsuccessful in the 1960s and 1970s in their efforts to influence U.S. school curricula, they now have the funding to move forward with the plans thanks to Bill Gates and a willing U.S. government. She explains:

> On November 17, 2004, at UNESCO's headquarters in Paris, UNESCO signed a 26-page "Cooperation Agreement" with Microsoft Corporation to develop a "master curriculum (Syllabus)" for teacher training in information technologies based on standards, guidelines, benchmarks, and assessment techniques. The Agreement states that . . . "UNESCO will explore how to facilitate content development."

> Following the signing of the Agreement, UNESCO Director General Koichiro Matsuura explained it in a speech. One of its goals, he said, is "fostering web-based communities of practice including content development and worldwide curricula reflecting UNESCO values." No doubt that is agreeable to Bill Gates because the Agreement states that "Microsoft supports the objectives of UNESCO as stipulated in UNESCO's Constitution."[110]

It's worth noting in 2010, the Gates Foundation received the "Population Award" from the United Nations Population Fund, which has also awarded Planned Parenthood for their abortion efforts. Congress investigated the UN fund and found it was facilitating the Communist Chinese's "one-child policy" which forced women to abort their babies if they already had a child. This barbaric population-control agenda is what drove people such as Adolf Hitler and Margaret Sanger.

Elites such as Bill and Melinda Gates use the same terminology, calling abortion and birth control "family planning" and "reproductive health."[111] These rich people have committed over $76 million to help

---

110   Phyllis Schlafly, "Bill Gates Teams Up With UNESCO," Eagle Forum, 11/3/2005, http://www.eagleforum.org/column/2005/nov05/05-11-30.html.

111   Anne Hendershott, "The Ambitions of Bill and Melinda Gates: Controlling the Population and Public Education," 3/25/2013 http://www.crisismagazine.com/2013/the-ambitions-of-bill-and-melinda-gates-controlling-population-and-public-education.

teachers implement Common Core, a Trojan horse for special interests and outside groups, including Planned Parenthood, the National Sexuality Education Standards, the UN (Agenda 21), and others such as textbook publishers.

Critics suggest Common Core is the attempt of Barack Obama's ED to force all states and schools to adopt national education standards for each grade level. Other critics of Common Core claim it represents the most comprehensive step in the agenda toward complete government control of children and their education.

If Common Core's implementation initiated a colossal shift in the entire education system in America, why did so few people know it was happening for the first few years? Didn't the majority of states that accepted the standards know what they contained? Why did the government initiate the adoption of Common Core standards under the radar?

As alluded to earlier, the federal government essentially deceived state governments into taking millions in taxpayer funding before states knew what the standards were *and* before they understood their future financial obligations to implement the standards. The complicit silence of the mainstream and local media allowed Common Core proponents to avoid early scrutiny which is one big reason it had been initiated unchecked. Backlash is growing as I write this, but it may be too late.

Common Core standards were adopted sight unseen by forty-six states in exchange for Race to the Top money or a waiver from No Child Left Behind. Alaska, Texas, Nebraska, and Virginia declined Common Core. Race to the Top funding was the initial vehicle used to impose Common Core on the state governments. If the federal funding was agreed to and accepted, the states were required to adopt the Common Core standards word for word. (A provision enabled states to "supplement the standards," but no provision was allowed for states to subtract any content from Common Core.)

> People who characterize Common Core as anything other
> than a national takeover of schooling are either unaware of
> these sweeping implications or are deliberately hiding this
> information from the public.
> —Joy Pullmann, Heartland Institute

CONCERNS, DANGERS, AND THREATS

One obvious danger of Common Core is having any alignment or partnership with UNESCO. Their goal is a New World Order through the vehicle of global socialism. To fulfill this agenda, education must be redirected and philosophies must be reframed to eliminate any remaining biblical values through the influence of the youngest among us. The strongest resistance to socialism and communism has always come from Christians and from older generations, those who were around in the early and mid-1900s and lived to see the devastating, tragic residual effects of brutal dictators and totalitarianism in the world.

In 1947, the first Director of UNESCO, Julian Huxley, said the task ahead for the organization is "to help the emergence of a single world culture with its own philosophy and background of ideas with its own broad purpose." Huxley's brother, Aldous, was raised among British elites who supported communist Russia, and he hoped for a global society controlled by an elite group of scientists. This theme recurs throughout history: Wealthy elites want more control and power over the working class. This "class system" ideology is a tenet of Marxism and should be cast from our shores forever, but many Americans have been manipulated by the marketing of class warfare and socialism.

Extremely wealthy families often have the attitude they were meant to rule while the rest of us were meant to work and serve society. The Carnegies, Fords, and Rockefellers are examples of families who have given grants to influence and nationalize American education. In the 1970s, the Ford, Carnegie, and Rockefeller foundations pushed education "equity" lawsuits in California, New Jersey, Texas, and elsewhere that led to enormous increases in state expenditures for low-income students.[112] Efforts such as these go back more than a half century.

Common Core is a very real threat to the basic freedoms we take for granted in America. How can a small number of rich elites, leftists, and government committees decide what American children K-12 will be fed in public schools? Aside from it being the furthest thing from what our founders envisioned for education, taxpaying citizens (including parents of young children) have had no say in the standards being

---

112   Jason L. Riley, "Was the $5 Billion Worth It?" Wall Street Journal, 7/23/2011, http://online.wsj.com/news/articles/SB10001424053111903554904576461571362279948.

implemented! The adoption of Common Core State Standards is flat-out government overreach. In addition to federal control comes a loss of state and parental input and local autonomy.

By imposing the Common Core Standards and aligned assessments on the states, the federal government is violating three statutes and has put America on the road to a national curriculum. With respect to the Race to the Top/Common Core scheme, Eitel and Talbert concluded "these standards and assessments will ultimately direct the course of elementary and secondary study in most states across the nation, running the risk that states will become little more than administrative agents for a nationalized K-12 program of instruction and raising a fundamental question about whether the ED is exceeding its statutory boundaries."

Tragically, states that have accepted Common Core money have ceded control to the federal government, taking it away from parents, teachers, and local school boards. Beyond the continuing educational mediocrity in public schools, elaborate plans are in place to use the required national assessments within the Common Core standards as a tool to institute massive data collection on American school children. This means an alarming amount of data collected that has nothing to do with education and everything to do with government intrusion.

As for homeschool and private school students, the expansion of statewide longitudinal databases is perhaps the most immediate threat. The designers of the new systems fully intend for homeschool and private school students to be part of the massive data collection. More parents are, therefore, voicing their concerns, raising awareness, and taking action.

Another area for alarm is the mandated cooperation of Common Core with the enforcement of ObamaCare. Even Nancy Pelosi probably didn't know the 2010 healthcare bill, aka the Affordable Care Act, includes mandates for assessing children's education and development records under the guise of health.

The 2009 Obama stimulus bill referred to earlier not only contained guarantees of grants from the government to selected recipients, but also had an earmark which required state databases to begin tracking students' religious affiliations, family income, family voting status, health care history, and disciplinary records. These will span pre-school to workforce entry and be linked to Common Core tests. The ED issued regulations allowing the sharing of personally identifiable student information (without the consent of parents) despite a law that prohibits such activity.[113]

Using school tests to collect information unrelated to education is a clever scheme, and data collected goes well beyond name, birthdate, and social security number. The government will now have access to private records and sensitive information about the student and his or her family including the following:

1. Political affiliations or beliefs of the student or parent.

2. Mental and psychological problems of the student or the student's family.

3. Sex behavior or attitudes.

4. Illegal, anti-social, self-incriminating, and demeaning behavior.

5. Critical appraisals of other individuals with whom respondents have close family relationships.

6. Legally recognized privileged or analogous relationships, such as lawyers, physicians, and ministers.

7. Religious practices, affiliations, or beliefs of the student or the student's parent.

8. Details of Income.[114]

You may be wondering if it is legal for government to gather and track personal data on students. No. The ED is prohibited by federal statute from maintaining a national student database. So how then can they do what Common Core requires? The feds get around the law by

---

113 Emmett McGroarty and Jane Robbins, "Controlling Education from the Top," 5/10/2012, Pioneer Institute public policy research, http://pioneerinstitute.org/download/controlling-education-from-the-top/.

114 Nancy Thorner and Bonnie O'Neil, "Common Core Violates Privacy of Students and Families," 6/23/2014, http://blog.heartland.org/2014/06/common-core-violates-privacy-of-students-and-families/.

making the states collect the data, and they in turn share it with the government.

Other examples of data mining methodology should be alarming to parents, including the use of facial expression cameras, posture analysis seat, pressure mouse, and wireless skin conductance sensor.

In a report released by the ED in 2013, "Promoting Grit, Tenacity, and Perseverance: Critical Factors for Success in the 21st Century," one section detailed how to evaluate a student's attitude and reactions through the use of "behavioral task performance measures." Some ways the government can capture data on students relating to their level of perseverance are: "associated emotional experiences, physical movements or facial expressions, physiological responses, and thoughts" that students exhibit. Understanding the emotions or physiological state of a student while they're presented with a challenge, the report said, can be measured through "analysis of facial expressions, EEG brain wave patterns, skin conductance, heart rate variability, posture and eye-tracking."[115]

Less alarming but no less concerning may be the fact Common Core has no track record, and many experts and educators have referred to the standards as "mediocre." Some have described them as "common" and even as a one-size-fits-all type of education. No state, school district, or individual school had previously tested any of the Common Core standards.

Most of us believe American children are too valuable to essentially allow a billion dollar experiment in which Common Core critics see them being used as lab rats or guinea pigs. Putting students in a test tube with new standards is not what most taxpayers would consider a wise investment of tax dollars. It is becoming clear why the ED did not want to take the necessary time to introduce and implement the changes in education curriculum incrementally. If parents, teachers, experts, and policy makers had time to review and evaluate the standards, we would not be having this conversation.

But how will this affect private and home schools? The control

---

115 Liz Klimas, "Eye Trackers, Wrist Bands, Posture Seats, 'Mood Meter'? A Close Look at the Tech Proposed to Track Your Kids in Schools, 3/28/2013, http://www.theblaze.com/stories/2013/03/28/eye-trackers-wrist-bands-posture-seats-mood-meter-a-close-look-at-the-tech-proposed-to-track-your-kids-in-schools/.

mechanism in the new standards is the tests. Because of these assessments, Common Core will control the curriculum of charter schools, private schools, Christian and Catholic schools, and homeschooling. Low or sub-par standards are irrelevant; kids will need to study and know Common Core requirements in order to do well on the tests. If they don't pass the tests, they won't receive a high school diploma or won't be admitted to college. Universities are being pressured to adapt the standards, and many publishers of textbooks and homeschool material have already aligned with Common Core.

The Home School Legal Defense Association (HSLDA) has been sounding the alarm about Common Core for several years. A federal law is prohibiting government education mandates from being applied to schools that do not receive federal funds (Section 9506, Elementary and Secondary Education Act, 20 U.S.C. 7886), but Common Core could eventually impact homeschool and private school students by affecting college admission standards.

Currently, no such protection exists for families who have enrolled their children in programs that receive federal funds, especially those who are using virtual charter schools that are run through the local public school for their home education. Though the specific provisions of Common Core only directly bind public schools, private schools that accept federal funding (through the Individuals with Disabilities Education Act, for example) may face a decision between foregoing federal funding and accepting the Common Core standards in the near future.

In addition, the SAT will be aligned with Common Core State Standards. Questions are being added to the ACT as well. The GED has been redesigned for the first time since 2002 to incorporate "practices and skills from the Common Core State Standards for Mathematical Practice." Students taking the redesigned SAT, ACT, or the Iowa Tests could soon encounter progressive ideologies, including social engineering and alternative lifestyles.

If you want to change society and worldviews, start with education and the tests. It has been said by many knowledgeable educators, "people who control the standards and control the assessments control education."

NOT EXACTLY "RIGOROUS" STANDARDS

The academic level of Common Core is even lower than what many states now use. For example, the new standards do not introduce the concept of money to children in math class until the second grade, whereas more successful educational programs have students encounter money in kindergarten. In those programs, by second grade they are learning multiplication while Common Core delays multiplication until third grade.

Dr. James Milgram is a professor emeritus of mathematics at Stanford University. The math standards are so inferior, Milgram, the only true mathematician on the Common Core validation committee, refused to approve of the standards and sign off on them, saying they are two years behind international expectations and fall even further behind in grades 8 to 12. Algebra is pushed back to ninth grade even though the highest achieving countries start teaching Algebra in eighth grade.

Several curriculum experts compared Common Core to the best international standards and found them to be not only deficient but "below the admission requirement of most four-year state colleges." Reading expert Dr. Sandra Stotsky served on the validation committee for Common Core and also refused to sign off on the standards. She noted the writers did not back up the claim "Common Core is benchmarked to international tests," and she said the English language arts standards were "low quality," "hard to follow," and they are composed of "empty skill sets that won't prepare students for college course work."

A friend of mine, a public school teacher, defended Common Core, suggesting the new curriculum would include all the important books necessary for quality English instruction. However, the best classics and historical books do not actually appear in the standards. They are on an accompanying list of *suggested* reading. In Common Core English and Language Arts, approximately 60 percent of the classic literature, poetry, and drama previously required has been stripped from the standards. In fact, this is one of the most frequent criticisms: The emphasis is on reading dry government documents and tech manuals such as the informational texts listed under suggested reading. Texts include stuff from the U.S. Environmental Protection Agency and the

Department of Energy. Historical texts like the Gettysburg Address are to be presented to students without context or explanation.

One book series on American history reveals not only liberal bias but factual and chronological errors. The Textbook League reviews educational material for accuracy and assigned Alice Whealey, author and historian, to examine the book *A History of US* by Joy Hakim. Noting there were also problems with terminology as well as "unjustified assertions," Whealey explained:

> Joy Hakim should not attempt to write about Western history, particularly the history of Europe, because she obviously hasn't had enough training in these subjects. It is a shame that Oxford University Press has let her get away with so many falsehoods and with such extreme exhibitions of bias.[116]

ONE SIZE NEVER FITS ALL — IN FREE SOCIETIES

Think about the diverse backgrounds, interests, personalities, and intelligence of kids who are the same age, and we can see potential problems with the collective nature of Common Core standards. Even if a single set of nationalized standards *could* be implemented effectively during grade school years, the same curriculum framework or guidelines cannot be supported at the high school level. A gap among individual students in abilities, development, talent, emotional needs and stability as well as capacity for learning is far too wide.

Two faulty and obvious assumptions made by the government in pushing centralized standards are: They know what curriculum is best for all students, and they are convinced theirs is the best model. It takes hubris and agenda-driven elites to think America is ready for Common Core. Good-bye innovation, hello uniformity. Apparently the government wants us to think teaching the same material, using the same methods for kids from upscale communities, rural areas, and inner cities is best. It doesn't matter if children are Jewish, Italian, Hispanic, black, white, Indian, or Asian; Atheist, Buddhist, Christian, or Muslim.

Like many of us, John Stossel questioned the federal government's

---

116   Alex Newman, "Common Core: A Scheme to Rewrite Education,"
       8/8/2013, http://www.thenewamerican.com/culture/education/
       item/16192-common-core-a-scheme-to-rewrite-education.

imposing a single teaching plan on 15,000 school districts across the country, saying Common Core is a "one-size-fits-all" government monopoly similar to public schools, public housing, the U.S. Postal Service, Department of Transportation, and others. Stossel explained:

> No Child Left Behind programs were an understandable reaction to atrocious literacy and graduation rates – but since school funding was pegged to students' performance on federally approved tests, classroom instruction became largely about drilling for those tests and getting the right answers, even if kids did little to develop broader reasoning skills. So along comes Common Core to attempt to fix the problem – and create new ones.[117]

Outcome-based standards will never pull American public schools up from low performance levels and mediocrity. They may however, help students do better on tests because out of necessity they will be instructed about what is on the tests. Remember, if students score higher on tests with Common Core standards and related tests, the teachers look good, and it would *appear* students are doing better and learning more. Teaching to the test helps kids test better; it does not necessarily help kids become better educated.

In addition, some states that have had better success in education and higher learning rates now have to lower their expectations to make Common Core fit into their standards. Minnesota is one state that had more rigorous math standards, and Massachusetts is one state whose existing English standards were higher than those contained in Common Core. Data-driven standards aim primarily for conformity which is exactly what the Left hopes will happen.

Speaking of Massachusetts, Education Secretary Paul Reville exposed his attitude toward public school students when he asked, "Why should some towns and cities have no standards or low standards and others have extremely high standards when *the children belong to all of us…*?" This is not an isolated case of "it takes a village" thinking. Big-government bureaucrats typically maneuver to gain power, and Common Core has

---

117 John Stossel, "The Latest Flaw in One-Size-Fits-All Public Schools," 1/1/2014, http://reason.com/archives/2014/01/01/common-core-the-latest-flaw-in-one-size.

been exposed as a political agenda that nearly eliminates parents' rights and state sovereignty.

Apart from being unannounced to the public, untested and unproven, opponents see the standards as another way for the government to increase the amount of liberal messages such as global warming, homosexuality, immigration, evolution, promiscuity, and abortion advocacy into curricula. What could go wrong?

The next time you hear someone say Common Core is good for kids, ask them to prove their claim by providing results or locations in which the standards were in place and tested. Be prepared for an uncomfortably long pause. Think of how absurd it would be if a different government agency such as the FDA (Food and Drug Administration) approved the use of a new drug for all American citizens – a drug that has not been tested – without being concerned about possible harm, side effects, or unintended consequences. Why would we play Russian Roulette with our children's education and future?

BROUGHT TO YOU BY STATES AND TAXPAYERS

We haven't heard much about the fact Common Core will cost states more money than they were aware of because many states signed up without any cost analysis. States will spend up to an estimated $10 billion up front for the standards. Not only that, states will pay as much as $800 million every year for the first seven years Common Core is fully implemented.[118] Among the costs are new textbooks, curriculum, teacher training, and technology upgrades.

The test creators have said that by 2016 they expect Common Core assessments to be taken online which is not only more expensive, but could present a whole new slew of problems for poorer and rural schools in particular. The online testing will require new hardware, such as computers, tech labs, microphones and earphones in addition to Internet connections, tech support, and upgraded operating systems.[119]

---

118 Perry Chiaramonte, "High cost of Common Core has states rethinking the national education standards, 2/5/2014, http://www.foxnews.com/us/2014/02/05/number-states-backing-out-common-core-testing-maryland-schools-low-on-funding/.

119 Sean Cavanaugh, "Consortium Releases Technology Guidelines for Common-Core Tests," Education Week, 12/21/2012, http://blogs.edweek.org/edweek/DigitalEducation/2012/12/consortium_releases_techology_.html.

In early 2014, *Fox News* reported that education officials in Maryland estimated it will require $100 million to upgrade computers statewide in order "to support the testing that is the centerpiece of Common Core." And Maryland is not that big of a state. Georgia and other states have found costs are far too high to implement the new standards, while California estimated about $35 million per year (about $30 per student in testing costs alone) due to Common Core.

The study done by Accountability Works, a nonprofit education advocacy group, estimated schools nationwide will need to fork out nearly $7 billion for technology, over $5 billion to train teachers, $2.47 billion for textbooks, and $1.24 billion for assessment testing over the first seven years Common Core is up and running. Sticking uninformed taxpayers with the bill for a government takeover of education is something progressives had dreamed about for decades.

Aside from the financial aspect, a greater and higher cost – freedom – will be due to the enormous transfer of power from local school districts to federal bureaucrats.

Mary Black, a veteran educator now with Freedom Project Education, has given seminars on Common Core, informing parents, teachers, and state representatives. Black stated:

> My review of the Common Core standards indicated that they were designed to teach students what to think and not how to think. Quite simply, control is the real goal … These people are socialists and globalists. The goal is not education but the production of compliant, dependent, uneducated citizens. This is the citizenry needed to implement the United Nation's Agenda 21 with the help of UNESCO's Education for All program.

AN EDUCATIONAL APPROACH INFUSED WITH SOCIALISM

In June 2006, the *Education Reporter* newspaper ended an article warning us about the potential consequences of American participation with international education reforms, suggesting the whole U.S. system – from preschool, elementary, secondary, and higher education

– "will encounter further upheaval and decline." This was fewer than ten years ago when George W. Bush was president and Margaret Spellings was U.S. Secretary of Education. Even though Common Core is being implemented by the Obama regime, several events took place under Bush's watch, such as No Child Left Behind (NCLB) and the "Moscow Declaration."

For a quick refresher, the NCLB Act of 2001 was a bipartisan Congressional Act reauthorizing the Elementary and Secondary Education Act, which supported standards-based education reform and required states to give assessments to students at select grade levels. NCLB also included Title I, the government program for disadvantaged students. Though states were responsible for developing their own standards, NCLB expanded the federal role in public education.

Since 1975, member nations of the international "Group of Eight" (G-8) have convened annually to discuss economic and political issues. The group includes Canada, France, Germany, Italy, Japan, the United Kingdom, and the United States. The Russian Federation became a member in 1997. The Moscow Declaration was adopted June 2, 2006, by G-8 Education Ministers who agreed to cooperate with the Russian education initiatives incorporated in the declaration. Secretary Spellings declared her strong support and said the declaration should be acted upon and lived by.

One week prior to the 2006 G-8 summit, Spellings and Russian Federation Minister Fursenko signed an agreement to partner in the field of education and expand cooperation between the U.S. and Russia. A May 31, 2006, U.S. Department of Education press release claims:

> This Memorandum of Understanding is the first of its kind between the U.S. Department of Education and the Ministry of Education and Science of the Russian Federation . . . and pledged to share best practices across borders to build education systems that can allow people . . . to live and contribute to a global society, and to work in a global economy.[120]

None of this is surprising when we consider the century-old movement

---

120 "Moscow Declaration" Adopted by G-8: Education Ministers—Secretary Spellings Commits U.S., Eagle Forum, U.S. Dept. of Education, June 2, 2006. http://www.eagleforum.org/educate/2006/june06/moscow.html.

toward global education and a New World Order. Obama's election, a Democratic majority, and the 2009 economic stimulus created the perfect storm from which Common Core could be carried out, leading to the end of state sovereignty over education. We need to understand the apparent agenda behind government education, the worldview upon which some decisions have been made, and where we're headed as a nation.

> Give me four years to teach the children and the seed I have sown will never be uprooted.
> —Vladimir Lenin

> Christians are not exactly bright, so it will be easy for socialism to lead them down the garden path through their ideals of brotherly love and social justice.
> —Victor Gollancz, British publisher and socialist

> Fundamentalist parents [read: Christian] have no right to indoctrinate their children in their beliefs. We are preparing their children for … life in a global one-world society and those children will not fit in.
> —Peter Hoagland, Former Democratic Senator, Nebraska

> The schools cannot allow parents to influence the kind of values-education their children receive in school; that is what is wrong with those who say there is a universal system of values. Our goals are incompatible with theirs. We must change their values.
> —NEA specialist Paul Haubner[121]

Is the expansion of socialism and humanism in American education a necessary step to ushering in the end times and the New World Order? It's been happening for over a hundred years. You're about to read some past selected events from history that have set the stage for Common Core today. As usual, godless, influential elites, businessmen, and politicians often call the shots.

The following is by no means an exhaustive list:

---

121   Joe Larson, "Why Our Schools Teach Socialism," September 2001, http://www.eagleforum.org/educate/2001/sept01/socialism.shtml.

- 1905 – The Carnegie Foundation for the Advancement of Teaching was founded by Andrew Carnegie and chartered in 1906 by an act of the United States Congress. Together with other Carnegie Foundations, it has been a major promoter and funder of socialistic global education projects.

- 1908 – John Dewey, known as the Father of Modern (i.e., progressive) Education, laid the foundations for a revolutionary transformation of American schools. In "Religion and Our Schools," he wrote, "Our schools . . . are performing an infinitely significant religious work. They are promoting the social unity out of which in the end genuine religious unity must grow.

- 1919 – The Institute of International Education was established with a grant from the Carnegie Endowment for International Peace . . . [S]ocialist John Dewey served on its National Advisory Council.

- 1933 – John Dewey, honorary president of the National Education Association (NEA), co-authored the first Humanist Manifesto, which stated: "Any religion that can hope to be a synthesizing and dynamic force for today must be shaped for the needs of this age."

- 1934 – In a report, Willard Givens (later NEA executive secretary) wrote: "all of us, including the 'owners' must be subjected to a large degree of social control . . . [T]he major function of the school is the social orientation of the individual. It must seek to give him understanding of the transition to a new social order."[122]

- 1942 – The editor of The Journal of the National Education Association, J. Elmer Morgan, wrote an editorial titled "The United Peoples of the World." In it, he explained that a world government would need an educational branch, a world system of money and credit, a world police force, and "a world bill of rights and duties."

---

122 Willard Givens, "Education for the New America" report; 72nd Annual NEA Meeting, July 1934, Washington, D.C.

- 1946 – "The establishment [of UNESCO] marks the culmination of a movement for the creation of an international agency of education . . . Nations that become members of UNESCO accordingly assume an obligation to revise the textbooks used in their schools. Each member nation . . . has a duty to see to it that nothing in its curriculum . . . is contrary to UNESCO's aims."[123]

- 1946 – In his NEA editorial, "The Teacher and World Government," J. Elmer Morgan wrote, "In the struggle to establish an adequate world government, the teacher . . . can do much to prepare the hearts and minds of children . . . At the very top of all the agencies which will assure the coming of world government must stand the school, the teacher, and the organized profession."

- 1947 – Julian Huxley wrote: "The general philosophy of UNESCO should be a scientific world humanism, global in extent and evolutionary in background . . . In its education program it can . . . familiarize all peoples with the implications of the transfer of full sovereignty from separate nations to a world organization . . . Tasks for the media division of UNESCO [will be] to promote the growth of a common outlook shared by all nations and cultures . . . to help the emergence of a single world culture."[124]

- 1948 – The NEA produced a set of international guidelines called Education for International Understanding in American Schools. It included this statement:

  The idea has become established that the preservation of international peace and order may require that force be used to compel a nation to conduct its affairs within the framework of an established world system . . . Many persons believe that enduring peace cannot be achieved so long as

---

123 I.L. Kandel, "National Education in an International World" (*The Journal of the National Education Association*, Vol. 35, 1946), p. 191.
124 Julian Huxley, "UNESCO: It's Purpose and its Philosophy," (Washington DC: Public Affairs Press, 1947). See http://www.crossroad.to/Quotes/globalism/julian-huxley.htm.

the nation-state system continues as at present constituted. It is a system of international anarchy.

- 1959 – Nikita Khrushchev, former General Secretary of the Communist Party of the Soviet Union stated:

  You Americans are so gullible. No, you won't accept communism outright, but we'll keep feeding you small doses of socialism until you'll finally wake up and find you already have communism. We won't have to fight you. We'll so weaken your economy until you'll fall like overripe fruit into our hands.[125]

- 1973 – The socialist authors (Paul Kurtz and Edwin H. Wilson) of the *Humanist Manifesto II* wrote: "We deplore the division of human-kind on nationalistic grounds. We have reached a turning point in human history where the best option is to transcend the limits of national sovereignty and to move toward the building of a world community."

- 1976 – An NEA program titled "A Declaration of Interdependence: Education for a Global Community" was made available to schools across the country ... The report said, "Educators around the world are in a unique position to help bring about a harmoniously interdependent global community."

- 1985 – The curriculum arm of the NEA, the Association for Supervision and Curriculum Development (ASCD), co-sponsored an international curriculum symposium in the Netherlands. According to *Education Week*, the ASCD executive director, Dr. Gordon Cawelti, urged representatives of other Western nations and Japan to press for the development of a "world-core curriculum" based on knowledge that will ensure "peaceful and cooperative existence among the human species on this planet."[126]

---

125 Nikita Khrushchev, "Dark Predictions of a KGB Defector," 1959 at http://frontpagemag.com/2010/10/19/dark-predictions-of-a-kgb-defector/2.

126 Susan Hooper, "Educator Proposes a Global 'Core Curriculum'" (*Education Week*, http://www.edweek.org/ew/articles/1985/11/27/06110023.h05.html).

- 1991 – On October 30, the U.S. Coalition for Education for All (USCEFA) convened a conference titled "Learning for All: Bridging Domestic and International Education" with First Lady Barbara Bush as the honorary chair. It would provide a vital link between the UNESCO plan and U.S. implementation. Partners in this venture included UNESCO, UNICEF, the World Bank, the NEA, and a long string of organizations involved in education at every level.

  The coalition was part of a 156-nation network working to reform education worldwide by bridging the gap between individual nations and UNESCO's Education for All. Keynote speaker Elena Lenskaya, deputy to the Minister of Education of Russia, spoke on the topic "Education for a New World Order."

- 1993 – "The 240 international affiliates of the NEA and the American Federation of Teachers joined to form Education International (EI)."[127]

  (*Thank you to Lighthouse Trails Research for making this information available.*)

This secular progressive agenda supports eradicating the Judeo-Christian worldview and has been carried out gradually, by design, through academia and government in America. The sooner we come to terms with the fact there is no going back, no rewinding history, and no reversing the damage that has been done, the better.

This is not to say those in the education system are hopeless; no one is outside of God's reach no matter how hardened and rebellious they may appear to be. However, the system as a whole has been lost to the other side and cannot be retrieved. We can debate or we can pray, but we have reached a point of no return.

When Kurtz and Wilson wrote the *Humanist Manifesto II* in 1973 for example, the groundwork had already been laid. Of the many, one statement revealing a man-centered philosophy is recognition of an individual's "right to die with dignity, euthanasia, and the right to

---

127 Berit Kjos, A "Common Core" for a Global Community: What's in Store for the Education of Today's Children?" (Lighthouse Trails Publishing) 11/16/2013, http://www.lighthousetrailsresearch.com/blog/?p=13825.

suicide." This thorough document also covered the subject of sexuality and objected to "intolerant attitudes" cultivated by religion because they "unduly repress sexual conduct." Naturally they fully endorse the recognition and "right to birth control, abortion, and divorce."

The manifesto was signed by 282 leaders, including university professors, scientists, wealthy businessmen, and executives wanting universal education and a socialist society. Today, approximately 3% of faculty at Ivy League schools identify themselves as conservative. It is not surprising thousands more eventually signed the Manifesto, agreeing to all the tenets and the vision of a New World Order. The separation of church and state was viewed as imperative. Many international humanists signed on as well, supporting those in America pushing "world community." Under the section on Religion, the *Humanist Manifesto II* reads:

> We believe … traditional dogmatic or authoritarian religions that place revelation, God, ritual, or creed above human needs and experience do a disservice to the human species. Any account of nature should pass the tests of scientific evidence; in our judgment, the dogmas and myths of traditional religions do not do so. Even at this late date in human history, certain elementary facts based upon the critical use of scientific reason have to be restated. We find insufficient evidence for belief in the existence of a supernatural.[128]

Similar to the previous chapter about creationism vs. evolution, this battle for the minds of youth is another aspect of the worldview war. Man's way always seems right to him, *but its end is the way of death* (Proverbs 14:12). Jesus said, *Whoever is not with me is against me* (Luke 11:23 NIV), so we cannot be ignorant regarding enemies of the cross of Jesus Christ any longer. Tragically, they have infiltrated America's education system and are headed for destruction (Philippians 3:19) unless they repent.

For those reading this and seeing for the first time how much anti-Christian influence John Dewey and his ilk have wrought on public schools in America, it is not the time to give up. Share the truth! One of our failures as a church was we didn't step in and get involved sooner

---

128 Paul Kurtz and Edwin H. Wilson, *Humanist Manifesto II*, Tenet #1, 1973. http://americanhumanist.org/Humanism/Humanist_Manifesto_II.

in education and government. We trusted political leaders and liberal teacher's unions as a whole, and as a result, conservative Christian teachers have been paying for it as their dues fund the advancement of evil, while they fear speaking up about their faith in the classroom or teacher's lounge.

Our society is paying a price as well. In the last fifty or more years, millions of youth have been educated with the liberal K-12 government school system and after that, higher (hyper-liberal) education at the university level. Many are today's workers, teachers, and business people helping further shape this country in the image of man. The same year the *Humanist Manifesto II* was published, Chester M. Pierce, M.D., Professor of Education and Psychiatry at Harvard University stated:

> Every child in America entering school at the age of five is mentally ill because he comes to school with certain allegiances to our Founding Fathers, toward our elected officials, toward his parents, toward a belief in a supernatural being, and toward the sovereignty of this nation as a separate entity. It's up to you as teachers to make all these sick children well – by creating the international child of the future.[129]

Socialism has no room for God, and we've seen its fruit not only in our schools but in our culture as well. The government replaced Christianity with the promotion or teaching of everything related to globalism and diversity.

REMOVE GOD AND ANYTHING GOES

Along with a lack of discipline, the new school environment has erupted with disrespect, profanity, cheating, violence, and even murder. Students drink, steal, and use drugs. These hyper-sexualized kids deal with rape, STD's, and unwanted pregnancies. In the face of depression, some turn to occultism and suicide. Maybe the Ten Commandments weren't so bad after all! Every other religion and practice is accommodated. Islam is often welcomed and even promoted. Our government and liberal media seem to cater (or cower) to Muslims regardless of the growing

---

129   Joseph R. Larson, "Why Our Schools Teach Socialism," *Education Reporter,* Issue 188, September, 2001, http://www.eagleforum.org/educate/2001/sept01/socialism.shtml.

news overseas about the beheadings of "infidels" and the dangers of ISIS and Sharia Law.

One incident in Texas reported by the *Washington Times* last year supports the fact that when Christianity is removed, anything goes. At Lumberton High School, female students in a geography class were asked to dress in a burka – a long, dark robe worn by many Muslim women covering them from head to feet. They were also told to refer to Muslim terrorists as "freedom fighters." The parents contacted the principal, who defended the program required under CSCOPE, a controversial electronic curriculum system that provides online lesson plans for teachers. (CSCOPE is Texas' version of Common Core and has since been rejected.)

Parents only found out about the school lesson because one of the girls posted a photo on Facebook showing the students dressed in Muslim garb. One girl's dad told *Fox News* he felt like the teacher crossed the line, and that parents are very sensitive to issues that appear anti-American – "that blames democracy for some sort of trouble in the world." He also said,

> Christian kids who want to pray have to do it outside of school hours – yet Islam is being taught to our kids during school hours.[130]

Many historians and critics of the education system in America refer to a turning point in 1898 when John Dewey launched the progressive education movement providing a road map for his socialist agenda in his essay "The Primary Education Fetish." Dewey was thirty-nine at the time and persuaded educators the only way to transform America from an individualistic society to a collectivist one was to dumb down the people. Is it possible the problem with literacy in America may be traced back to this deliberate attempt to lower education standards?

The situation with declining literacy was addressed in an April 1, 1996, issue of *U.S. News and World Report* in the article "Dumb and Dumber." This article stated 23 million Americans – one out of every five – did not know how to read and write well enough to meet the demands of

---

130   Jessica Chasmar, "Texas students dress in burqas, taught to call Muslim terrorists 'freedom fighters'" 2/25/2013, http://www.washingtontimes.com/news/2013/feb/25/texas-students-dress-burqas-taught-call-muslim-ter/.

daily life as an adult. Children in public schools were not learning the basics, and the solution was to spend more money on education and raise the standards. That was nearly twenty years ago. Has it worked?

John Dewey was able to influence public school curricula with the help of grants from the Carnegie and Rockefeller Foundations through which he implemented teacher training programs. It appears several of the goals of these foundations were similar to Dewey's agenda to mold young people through the public school system, eliminate tradition and scholarship, create a strong class (or caste) system, overthrow faith and family values (the influence of Christianity), and prepare children for a future global job market.

World history reveals totalitarian leaders, including Adolf Hitler and Joseph Stalin, murdered millions of their own people after successfully centralizing and controlling education. Stalin once said, "Ideas are more dangerous than guns. We don't let our people have guns. Why should we let them have ideas?"

Some of the most powerful and evil world leaders understood that whoever fills and shapes the minds of young people could dominate and rule the masses. Karl Marx, Hitler, Antonio Gramsci, and others left marching orders in their writings explaining why government-controlled education is imperative to reach the objective of socialism.

These marching orders start with children. Atheists, humanists, and secularists understand this fact: Influence changes everything. Liberals have been much more intentional and persistent than conservatives when it comes to influencing culture. Self-avowed secular humanist, John Dunphy, wrote an essay entitled "A Religion for a New Age" that speaks volumes. It can be found in the January/February 1983 edition of the *Humanist* magazine. He stated:

> I am convinced that the battle for humankind's future must be waged and won in the public school classroom by teachers who correctly perceive their role as the proselytizers of a new faith: a religion of humanity that recognizes the spark of what theologians call divinity in every human being. There teachers must embody the same selfless dedication of the most rabid fundamentalist preacher, for they will be ministers of

another sort, utilizing a classroom instead of a pulpit to convey humanist values in whatever subject they teach, regardless of the educational level – preschool, daycare, or large state university. The classroom must and will become an arena of conflict between the old and the new – the rotting corpse of Christianity, together with all its adjacent evils and misery, and the new faith of humanism, resplendent in its promise of a world in which the never-realized Christian ideal of "love thy neighbor" will finally be achieved.[131]

Humanists are not all bad, evil people; many are deceived and have accepted a faulty premise of a hopeless, godless religion. They may be somewhat ethical according to man's morality, and they may even do some good in society, but their motive is to please themselves, not God. The slogan for the American Humanist Association is "Good Without a God," and their mission is "advocating progressive values and equality for humanists, atheists, and freethinkers." They have presented an annual award to the Humanist of the Year since 1953. Last year's winner was the radical homosexual Dan Savage, and in 2010 the award went to Bill Nye, the "Science Guy."

> But we can discover no divine purpose or providence for the human species. While there is much that we do not know, humans are responsible for what we are or will become. No deity will save us; we must save ourselves.
> —*Humanist Manifesto II*, 1973; Tenet 1

BACKLASH: THE GROWING RESISTANCE TO FED ED & COMMON CORE

By this time, I trust you are more than ready for some good news as the information presented here can be overwhelming. Results of a Rasmussen poll released June 26, 2014, found support for Common Core standards among parents with school-age children at its lowest point, having dropped dramatically. The survey revealed only 34% of American adults with children of elementary or secondary school ages

131 John Dunphy, A Religion for a New Age, Humanist, Jan.-Feb. 1983, p. 26, http://creationrevolution.com/john-dunphy-on-public-schools/#hIEU4GCBvZ9tblLY.99.

support the requirement that all schools nationwide must meet the same Common Core education standards.

This was a big decline of support, an 18-point drop from the major survey taken seven months earlier. With 19% undecided – meaning perhaps they know nothing about what's going on or need more information – nearly half of those surveyed oppose the controversial standards compared to 32% in the prior survey. Since this Rasmussen survey was the first major poll done on "support for Common Core," it shows the more people learn about the content and quality of the standards, the less they approve of them.[132]

The rollout of the standards was purposely rushed. Then, when concerned citizens started learning about it, Democrats went into marketing mode, paying for push polls to make it appear Common Core had public support. Does it not minimize the credibility of Common Core the way the standards were hurried into classrooms across America? Those who understand the educational process wonder why the approach to implement the standards did not include pilot programs allowing for the necessary time and money to evaluate them at a reasonable pace.

At the time of this writing, more concerned Americans seem to be resisting the White House's attempt to corral the states into this controversial education scheme. Let's take note of New York where typically loyal teachers' unions pulled their support from Common Core to the tune of over 600,000 members. Though some are struggling with how to deal with the problem, this is a good sign. Loyal allies of President Obama, such as the New York State United Teachers (NYSUT), voted unanimously to pull their endorsement for Common Core.

Also, the NEA, which is the largest teachers' union in America, also withdrew their support of Common Core as NEA President Dennis Van Roekel blamed the government for another botched rollout. Van Roekel's issue seems to be more with the implementation than the standards themselves. Nonetheless, 70 percent of NEA teachers (according to their own internal polling) object to how Common Core is being introduced in schools.

---

132   Dr. Susan Berry, ""Rasmussen: Common Core Support Plummets Among Parents with School-Age Children," 6/26/2014 http://www.breitbart.com/Big-Government/2014/06/26/Rasmussen-Common-Core-Support-Plummets-Among-Parents-with-School-Age-Children/.

Many are upset they were not able to provide any feedback or give input, but one of the teachers that did participate as the standards were being written suggested he was only used as "window dressing." Other teachers are angry about the apparent lack of commitment by the government to implement Common Core properly. Yes, it is good they understand the importance of a smooth process; it should raise eyebrows if they are *not* as concerned about what is actually in the standards.

A sneaky tactic has been used by a few states due to the growing unpopularity of Common Core: changing the name of the standards. In Arizona the new program is called "College and Career Ready Standards," and believe it or not, in Florida, "Next Generation Sunshine State Standards." Then there is "Idaho Core" and "Iowa Core." Changing the name on a case of radioactive material won't make it less dangerous.

The objections are coming from more than individuals, teachers, and a few unions; more states are working toward dropping the standards. Parents are also putting two and two together (pun intended): If a government is not competent enough to create and launch a simple health care website without massive delays, glitches, and millions of dollars in attempted fixes, how can they possibly be trusted with nationalized education? Tell me again how the federal government is qualified to run education.

In 2014, Indiana's Governor Mike Pence signed a bill to drop Common Core, and South Carolina's Nikki Haley stressed the fact her state doesn't want "to educate South Carolina children like they educate California children." Haley and Oklahoma's Mary Fallin have both signed laws pulling their states out of the suffocating standards. Fallin's decision is key because she is chairwoman of the National Governor's Association, one of the private groups holding the copyright for Common Core. (Fallin was not governor at the time the standards were created and written, and she was heavily influenced by concerned, persistent parents.)

North Carolina passed legislation to repeal parts of Common Core; Alabama and Utah had already quit, while North Dakota dropped out of the testing. Louisiana's Governor Bobby Jindal signed an executive order dropping out of the federally funded testing consortia and requiring his state to develop its own standards.

Missouri legislators have passed HB 1490 to repeal and replace Common Core in their state, and surprisingly, Democratic Governor Jay Nixon signed the bill. One representative said, "HB 1490 can be simplified to three words: sovereignty, privacy, and flexibility." As rallies against Common Core grew in Ohio, a representative in that state said the reason Common Core standards were originally accepted was money, politics, and failed leadership. It appears nearly two dozen states have pending bills rejecting parts or all of the standards.

While this is good news and more states may follow, the primary ways to resist further government influence and control are to repeal Common Core completely, eliminate the U.S. Department of Education, and vote conservative in elections. Education is a Christian, ethical, and moral issue: Schools are teaching kids an anti-biblical worldview.

President Obama is a committed leftist supported and surrounded by globalists and progressives. He is influenced by powerful lobbyists, anti-American radicals, and wealthy foundations and organizations. Education will continue to be a primary focus for them.

State and local governments are relying on concerned parents and citizens to help inform others. Many encouraging signs that the public is catching on are appearing, but still not enough. The truth must be exposed about Common Core including the "lynch pin" testing mandates, special interest groups, lack of accountability, immoral and propagandized curriculum, lack of individual creativity, and of course, government intrusion on student's lives. Federal education mandates don't work because every child is unique.

We can't force people to care, but we can work to raise awareness. Parents need to get involved in the community, attend school board meetings, and rally other parents. We cannot remain silent.

In an extensive article on education for the *New American* last August, Brain Farmer reiterated the fact that for centuries parents educated their children on the Bible, which was the pillar of our republic. The good news that does not make the headlines is millions of young minds are currently instructed on Christian principles and history by godly parents in private schools and in home schools. Farmer writes that those children "are being taught to apply the cause and effect principles of Scripture to family, economics, government, and all areas of life and society."[133]

Through the centuries, children have been the main target of all kinds of evil. One way we can look at it is the end times are drawing much closer. Again, author and researcher Berit Kjos helps put this in perspective:

> We can no longer count on the American Constitution, which was based on moral and just values, as it is daily being redefined … May God show us how we can best equip our children to stand firm in Christ in the midst of the coming battles. Let us remember that our Lord still reigns! In the midst of this spiritual war, He will surely provide His strength, wisdom, and comforting nearness to all who choose to trust and follow Him![134]

Being informed and willing to participate in the political process is good, and the people may be gaining some ground back, but as vital as these surface battles are, they are merely symptoms of an underlying worldview war. Regardless of what happens in education, government, media, politics, or culture in the future, we trust in a sovereign God and have assurance we are on the side of Truth. May we speak the truth we know.

> Give ear, O my people, to my teaching; incline your ears to the words of my mouth! … things that we have heard and known, that our fathers have told us. We will not hide them from their children, but tell to the coming generation the glorious deeds of the LORD, and his might, and the wonders that he has done. He established a testimony in Jacob and appointed a law in Israel, which he commanded our fathers to teach to their children, that the next generation might know them, the children yet unborn, and arise and tell them to their children, so that they should set their hope in God and not forget the works of God, but keep his commandments (PSALM 78:1, 3-7 ESV).

---

133 Brian Farmer, "New Public School Policy," 8/14/2013, http://www.thenewamerican.com/culture/education/item/16194-new-public-school-policy.

134 Berit Kjos, Lighthouse Trails Publishing, 11/16/2013, http://www.lighthousetrailsresearch.com/blog/?p=13825.

CHAPTER 13

WITCHCRAFT IS OUT OF THE (BROOM) CLOSET

When you enter the land the LORD your God is giving you, do not learn to imitate the detestable ways of the nations there. Let no one be found among you who sacrifices their son or daughter in the fire, who practices divination or sorcery, interprets omens, engages in witchcraft, or casts spells, or who is a medium or spiritist or who consults the dead. Anyone who does these things is detestable to the LORD; because of these same detestable practices the LORD your God will drive out those nations before you.
Deuteronomy 18: 9-12 (NIV)

It is hard not to notice the rapidly growing fascination in America with zombies, vampires, death, the occult, and the supernatural. Witchcraft has gone mainstream; casting spells is cool, black magic is exciting, fortune telling is fun, and killing zombies is sport. Are these just harmless, innocent fads or is there something more – something evil – behind the fascination? We need to determine what is behind it and understand what the Bible teaches.

As we look at secular entertainment and note the open rebellion against God and His Word, we must also recognize pop culture has crept into the church. I don't expect unbelievers to appreciate Scripture, but Christians should strive to obey the commands and warnings throughout the Bible regarding the occult, witchcraft, and idolatry. We should avoid any form of spirituality or godliness that denies Jesus is Lord Savior.

The apostle John tells us *every spirit that does not confess Jesus Christ is not from God* (1 John 4:3). Must we point out the obvious? The modern spirits behind the ideas, practices, and products of Hollywood and the gaming industry certainly are not acknowledging Jesus as Lord and God. The Bible cautions us about the dangers and subtleties of sin and its practices. John also writes, *Do not believe every spirit, but test the spirits to see whether they are from God* (1 John 4:1). How do we test spirits?

We need to be walking closely with the Lord, seeking Him first, and allowing the Holy Spirit to give us discernment. In many entertainment products from *Charmed* to *Harry Potter* to *Sabrina the Teenage Witch*, the heroes are typically good people – you know, the ones using witch-craft and the occult – while the average person is portrayed as ordinary, weak, or even bad, partly because they do not have any magic powers. Therefore, the occult, the satanic, and anything related to it are looked at as beneficial and desirable, which is a complete twisting of the con-cept of good and evil. We are to resist, expose, and stand against sin, not invite it into our homes.

The apostle Paul wrote,

> *But examine* [test] *everything carefully; hold fast to that which is good; abstain from every form of evil* (1 Thessalonians 5:21-22).

Some say it isn't blatant in-your-face evil and it's just entertainment, but if the Bible considers something to be sin, we had better decide to align ourselves with Scripture. Appearing harmless and sold as benefi-cial, sin often attracts the youngest, most innocent, and gullible. This is only part of the problem when we let down our guard over what the world considers good entertainment.

Occult themes dominate books, movies, marketing campaigns, the Internet, and primetime television. And the children are playing right along. The darkness of the occult and witchcraft has to a great degree been accepted in our society, but the question we should ask is to what extent has it seeped into our churches? That may sound extreme to those who have bought what the world has been selling, but for Christians, we are instructed to not conform to this world (Romans 12:2).

Here's some food for thought: Public schools do not allow Christianity to be taught or promoted. However, they accept the religions of athe-ism, Humanism, evolution, environmental extremism (earth worship),

Buddhism, Islam, and of course the religion of Wicca – the practice of witchcraft. Kids have sat through readings of the *Harry Potter* books, watched the movies during class instruction times, and have even discussed the details of casting spells. Someone may argue Wicca is not a religion and Harry Potter has nothing to do with the occult.

First, on the bottom of its home page, the Church of the Wiccan Interfaith Council (aka Wiccan Interfaith Council International) describes itself as a "nonprofit religious, educational, and charitable organization" holding a 501(c)(3) status with the federal government as a "church or conventions or association of churches."[135] So don't give me the separation of church and state line as the reason for banning God, Christian prayers, and the Bible. Public schools openly discriminate by allowing anything *except* biblical Christianity.

I have nothing against Wiccans themselves; some of them left the Christian church for various reasons and I pray they come back to Jesus. Wiccans are free to believe and practice whatever they want under the Constitution in America and are thankful for religious freedom as well as their tax-exempt status. But unlike Christians, their influence and teachings will not be kicked out of government-controlled schools.

Second, even many well-meaning parents have said, "at least the kids are reading," as if to imply the occult influence in *Harry Potter* is not as blatant and reprehensible as so much of what we see in culture today. This argument merely shifts the line of acceptance which most always leads to compromise. This includes questionable computer and video games, kids' books, and naïvely dressing up the kids as *Harry Potter* characters and witches for Halloween.

"It's all harmless and innocent," you've probably heard someone say. "My kids aren't going to sacrifice any cats or babies." These are the folks who are uninformed, spiritually immature, or simply unwilling to take the time to research the truth for themselves and their children. This is one reason I believe God put it on my heart to write this chapter.

NOT JUST FICTIONAL CHARACTERS

In a 2008 interview with several young witches, Abel, a teenage boy,

---

135   The Church of the Wiccan Interfaith Council, http://wiccaninterfaithcouncil.org/.

explained, "In the Craft, no matter who you are, you are divine ... However you interact with the world, you are sacred." A 16-year-old girl talked about how she hides the fact she practices witchcraft: "If I'm put on the spot and kids ask, 'Why don't you go to church?' I say, 'I worship my own way.'"[136] One young man suggested Paganism is a "healing spiritual path." Many witches' beliefs indicate that organized religion is bad, but then include ultimate respect for nature, hyper-tolerance, equality of the sexes (male gods are not superior), worship of a deity, and karma.

Pastor Joe Schimmel of Good Fight Ministries suggests the sharp increase of young people identifying themselves as neo-pagans and Wiccans is mainly due to the media's propagandizing and the glorification of occult themes in Hollywood, which has a long history of providing fuel for the lie that there are both good and bad witches. Schimmel added, "*Harry Potter* is a doorway to the occult," and "even MTV has acknowledged that such movies [including the *Twilight* series] have played a surprising role in making Wicca [witchcraft] one of the fastest growing religions in America."[137]

The *Harry Potter* brand is worth about $15 billion due to the popularity of not only the books, but movies and merchandise. Over 400 million books have been sold worldwide in sixty-seven language translations representing readers in over 200 nations, and a U.S. consumer research survey reported "over half of all children between the ages of six and seventeen have read at least one *Harry Potter* book."

Christian parents, we cannot be naïve any longer about subtle satanic influences. The enemy rarely tempts us with something so obviously evil and wicked that we know immediately it is his doing. Make no mistake: *Harry Potter*, along with many other accepted forms of entertainment, is an entryway into the occult through the hearts and minds of trusting children as well as plenty of adults. The first *Harry Potter* book was released in June 1997, and tragically documented cases now exist of kids who have died or have committed suicide as a result of their occult

---

136 Alex Mar, "Far From Devil Worship and 'Harry Potter,' Young Witches Explain What They're Really About," 3/5/2008, http://www.mtv.com/news/1584096/far-from-devil-worship-and-harry-potter-young-witches-explain-what-theyre-really-about/.

137 Pastor Joe Schimmel, "Twilight, Harry Potter, The Wizard of Oz, and the Wiccan Revival," Good Fight Ministries, http://www.goodfight.org/a_co_twilight_harrypotter.html.

activity and the darkness and depression that enveloped their lives. You decide after reading this chapter if there might be any connection.

God created mankind in His image. He rules and is sovereign over all He created. He has authority over all powers in the universe, and He is a personal Being of infinite love, wisdom, and power. Human beings – every one of us – are accountable to Him whether we choose to accept His existence or not.

Occultism, however, promotes the idea every individual can acquire supernatural powers and become his or her own god. This is similar to what Buddhist and Hindu missionaries to America – yes, their goal is to convert the West – have taught through meditation techniques and various forms of yoga which are welcomed in many American churches. Yoga is a Sanskirt (primary language in Hinduism) word meaning to "yoke," and the whole idea behind yoga is to join with the Hindu concept of God to achieve "enlightenment" and realize the individual soul (atman) is identical with the universal soul (Brahman).

Eastern mysticism invaded Christianity through the drug and hippie movement in the 1960s and 70s when unsuspecting Americans opened up their minds, hearts, and wallets to welcome the new cosmic consciousness. People got by and got high with a little help from their friends: *The Beatles*. One of the largest missionary organizations in the world is India's Vishva Hindu Parishad (VHP). Hindus freely evangelize in America with the goal of replacing Christianity as its foundation; however, by law, Christian missionary activity is not allowed among Hindus in India.

Many occultists also believe in a dark side and a light side of energy forces in the universe. In witchcraft, they may refer to this in terms of "black magic" or "white magic." Some occultists attribute their powers to different deities or even to a "Force" inherent within the universe. Sorry friends, these ideas didn't originate with *Star Wars*.

Other occultists believe they must look to the spirit entities who have some sort of authority and who control this force. They developed chants, practices, and rituals through which man-made gods might be pleased and grant them favors. Their goal is to tap into these powers in order to use them for their own benefit.

Looking at definitions of the word *occult*, the meaning goes beyond dealings with the paranormal, the "psychic," or supernatural even though the word is generally associated with secret knowledge and rituals. The essence of the occult is rooted in paganism and nature-based philosophies. Modern interest has been generated by the New Age movement. Words defining the occult can include: hidden, concealed, secret, and mysterious. One source described the occult as pertaining to magic, astrology, or any system claiming use or knowledge of secret or supernatural powers or agencies.

In his extremely thorough and research-packed book, *Occult Invasion*, internationally-known author, Dave Hunt, explains:

> It involves mystic knowledge and magic powers and revelations received from the spirit world and dispensed for the benefit of devotees or directed destructively at enemies by those who have been initiated into its secrets. The masters of occult power are known as medicine men (or women), witch doctors, witches, psychics, priests, sorcerers, astrologers, gurus, yogis, shamans, mediums, seers, or healers.[138]

Until recently, most occult activities, including black magic practices involving demons or spirits, were carried out in secret and often at night. With the widening acceptance of the occult, people have become less sensitive to its influence, and we often fail to recognize some of the dangers. Though most practices are spiritually based, Wiccans tend to follow what is known as the "Rule of Three" so as to do no harm to others. The rule basically suggests that whatever you do to another will return to you three-fold. It's a counterfeit of the biblical principle of reaping and sowing as well as an offshoot of the concept of karma.

Let's look at how some in the *Harry Potter* and *Twilight* generation have grown up. In a *Newsweek* article called "Hexing and Texting," some of the young people interviewed said they "enjoy dabbling in different metaphysical practices without subscribing to one doctrine," while others are more dedicated to a specific craft or are literally experimenting with sorcery. One twenty-eight-year-old tarot card reader said every reading is "kind of like a snowflake," and the article states, "more and

---

138   Dave Hunt, *Occult Invasion*, 1998 Harvest House Publishers, Eugene, OR, p. 39.

more smart, savvy and usually cynical eighteen- to thirty-year-olds are dabbling in the occult, from astrological natal charts and tarot to séances and full-moon ceremonies."[139]

One college professor admits we're in the middle of an occult revival, and these kids are not just wearing black lipstick, nail polish, and dark clothes while watching witches hex each other on screen; they're practicing it themselves. Twenty-seven-year-old Hilary Pollack reveals the heart of this generation and the ignorance about authentic Christianity by stating, "It's embarrassing to admit you're religious … spirituality is a lot cooler."

Another young woman said she turned to tarot cards and astrology when things were difficult in her personal life. If only she would turn to the Maker of the stars and read the truths in the living Word instead of tarot cards! Rebecca, a twenty-five-year-old, said lesbian women are drawn to the occult because they "seek outside validation" but don't want to answer to pastors or priests. Lynsey, twenty-two, declares she wants nothing to do with a church where a man is in a position of authority. Another young woman said when she reads ritual instructions, it makes her feel "grounded." Isn't it interesting many Christians say the same thing about reading the Bible regularly?

Before we investigate some of the history and influences behind J.K. Rowling's works and her fame, we must acknowledge that long before *Harry Potter*, practically everyone in America fell in love with Glinda, the "Good Witch of the North," from the classic movie *Wizard of Oz*. You're not going to want to hear this: As its author, Frank Baum claimed he channeled the *Wizard of Oz*, saying it came to him "out of the blue," and "I happened to be that medium and I believe the magic key was given to me." Baum belonged to Helena Blavatsky's Theosophical Society. Blavatsky claimed she was a "Buddhist pilgrim" and admired Satan.

Since the early days of Oz, America has been subjected to an endless smorgasbord of cult films in the science fiction and horror categories along with everything in between. Many adults today may not realize or be willing to acknowledge that as children, they were targeted by

---

139 Katie J.M. Baker, *Newsweek*, "Hexing and Texting," 10/24/2013, http://www.newsweek.com/hexing-texting-243730.

Hollywood and the entertainment industry through media, movies, and music promoting the occult.

We could probably do an entire chapter on, believe it or not, Disney movies and cartoons, many of which glorified magic, witches, wizards, and the casting of spells. More recently, some of us remember titles such as *Charmed, Buffy the Vampire Slayer, The Craft, Practical Magic, Ghost, True Blood, Interview with a Vampire, Sabrina the Teenage Witch, Hex, Eastwick, Blood Ties, Secret Circle, Witches of East End, Wizards of Waverly Place,* and *American Horror Story.* This is not at all an exhaustive list.

Curiosity and intrigue have also helped open the door of minds and hearts to supposedly investigate the paranormal through so-called reality shows such as *Ghost Hunters, Most Haunted, Paranormal Challenge, Extreme Paranormal, Ghost Stories, Psychic, Medium, Haunted Hotels,* and *Ghost Hunters Academy.* I refer to this as "imagination programming." We can trick ourselves into believing something is real and present, or into being genuinely scared by what is already in our own thoughts.

Entire books have been written on these subjects, and documentaries have been done, so understand we're merely touching the surface here. Pastor Joe Schimmel says Hollywood uses whatever it can to reach people and the "products" we are discussing have been powerful weapons in Satan's arsenal, "used as evangelistic tools to seduce our impressionable youth into *his* kingdom." Schimmel elaborates on his concerns:

> Tragically, many Wiccans have been deceived into believing they can have relationships with "good" spirits and cast "good" spells, when in reality they have opened the door to demonic oppression and even demon possession. After many Wiccans open the door to the demonic realm, they are then taught that they can use counter spells to summon "good" spirits to protect them from evil spirits. This device has been effectively utilized by Satan to delude the prospective Wiccan by promising power, while enslaving them to an occult construct.
>
> God has revealed in His Word that spirits contacted by occult means are evil and part and parcel of Satan's original rebellion

(Ephesians 6:10-12). God's Word is saturated with categorical warnings against all forms of the occult, including astrology, sorcery, divination, magic, and witchcraft (Gen. 3:1-6; Ex. 22:18; Lev. 19:26, 31-32; 20:6, 27; Deut. 18:10-12; 1 Sam. 15:23a; 2 Kings 21:6, 23:24; I Chron. 10:13; Isa. 2:6; 8:19-20; 19:3; 47:13-14; Ez. 13:20-23; Dan. 2:27-28; 5:15-17; Mal. 3:5; Acts 13:7-10a; 16:16-18; 19:19; Gal. 5:19-20; Rev 9:19-21; 21:8; 22:15, etc.).[140]

Would millions of people have been introduced or desensitized to the occult and various forms of witchcraft had it not been for the influence of *Harry Potter* and *Twilight* series? Would today's shows have made it to television, would video games have taken such a dark and dangerous turn, and would countless young people be dabbling with astrology, tarot cards, Ouija boards, magic spells, séances, and fortune telling? We may never fully know.

The story of *Harry Potter* begins on Halloween night when his parents are murdered by the dark Lord Voldemort. Through the sacrificial goddess magic in Harry's mother's life, the young boy is saved, and his blood given magical powers. Because of this, Voldemort sears a death curse in the form of a lightning bolt on Harry's forehead.

The name of the Hogwarts "School of Witchcraft and Wizardry" is telling enough, but a few red flags should fly when an eleven-year-old orphan is taught by the faculty's wizards and witches how to properly use magic, rituals, and cast spells. One of the tools used is a tail feather from a mythical Phoenix bird, symbolizing resurrection. Harry Potter and master of "dark arts," Lord Voldemort, use the feather in their wands. Hogwarts also offers a special class in which one may learn to communicate with spirits by tapping into their "mind's eye."

Let's go back to that mark given to Harry on his forehead. Only J.K. Rowling knows the true intention of the mark on the story's hero, but countless young fans idolized Harry Potter by giving themselves a lightning bolt mark on their own foreheads. The lightning bolt is also known as the Satanic *S*, symbolizing Lucifer being cast out of heaven and

---

140 Pastor Joe Schimmel, "Twilight, Harry Potter, The Wizard of Oz, and the Wiccan Revival," Good Fight Ministries, http://www.goodfight.org/a_co_twilight_harrypotter.html.

his transformation into Satan. Jesus told His disciples, *I was watching Satan fall from heaven like lightning* (Luke 10:18). We also know in the end times, the Beast will cause all people wanting to buy and sell to be *given a mark on their right hand or on their forehead* (Revelation 13:16).

Representing one of the most evil empires in world history, the double *S* was used by Adolf Hitler's Schutzstaffel (SS), and the swastika (two crossing lightning bolts) represented Germany's Nazi Party whose aim was world domination by government. In mythology, some gods used the power of the lightning bolt to punish or scare mortals on earth, and one of the most powerful Greek gods, Zeus, wielded the double bolt at times.

Even Lady Gaga made lightning bolt necklaces and make-up kits popular, as the occult-influenced superstar wore them on and off stage, as have other Satan-worshipping artists.

In real life apart from books and the big screen, the big lure in the occult is the possibility of gaining access to power in the universe or becoming like God. Some occultists believe they are already gods or are part of God. To understand the intrigue that attracted many Christian kids, we need to research and evaluate the progression of ideas and the people involved.

AUTHORS WHO SEDUCED A GENERATION

Harry Potter author, J.K. Rowling, has been interviewed quite a bit since becoming famous and admits she received inspiration for the characters from spirit communication through a stream of consciousness:

> Harry as a character came fully formed, as did the idea for his sidekicks, the characters of Ron and Hermione, who is the brains of the threesome; The character of Harry just strolled into my head … I really did feel he was someone who walked up and introduced himself in my mind's eye.

Rowling marveled at the appeal of the whole idea of a child escaping "the confines of the adult world" and going to a place where "he has power, both literally and metaphorically."

You may be reading this and thinking this is quite a stretch and I am nitpicking or even going on a witch hunt – pardon the pun. J.K. Rowling has defended her books and characters as being "highly moral," and yet from the *Harry Potter* series, children have learned about demons, werewolves, and other monstrous creatures along with magic, spell casting, levitation, animal sacrifices, astral projection, crystal gazing, and communing with dead souls.[141]

When we realize Satan and his demons are very real and they hate human beings, especially Christians, we'll understand this is not fantasy but rather an organized power with plans only for evil. The occult movement is basically a substitute religion; even the Bible teaches that Satan, *the god of this world has blinded the minds of the unbelieving so that they might not see the light of the gospel of the glory of Christ, who is the image of God* (2 Corinthians 4:4).

If the craft was not represented accurately in *Harry Potter*, real life witches would have pointed it out. Instead, some have stated J.K. Rowling did her research and has represented witchcraft, black magic, and the black arts very well. We must mention that Rowling has admitted there are Christian overtones in the series, but none clearly point to the redemption by Jesus Christ, and any comparison between the world of witchcraft and the kingdom of God is useless. The fruit of Harry's actions reveals an occult context that is abhorrent to a holy God. Everything he does is an extension of his (and perhaps Rowling's) belief system.

Dr. Alan D. Ingalls, a professor at Baptist Bible Seminary in Pennsylvania, wrote that the pagans are delighted Rowling's Harry Potter, "the poster-boy for witchcraft," is creating a good image for them.

> This poses a serious danger for the undiscerning who read *Harry Potter* because they will be desensitized to a way of life that God condemns in the strongest possible terms. Though Harry is not the only source of such desensitization, he is, at the moment, one of the most prominent and popular.[142]

Reading fantasy and fiction books or watching television programs

---

141   Dennis Leap, "It's Baaaack ... the Occult Revival," May/June 2014 theTrumpet. com Print edition, https://www.thetrumpet.com/article/11529.31725.164.0/world/ its-baaaack-the-occult-revival.

142   Dr. Alan D. Ingalls, "A Christian Perspective on the Harry Potter Phenomenon." Journal of Ministry & Theology 5:1 (Spring 2001): 69-88.

and movies dealing with the occult is dangerous because little by little it wears down barriers in our minds and hearts while opening us up to the demonic realm. The bottom line is the enemy uses entertainment to lure people and portray occult practices as normal or good.

Though Rowling's *Harry Potter* series may not directly open the door to destructive patterns including depression, narcissism, drug use, and sexual promiscuity; the spirit world of the occult is almost guaranteed to lead kids down these paths.

> *Then I will draw near to you for judgment; and I will be a swift witness against the sorcerers and against the adulterers and against those who swear falsely* (Malachi 3:5).

It makes sense to mention sins of sorcery and adultery together. This destroys the argument that mild interest in sorcery and witchcraft falls under the category of things that are permissible to Christians.

Next, very similar to J.K. Rowling, Mormon author Stephanie Meyer, a housewife and inexperienced writer, explained how she "woke up from a very vivid dream" and described a conversation in the woods between an average girl and a "fantastically beautiful, sparkly" vampire. She said she heard voices in her head that would not stop until she would type what they were saying. *Twilight* was born. Meyer also talks about the character Edward coming to visit her in a dream after she completed *Twilight,* saying they had a conversation and "he was terrifying."

Overall, the *Twilight* saga films have earned over $2.5 billion at the box office, and DVD sales, cable TV showings, and millions in merchandise are in addition. The four *Twilight* books have sold well over 120 million copies worldwide and have been translated into more than thirty-eight different languages. The series won the 2009 Kid's Choice Award in the Favorite Book category, set records on the *USA Today* Best-Selling Books list, and spent 235 weeks on the *New York Times* Best Seller list for Children's Series Books. *Twilight* has over 100 million fans and "likes" on Facebook alone as well as approximately 350 fan sites on line.

"Twilighters" are encouraged to write their own fan fiction stories about *Twilight* characters and conjure up their own reality. Hard core fans, also known as "Twi-hards," are just as obsessed with the series characters and concepts of the occult as *Harry Potter* fans are with its characters, sorcery, and the religion of Wicca.

Fans established and organized a nationwide "Stephenie Meyer Day," and in 2014 it was held on September 11th to honor the birthday of *Twilight* character Bella Swan. The main event is held each year in Forks, Washington, the location for much of the *Twilight* series filming. The town of Forks now enjoys perhaps tens of thousands of new tourists each year due to the series' popularity. Similar to Halloween, fans dress up like the characters in the book. Interestingly, the majority of fans seem to be young girls.

Meyer admits the fame came quite suddenly and "miraculously," her work was published. It is interesting a woman who worked as a receptionist with little writing experience and three young children at home wrote and edited the completed novel, *Twilight*, in just three months after receiving the first dream. Within three weeks Meyer signed a three-book deal with Little, Brown and Company for an unusually large sum of money ($750,000) according to industry standards.

Not exactly Holy Spirit inspired, some believe Meyer was chosen to be the instrument through which the concepts and dialogue were channeled. By whatever power and for whatever reason, *Twilight* was selected to influence millions worldwide. Was it through the process of illumination that she heard the voices?

Conversations and dream visitations by spirits are part of occult communication. Meyer's spiritual experiences could well be influenced by her Mormon faith, which allows for communication with "the dead" of former generations, those who were baptized into Mormonism in the Mormon Temple ritual. Mormon founder Joseph Smith was "visited" by a communicating "angel" named Moroni who stands atop all Mormon Temples.[143]

Plenty of romance novels are out there with themes similar to those found in *Twilight*, such as submission and surrender, obsessive love, and even some with characters fantasizing about having sex with vampires. The problem occurs after young girls read this stuff or see the movies - and they fantasize about having sex with vampires.

---

143   Amos 3:7, "Twilight Occult Examined," 2/25/2010, http://amos37.com/2010/02/25/twilight-examined/.

In *The Guardian*, logical questions were asked to young girls as to why they responded to *Twilight* so wildly and why they are so intrigued about a "potentially violent romantic hero."

> In a world where porn is ubiquitous, where there do seem to be new sexual pressures on young women – demands for them from boys to take naked pictures, for example – is a chaste but adoring partner especially appealing? Do young women still yearn for a dominant man? Do they identify, more than ever, with an awkward, unconfident female protagonist? Bubbling away in a generation's subconscious are some troubling answers.[144]

Also, Stephenie Meyer claims she is a feminist, but a few portrayals in the books and movies seem to oppose the message of feminism. For example, Bella became pregnant, and apparently the vampire fetus endangered her life as a mere mortal, and yet she refused an abortion, the opposite choice die-hard feminists endorse.

And the most obvious idea that rubs true feminists the wrong way is that after having sex with a rough, potentially dangerous, much stronger being, Bella had bruises and marks on her body but couldn't wait to have sex again. This resembles somewhat of an abusive relationship. In the book version of *Breaking Dawn*, Bella explains a slight mark on her cheekbone and her swollen lips, and she was "decorated with patches of blue and purple. I concentrated on the bruises that would be the hardest to hide – my arms and my shoulders."

Nonetheless, in the *Guardian* interview mentioned earlier, Meyer exclaimed:

> I love women, I have a lot of girlfriends, I admire them, they make so much more sense to me than men, and I feel like the world is a better place when women are in charge. So that kind of by default makes me a feminist. I love working in a female world.

I have no doubt Meyer has high respect for women, but do you find it slightly disconcerting the public accepted the storyline about a

---

144   Kira Cochrane, "Stephenie Meyer on Twilight, feminism, and true love," 3/10/2013, http://www.theguardian.com/books/2013/mar/11/stephenie-meyer-twilight-the-host.

young teenage girl (Bella) falling in love with a 108-year-old vampire and their infatuation with each other? Okay, apparently he was "frozen" outwardly at seventeen, and he appears human in his handsome whiteness. However, isn't this a little odd to you? The focus is supposed to be on their intoxicating, lustful obsession with each other, and apparently, age shouldn't matter.

Let's talk about the name given to the hero vampire, Edward Cullen. Infamous Satanist and bisexual occult leader Aleister Crowley's birth name was Edward Alexander Crowley. Coincidence? As a Free Mason, Crowley was initiated to its highest levels, hated God and Christianity with a vengeance, and was reported to have been involved in the gruesome practice of child sacrifice. Also of interest is that Edward's pre-vampire name was Edward Masen, spelled with an *e*, son of Edward and Elizabeth Masen.

Naturally, Stephenie Meyer portrays the vampires as well meaning, goodhearted, and even trustworthy. Even though Edward and his "coven" of vampires do their best to resist drinking human blood, they exist on the blood of animals, which is clearly forbidden by God in Scripture. As far as acceptable forms of entertainment, opinions vary even among Christians, so each of us must decide and discern the spirits.

> *Do not be deceived: God cannot be mocked. A man reaps what he sows. The one who sows to please his sinful nature, from that nature will reap destruction; the one who sows to please the Spirit, from the Spirit will reap eternal life* (Galatians 6:7-8 NIV).

What is so appealing in *Twilight* is a counterfeit of the truth, and we cannot complete this section without mentioning the book cover Meyer chose featuring the "forbidden fruit." Pictured on the first cover are a woman's hands cupping a bright red apple, perhaps signifying the original temptation and fall of mankind.

Meyer may well have been influenced by Mormon teachings about the apple. For example, the most revered Mormon prophet after Joseph Smith, Brigham Young, called Eve "Mother Eve" and said he did not blame her for disobeying God. He stated, "I would not have had her miss eating the forbidden fruit for anything in the world."[145]

---

145   *Deseret News*, 6/18/1873, from the pulpit of the Mormon Tabernacle in Salt Lake City, Utah.

According to Pastor Joe Schimmel:

> Like ancient Gnosticism and the new spirituality, Mormonism teaches that one may become a god through secret knowledge. Ancient Gnostics venerated the serpent and celebrated Eve's partaking of the forbidden fruit in Eden. In the Mormon Church, achieving godhood comes through the temple endowment and secret Mormon rituals.
>
> Tragically, Mormon leaders, like their Gnostic predecessors, have twisted the Genesis account and made Eve's fall, when partaking of the forbidden fruit, a heroic step ... upward to godhood. Mormon leaders have contradicted God's own testimony as recorded in the book of Genesis and have taught that Satan told Eve the truth in offering humanity deification ...

Former LDS President, Joseph Fielding Smith, declared:

> "The fall of man came as a blessing in disguise ... I never speak of the part Eve took in this fall as a sin, nor do I accuse Adam of a sin ... it is not always a sin to transgress a law ... We can hardly look upon anything resulting in such benefits as a sin." (Joseph Fielding Smith, *Doctrines of Salvation*, Vol. 1, pp. 113-115)

The sad and tragic result is that many have been deceived to the point of becoming spiritually blind. Dear friend, I encourage you to turn from *Twilight* to the true light, Jesus Christ, who died for the sins of the world and rose from the dead to conquer death and the grave.[146]

Other leaders in the Mormon Church have said the doctrine of original sin causes problems because it is "built around the idea of man's natural depravity and weakness inherited from Adam." Assistant to the Council of the Twelve Mormon Apostles, Sterling Sill, said that when Adam fell, "he fell in the right direction" and also declared, "Adam was one of the greatest men who has ever lived upon the earth."[147]

Stephenie Meyer may see the *Twilight* characters as heroic, similar to how Mormon leaders see Adam and Eve.

---

146 Pastor Joe Schimmel, "Twilight, Harry Potter, The Wizard of Oz, and the Wiccan Revival," Good Fight Ministries, http://www.goodfight.org/a_co_twilight_harrypotter.html.

147 *Deseret News*, Salt Lake City, Utah; Church Section, 7/31/1965, p. 7.

But I am afraid that, as the serpent deceived Eve by his crafti-
ness, your minds will be led astray from the simplicity and
purity of devotion to Christ (2 Corinthians 11:3).

The cowardly, the unbelieving, the vile, the murderers, the sexu-
ally immoral, those who practice magic arts, the idolaters and
all liars – their place will be in the fiery lake of burning sulfur.
This is the second death (Revelation 21:8 NIV).

I think the main fascination with this darkness that includes zombies and vampires is the idea of a man-created afterlife. Though it is a
counterfeit of the truth and of the biblical concept of eternity, theirs
is based on life with no need for God and no accountability. Worldly
religions, practices, and philosophies often lead people away from the
only One who can save them, the living God and Lord of all.

Thankfully, followers of Jesus Christ have the victory over death
based on our faith in Him and in His resurrection from the dead. He
overcame the enemy and provides a way for "whosoever" will believe
in Him.

Two major sources admitting there is no distinction between black
and white magic are Doreen Valiente, author of *An ABC of Witchcraft*,
a Wiccan high priestess who has had perhaps more influence on Wicca
than any other woman, and Anton LaVey, founder of the Church of
Satan in 1966 and author of *The Satanic Bible* in 1971. LaVey also
explained there is no difference between black and white magic "except
in the smug hypocrisy, guilt-ridden righteousness, and self-deceit of
the 'white' magician himself." LaVey believed all witches make a pact
with the devil to some degree and said he was thrilled more people
were being drawn to Satanism through movies and television because
of their sugarcoating of witches and their craft:

> White magic is supposedly utilized only for good or unselfish
> purposes, and black magic, we are told, is used only for self-
> ish or evil reasons. Satanism draws no such dividing line.[148]

America has come a long way from the 1960s and the days of the

---

148 Anton LaVey, *The Satanic Bible*, New York: Avon Books, 1971, p. 110.

first "likeable" witches, Samantha Stevens on *Bewitched* and Jeannie on *I Dream of Jeannie.*

In more recent years, one of the most influential people in America has been New Age proponent, Oprah Winfrey. I came across clips of the "Super Soul Sundays" program on her network, OWN TV, and while discussing *The Wizard of Oz* in an interview with spiritual teacher and mystic, Jean Houston, Winfrey said, "It's one of my favorite spiritual teachings." Looking into the camera as she introduced a segment on the show, she told the audience one goal of her TV show is "to help you find your soul's desire." Winfrey continued:

> I always say, "Glinda the good witch says, you've always had it my dear; you've always had the power."[149]

The point being made is that if the power was within us all along, then we don't need God – a "higher power." In this fascinating interview, author Jean Houston said the yellow brick road in the movie represents "the road of spiritual power." She said through her 2012 book, *The Wizard of Us,* her desire "is to show people how to enhance their minds" and their brains. In the book description page, it says "you'll begin to expand your thinking, open your heart," and understand the importance of myth. It further states, "The Wizard not only calls us forth, but he has called forth the journey itself."

This is another reminder to pray for those who are deceived or are deceivers themselves.

GRAMMYS GONE WILD

One last observation that needs to be made is that the anti-Christian and occult influences in the music industry, particularly at the 2014 Grammy Awards were not only glaring but accepted by people across America. As we have seen for over a decade, pushing the envelope of decency is now the new normal for Hollywood award shows. They have gone beyond the generally accepted and normalized profanity, semi-nudity, crass behavior, and promotion of the perverse. Last year's Grammys had

---

149 Oprah Winfrey, "The Mile Markers of Every Life Journey - Super Soul Sunday," Oprah Winfrey Network, http://www.youtube.com/watch?v=FqydlrKJbaA.

it all – including a same sex marriage ceremony, seductress Beyoncé's "adults only" performance, and Katy Perry glorifying Satan.

It appeared to be a desperate attempt by Grammy organizers to get ratings and make headlines. Christian friends, if we don't teach our children to believe in and follow Jesus Christ, the world will definitely teach them not to. Hollywood makes no apology for offending traditional Americans and for mocking Christianity; their hostility has become open rebellion. Will we continue being silent?

You might be thinking I need to lighten up because the entire show was not offensive, and Hollywood is only giving America's culture what it wants. You may be right about the latter, but that doesn't mean we should go along with it. Christians have been especially guilty of this.

Too many families have given in to the no-holds barred, secular "programming" and have conformed to the world where entertainment is concerned. We cannot protect our hearts and minds while filling them with trash. A more accurate description of this type of programming is "soul pollution."

So what was so bad about this particular Grammys' show? They may have reached a new demonic low – and smack in the middle of prime time hours for the whole family to see.

Beginning with Katy Perry (aka Illuminati Priestess) and her performance of what appeared to be a black magic witchcraft ritual to her song "Dark Horse." It began with a sinister voice saying, "She casts spells from crystal balls. Invoking spirits. She put me in a trance." From inside a crystal ball, Perry sang while four horned, demon-like figures rose above her.

Wearing black witches clothing emblazoned with a glowing red Knights Templar cross on her chest, she emerged from the crystal ball while demons danced frantically around her. The Knights Templar were a medieval occult society some consider to be the originator of Freemasonry, the Bavarian Illuminati, and the keepers of "sex-magick" secrets as practiced by Aleister Crowley's O.T.O. (Ordo Templi Orientis).

As she sang about playing with magic, "once you're mine, there's no going back," Perry and fellow witches used their brooms to perform a pole dance of sorts. The act featured a beast with Moloch horns and dark-robed dancers with devil horns. "Dark Horse" ended with a circle of fire around her, apparently symbolizing her being burned at the stake, which could have represented her take on the 1692 Salem Witch trials. *E! Online* even tweeted, "Um, did we just witness actual witchcraft during Katy Perry's #Grammys performance?"

Sadly, Perry's music and videos are being used to seduce young fans into the demonic realm. This is no joke and it goes far beyond entertainment. Perry now seeks spirituality in the writings of people such as neo-gnostic medium, Echart Tolle, who channels demonic forces and teaches we can realize our own inner divinity through occult knowledge.

Growing up in a Christian home and even releasing an album as Katy Hudson early in her career called "Keep the Faith," Perry admitted, "I sold my soul to the devil" after her original goal to make it in Christian music did not work out. Her first big hit after that was the lesbian-promoting song "I Kissed a Girl." No longer believing in Jesus, heaven, or hell, Perry admits she now looks elsewhere for answers. This is a reminder to pray for those who look to "the universe" or to other gods for answers.

Shortly after her transformation to the dark side in an article in the UK's *Sun Online*, Perry's father, an evangelical minister, pleaded for congregations to pray for his daughter. Keith Hudson revealed his grief saying:

> I was at a concert of Katy's where there were 20,000. I'm watching this generation, and they were going at it. It was almost like church ... I stood there and wept and kept on weeping and weeping. They're loving and worshipping the wrong thing.

The music industry today features many performers engaging in Satanism and witchcraft in an effort to summon and utilize demonic powers to ensnare their followers. We cannot expect unbelievers to act like Christians, nor should we judge them. They need Jesus. We can, however, overcome our silence by warning, informing, and encouraging fellow believers to be more discerning and avoid the garbage this world often produces and promotes.

The Bible teaches that friendship with the world is hatred toward

God and *Therefore whoever wishes to be a friend of the world makes himself an enemy of God* (James 4:4).

We forget there are a few Christian artists nominated for secular awards and who also attend the Grammys, and I used to wonder how they feel while watching such world-glorifying performances. During this program, contemporary Christian artist, Natalie Grant (nominated for two Grammys) decided not to stay to the end. (Do you blame her?) Here's what she tweeted that night:

> We left the Grammys early. I've many thoughts, most of which are probably better left inside my head. But I'll say this: I've never been more honored to sing about Jesus and for Jesus. And I've never been more sure of the path I've chosen.

Evidently, some folks thought that was quite intolerant, and after getting hammered by certain media and critics the next day, she posted a response on the Natalie Grant Music Facebook page that included the following:

> What I DID say is this: I am honored to be a part of the Christian music community. I've had many people throughout my career ask why I never tried to go in to mainstream music and last night was a beautiful reminder that I love singing about Jesus and FOR Jesus. I've judged no one. I hate no one.

> And I believe that every person has been created in the image of God … I do have my own personal convictions that I live by, and I will continue to work out my own salvation with fear and trembling before the Lord (Philippians 2:12). My last thought:

> *I am not ashamed of the gospel of Jesus for it is the power of God who brings salvation to ALL who believe* (Romans 1:16).

Kudos to her. What Grant experienced should remind us to pray for Christian artists and those on the frontlines in ministry who are committed to the cause and message of Jesus Christ without apology or compromise.

POSSESSED TO PERFORM?

We also need to touch on the worldwide influence of Beyoncé, who opened the 2014 Grammys with her song "Drunk in Love" while gyrating sensually, touching herself, and spreading her legs on national television while children watched. What a way to start the show. Right then, we could realize the direction the Grammy Awards was taking.

While some of the explicit lyrics had to be bleeped out, she sang about drinking and how "filthy" she gets when liquor gets into her. Her husband, Jay Z, later joined her on stage during the performance some described as leaving little to the imagination. So much for family-friendly television.

Not surprisingly, Jay Z has also been linked to the Illuminati and Aleister Crowley's OTO. We should note that Crowley, who was born into an upper-class British family in 1875, styled himself as "the Great Beast 666." Jay Z has worn a hooded sweatshirt with "Do What Thou Wilt," on the front, which is known as the law of Thelma that Crowley developed. Jay Z's "Roca Wear" apparel features shirt designs with the satanic all-seeing eye (the Eye of Horus, an Egyptian solar god) and a "Masters of the Craft" shirt displaying occult symbols.

Having invited Beyoncé to the White House for parties and performances, including Michelle Obama's 50th birthday bash, President Barack Obama believes she is a good role model for his girls, Malia and Sasha. He said so publicly. The definition of a good role model varies drastically depending on your worldview.

Beyoncé's spellbinding performance at the 2013 Super Bowl had some asking why she was flashing the "devil's triangle" (Illuminati) and looking so angry. Beyoncé entered a circle with an inverted pentagram and lay down, inviting a spirit named "Sasha Fierce" to take over her body. Beyoncé claims Sasha Fierce possesses her, enabling her to perform the way she does.

Also in that Super Bowl performance, we saw imagery of four arms on each side representing the mysterious Hindu goddess, Kali, a dark goddess of empowerment, time, and a fierce warrior. Having said, "I want the whole video to feel possessed," Beyoncé now thinks Sasha

Fierce is part of her and tells people she can do things on stage she wasn't able to do before.

She enjoys being possessed by Sasha Fierce. The following quotes are from an interview on *BET* (Black Entertainment Television) in which she reflects on the first time she invoked the spirits and joyously described how the demon helps her perform:

> Sasha comes out and she's fearless. She can do things that I cannot do [during the performance] when I'm in rehearsal. I can try, but it just doesn't happen…
>
> I remember right before I performed, I raised my hands up and it was kind of the first time I felt something else come into me.[150]

Admitting she has out-of-body experiences, Beyoncé has claimed she wouldn't like Sasha if she met her off stage, and in a 2003 interview she exclaimed, "When I see video of myself on stage or TV, I'm like 'Who is that girl?' That's not me, I wouldn't dare do that."

During the Super Bowl half-time show performance, immediately after she exits the circle and Sasha takes over, a warped, striking change occurs in her facial expressions from that point forward. Photo images from the performance seemed to reveal the evil manifestation of Sasha Fierce even to the shock of Beyoncé herself. Even her publicist told BuzzFeed to remove the unflattering images from the Internet. Toward the end of the performance, flames shot up from the stage in front of and behind her, which almost looked like another witch's circle of fire.

There are many influential artists we could also discuss in this chapter. From self-admitted Satan worshipper, Kesha; to promoter of homosexuality and the occult, Lady Gaga; to former Disney star, Miley Cyrus, glorifying profanity, sex and drugs; we have a problem with what is considered acceptable entertainment today. Many of today's youth are following these idols.

Pray for them, yes, but we should be much more protective of what goes into our hearts and minds. It doesn't matter if you think your kids are not into this stuff. Many of their friends and peers are, and

---

150 "Beyoncé, The Super Bowl, Sasha & Satan," Good Fight Ministries, 2/16/2013, http://www.youtube.com/watch?v=21GOSnJc4Mg.

they spend nearly triple their waking hours with friends, media, and technology than they do with you, their parents. Who is winning the battle of influence in *your* family?

RECAP AND CONCLUSION

Witchcraft is the fastest-growing offshoot of paganism today as hundreds of thousands of children and teenagers have joined its ranks. The Pagan Federation claims their mail bags swell by the thousands every time an article on witchcraft is published in a teen magazine. Wiccans revere the mother goddess, the global environment, feminism, and nature; and kids are learning it from several places.

Author and researcher, Caryl Matrisciana, is a well-known authority on ancient and modern world religions, contemporary cults, paganism, and the occult. In a video about the repackaging of witchcraft and making evil look innocent, Caryl and Robert S. McGee point out a wide variety of witchcraft techniques offering powers of control for personal gain are readily available today through many bookstores, on the Internet (aka "the portal of transcendence"), in public schools and libraries, and throughout the media as an aggressive marketing campaign to young people.

> Hollywood's presentation of witchcraft as exciting and glamorous has further increased its appeal to young audiences. Enhanced by digital technology and revolutionary special effects, cultic spells and rituals are given visually stunning portrayals as are the depictions of supernatural beings: ghosts, demons, vampires, mythological characters, and even Satan.

A growing number of cartoons and television dramas aimed at increasing younger audiences further seduce children with the allure of sorcery and divination. Cultic themes are frequently woven into the storylines of prime time series, which has undoubtedly contributed to the practice of magic as being the fastest growing mystical attraction among teenagers.[151]

On Amazon.com alone, kids can find nearly 2,000 books on witchcraft

---

151 Caryl Matrisciana, "HARRY POTTER: Witchcraft Repackaged – Making Evil Look Innocent," CarylTV, 7/04/2009, https://www.youtube.com/watch?v=0SWr0T0o9E0.

and hundreds of websites are dedicated to selling it specifically to children. Young people are turning away from Christianity and traditional religion and joining witches' covens in order to learn spells to help them pass tests in school, attract boyfriends (or girlfriends), and get rich.

Formed in 1996, The Magic Circle, known as the Young Magician's Club, calls itself "the world's premier magical society." The club's mission is "to promote the performance of magic by the young people of today (aged between 10 and 18) and encourage them in their chosen art form ..." The secretary of the club credits the *Harry Potter* books for rekindling a love for magic and for the impossible. Kids may not realize what they are getting into, but most pagans and witches believe they must communicate with supernatural spirits they consider "forces of nature." From these spirits, they receive power and magical skills.

For adults, the practices of Wicca lure the "me" generation by promoting self-gratification, self-centeredness, and rebellion and preaching of the "do whatever you want" philosophy. There is no absolute truth, no sin, and no need for God the Creator or for Jesus Christ the Savior because the patriarchal God of the Bible has been removed.

Finally, the spirituality behind contemporary feminism often comes in the form of goddess worship. The more radical feminists seem to believe in an internal god, if they believe in any at all, and have a desire to overthrow the patriarchal structure in society. Some New Age proponents teach that Wicca, goddess worship, paganism, and witchcraft are all centered on a religion involving the mystery and sexuality of the female. The idea is for women to regain their natural power and to have authority over men. In order to accomplish this dominance, they must invoke certain spirits to help destroy the Judeo-Christian religion. God can no longer be "Father."

In our power-hungry, self-seeking, post Christian culture, many fall for teachings that self-realization is attainable through various methods of meditation, visualization, and other mind-altering techniques of self-hypnosis. It must be emphasized all Wiccans and pagans are *not* demonic or Satan-worshippers. Yes they can open doors to demonic spirits, but most are concerned for others, have respect for the earth, and try to maintain a form of *human* morality and accountability.

We're all in need of the Savior. For those of us thankful enough to be forgiven and saved from eternal separation from God, we need to pray for the lost souls in Hollywood and the music and publishing industries. Imagine the influence if some of the top producers, authors, and executives trusted in Jesus Christ. If they don't turn to Him soon, their rewards end in this life. Isaiah 47:11-14 states:

> But evil will come on you Which you will not know how to charm away; And disaster will fall on you For which you cannot atone; And destruction about which you do not know Will come on you suddenly.

> Stand fast now in your spells And in your many sorceries With which you have labored from your youth; Perhaps you will be able to profit, Perhaps you may cause trembling. You are wearied with your many counsels; Let now the astrologers, Those who prophesy by the stars, Those who predict by the new moons, Stand up and save you from what will come upon you.

> Behold, they have become like stubble, Fire burns them; They cannot deliver themselves from the power of the flame;

Secular entertainment can open us up to demonic spirits and move us away from the truth of Jesus Christ. Satan will take every opportunity and use people to fill us with the things of this world. We are not unaware of the schemes of the enemy. The Bible instructs us to meditate on the Word of God "day and night" for good reason.

Entertainment is not all bad or evil; it is often simply a distraction and an escape from reality. In essence, we are switching our brain off. The problem is our hearts remain open. When we turn the TV on, go to a movie, concert or sports event, read a fantasy or fiction book, we should think twice about our options. Let's be more discerning and guard our hearts, protect our children, and not be silent.

CHAPTER 14

STORMING THE GATES OF HELL

*He said to them, "But who do you say that I am?" Simon Peter
answered, "You are the Christ, the Son of the living God." And
Jesus said to him, "Blessed are you, Simon Barjona, because
flesh and blood did not reveal this to you, but My Father who
is in heaven. I also say to you that you are Peter, and upon
this rock I will build My church; and the gates of Hades will
not overpower it.*
Matthew 16:15-18

*Suffer hardship with me, as a good soldier of Christ Jesus.
No soldier in active service entangles himself in the affairs of
everyday life, so that he may please the one who enlisted him
as a soldier.*
2 Timothy 2:3-4

B ecause we're believers, Jesus Christ enlisted us in active service,
and we are to make it our goal to obey and please Him (2 Corinthians
5:9). Soldiers cannot afford to be indifferent or ignorant about the battle
around us. When we are silent and fail to engage, we become ineffective for God's kingdom.

Much of this book has been about the intensifying cultural battle
being fought in every area of society, but what we are talking about here
is the ongoing spiritual war affecting every one of us. This epic battle
between the kingdom of heaven and the kingdom of darkness is real
whether you believe the Bible or not. Jesus came to earth to destroy the
works of the devil (1 John 3:8), and when He returned to heaven, He
sent the Holy Spirit to help us fight (John 16:7; 14:12).

The leaders of the armies are Jesus Christ whom God has exalted forever *far above all rule and authority and power and dominion, and every name that is named, not only in this age but also in the one to come* (Ephesians 1:21), and Satan, the temporary ruler of this world (John 12:31) whose time is short (Revelation 12:12).

God allows us to choose what part we will play in advancing His kingdom. We can choose indifference and do nothing or respond to His call and fight the good fight of faith. Yes, it is risky, certainly unpopular, and potentially dangerous. Yes, it may sometimes feel scary, but *without faith, it is impossible to please Him* (Hebrews 11:6). Without risk, we experience little reward and often suffer repercussions for not taking action.

Lord of the Rings' fans will remember the scene in *The Two Towers* in which the massive, evil army of Mordor was on the move toward Gondor in their quest to wipe mankind off the face of the earth. After being warned about the enemy advancing, Théoden, King of Rohan, declared, "I will not risk open war."

Aragorn replied with truth, "Open war is upon you whether you would risk it or not," and he encouraged the king to ride out and face the enemy head on.

Instead, the king ordered the city to evacuate and retreat to Helm's Deep, a fortress that had kept them safe in the past. Questioning the king's decision, Gimli said, "They flee to the mountains when they should stay and fight."

Even though the king was doing what he thought was best for the people, Gandalf believed Théoden was walking into a trap because there was no way out of the ravine of Helm's Deep, and he stated, "He thinks he is leading them to safety, but what he'll get is a massacre." As a result of not staying to fight, many lives were lost.

> *Finally, be strong in the Lord and in his mighty power. Put on the full armor of God so that you can take your stand against the devil's schemes. For our struggle is not against flesh and blood, but against the rulers, against the authorities, against the powers of this dark world and against the spiritual forces of evil in the heavenly realms* (Ephesians 6:10-12 NIV).

Are we prepared for spiritual warfare or do we avoid conflict and run away when life gets difficult and we are faced with opposition? For some, their security is money; for others, that security comes from family, a job, a relationship, the Internet, or even church activity. Some escape to entertainment; others to whatever provides immediate gratification. Our culture will only get worse if Christians continue to seek comfort, worldly things, or our own happiness while avoiding the battle and ignoring our mission.

Most of us would acknowledge the enemy's army of wickedness has wreaked havoc in our country by chipping away at its Christian foundation. What we see today is the result of our silence and inactivity, but the Bible teaches that when we choose to take a stand for righteousness, we have the power in Christ to overcome Satan and his minions.

The question is: Do we have the will?

Christians are instructed to *Resist the devil and he will flee from you* (James 4:7). We are not to be the ones who run away. Peter reminds us that other true believers around the world are resisting the enemy by standing for Christ in the face of persecution , and they are enduring *the same experiences of suffering* (1 Peter 5:9) we are; and much worse.

After we spend time in the Word and in prayer and put on the armor of God and after we do everything we can to prepare for the attacks of the enemy, Paul tells believers to stand firm.

> *Therefore, take up the full armor of God, so that you will be able to resist in the evil day, and having done everything, to stand firm* (Ephesians 6:13).

You and I have three possible choices:

1. We will put on our spiritual armor, engage in battle, and not only stand against the enemy but stay on offense by wielding the sword of the Spirit. We will stand on God's Word in all things and battle until the end, hoping to hear the Lord say to us, "Well done, good and faithful servant."

2. We will refuse to take our faith and God's Word seriously, perhaps even suggesting the Bible is not literal, but figurative. As a result – though we profess to be Christian – we fail to build on a proper foundation, and

we conform to the world, falling prey to the devil's schemes. This will have repercussions on many souls in our sphere of influence.

3. (Most common) Though we trust God, believe the Bible, and are somewhat aware of the battle, we will avoid or ignore it and live this temporary life for ourselves and our earthly families. We *may* do some good works, but fail to see the big picture. This will often produce an empty, mundane existence, and as our faith becomes lukewarm, our lives will be of no consequence where God's purposes and eternity are concerned.

The apostle Paul describes all the pieces of the armor of God, and everything we need for battle is provided for us. Each piece of armor represents a blessing in Christ: Salvation, righteousness, truth, the gospel, faith, and the Word of God. In that order, we have helmets, breastplates, belts, shoes, shields, and swords, but one area is left uncovered – our backsides. Why?

Two reasons: We are only supposed to be moving forward, and God has our backs! He will not only lead us, but He is our rear guard as well.

> *The LORD has bared his holy arm before the eyes of all the nations, and all the ends of the earth shall see the salvation of our God … For you shall not go out in haste, and you shall not go in flight, for the LORD will go before you, and the God of Israel will be your rear guard* (Isaiah 52:10, 12 ESV).

In Isaiah 58:8, the Bible states, *the glory of the Lord* will be our rear guard.

But what if the battle heats up and the fighting intensifies? What happens when our armor gets dinged, we get tired, our sword and shield get heavy, and we feel like retreating? Stand! The natural reaction is to flee, but we can *do all things through Christ who strengthens us* (Philippians 4:13).

The path of least resistance (#3 above), however, has been to not even show up for the battle and not let anyone else know what side we're on. Rather than stand firm when opposition increases, many of us duck conversations about the Bible or our faith so we do not ruffle any feathers. Thus, we avoid the very mention of Jesus' name in public.

Therefore everyone who confesses Me before men, I will also confess him before My Father who is in heaven. But whoever denies Me before men, I will also deny him before My Father who is in heaven (Matthew 10:32-33).

What if we get laughed at or ridiculed for being a Christian? Press on.

What if they claim we're intolerant because we say Jesus is the only way? Press on.

What if people say we hate women because we are pro-life? Press on.

What if the most conservative Christian candidates do not get elected? Press on.

What if judges overrule marriage laws the people voted for? Press on.

What if they say we're racist for opposing the policies of a progressive president? Press on.

What if homosexuals call us hateful for saying their lifestyle is a sin? Press on.

What if we get arrested or fined for preaching the gospel? Preach on.

And what if people in our own church say the Bible is not inerrant, there are no moral absolutes, and we are taking our faith too seriously? Press on!

Please do not take any salt out of your shaker, do not hide your light nor back out of our godless culture completely when hostility increases. We need you, God can use you, and the lost need to hear of the hope you have in Christ.

We're not to be overcome by evil; we are supposed to overcome evil with good (Romans 12:21). Today's remnant of committed believers must not follow the pattern of the church in the last hundred years. We will reap a harvest if we do not grow weary of the battle and give up (Galatians 6:9).

There *is* no retreat! There *is* no waving the white flag. Nothing in the soldier's instruction manual, the Bible, explains how to run away from conflict and avoid the fight. Doing so gives the enemy ground. Okay, I'm sure if we could get a glimpse into the spirit realm for just a few seconds, we might see some Christians with fiery darts sticking out of their backsides, but that is because we are not supposed to have our backs to the battle.

But what about concept of turning the other cheek? Jesus gave some examples of physical non-retaliation including the teaching: *Whoever slaps you on your right cheek, turn to him the other also* (Matthew 5:39). To the Jews of Jesus' day, a slap in the face was a great insult and meant to dishonor a person. In some cultures today, a slap is a demeaning act. When we are treated with contempt, we are not to run, back down, or compromise our convictions and position, but to stand; and when necessary, offer them our other cheek as well.

God does not discuss the option of quitting. Jesus, the Lamb of God, has overcome the world. He has beaten death, and in the end when the beast wages war against Him one last time, *the Lamb will overcome them because He is the Lord of lords and King of kings* (Revelation 17:14). Through the power of the Holy Spirit, our faith in Him is the victory that helps us overcome as well (1 John 5:4).

I agree with Charles Spurgeon and others who believe we are foolish to expect to serve God without opposition. In fact, Spurgeon stated, "the more zealous we are, the more sure are we to be assailed ..." But he always kept the victory in sight:

> Glory be to God, we know the end of the war. The great dragon shall be cast out and forever destroyed, while Jesus and they who are with him shall receive the crown. Let us sharpen our swords tonight, and pray the Holy Spirit to nerve our arms for the conflict. Never battle so important, never crown so glorious. Every man to his post, ye warriors of the cross, and may the Lord tread Satan under your feet shortly!

The Bible teaches that though we live in this world, *the weapons of our warfare are not of this world* but are spiritual, and we have the ability to not just survive but to crush the enemy. Paul wrote to the Corinthian church that we do not wage war according to human standards because our spiritual weapons have *divine power to demolish strongholds* (2 Corinthians 10:3-4 NIV).

Jesus used Scripture to refute the enemy – and He *is* the Word, so we would be wise to know the Bible and follow His lead.

Then Jesus said to him, "Be gone, Satan! For it is written,

"'You shall worship the Lord your God and him only shall you serve.'" Then the devil left him, and behold, angels came and were ministering to him (Matthew 4:10-11 ESV).

We have the most powerful weapon in the world – the Word of God! An offensive weapon, God exalts His Word and His name above all things (Psalm 138:2). In the book of Hebrews, the Word is described as being *living and active and sharper than any double edged sword* (4:12).

Jesus said the gates of hell would not prevail against us (Matthew 16:18). Think about what gates are used for. Christians will overpower the enemy's gates in the end. Did you get that? Though Satan constantly attacks believers, the Bible never refers to the enemy storming the gates of heaven!

One of the keys to our success in spiritual warfare is this pearl of truth: Gates are defensive!

All hell should be on guard, and a strong, armor-wearing, battle-tested church should be on offense, attacking the enemy with God's Word. Preaching the gospel is one way to stay on offense and help rescue people from the camp of the enemy.

Moreover, gates don't chase people down, and we are not supposed to be on defense as the church in America has been when it comes to the culture war. Ephesians 6:17 tells us that the sword of the Spirit is the Word of God. Too many of us leave our swords at home on a dusty shelf. We forget Satan is a defeated foe, and one day Jesus will cast him into the lake of fire to be tormented forever (Revelation 20:10).

We must know Scripture, apply it to our lives, and stay on offense by speaking its truth. Remember the power of Christ and His Spirit. John said, *Greater is He who is in you than he who is in the world* (1 John 4:4). The same power that defeated Satan dwells in converted believers. Consequently, we are never alone or without divine resources.

OPPORTUNITY TIME

Though Israel is of utmost importance, as one of the great obstacles in the enemy's way, America has become one of the key epicenters of spiritual warfare. World events and cultural chaos reveal evidence of the battles being fought. Most of us know how this will end, but for those who don't know or believe the Bible, they only have a shaky confidence in their own ability to save themselves. Being unfamiliar with Scripture, they fail to understand the times and the Bible prophecies being fulfilled, and many are overcome by fear or uncertainty in these dark days.

During seasons such as this, more people are looking for hope and peace. Because of this, we have the unique opportunity to share some great news with them, because we have the answer to every problem facing mankind. They, too, can be forgiven! True hope and lasting peace can be acquired by knowing Jesus Christ and trusting in Him.

On the other hand, desperate times often pave the way for anger toward God, because people fail to discern the spiritual nature of events surrounding them. They blame a God they don't know and don't believe in when life gets hard and trouble increases. Trials bring some to their knees in surrender, yet cause others to stand in defiance, shaking their fist at the heavens. Some will hunger for the truth and receive salvation, while others will hate those who proclaim it.

The lines have been drawn and attacks are going to increase against the church, forcing many Christians to make a decision: Take a stand, retreat, or compromise. Are we ready? Let's tighten our armor and sharpen our swords. There is no middle ground; Jesus said we are either with Him or against Him (Matthew 12:30).

Pick a side: Culture or Christ!

We need to get on our knees and pray hard; then get up and go as the Lord leads. Our actions reveal our true faith, and our obedience reveals our love for God (John 14:15). Are we contenders or pretenders? Since we are living in the last days, it is time to counter the anti-Christian movements in our culture with our own revolution of righteousness.

The good news is Jesus will soon return as a conquering King, as He promised.

> *And I saw heaven opened, and behold, a white horse, and He who sat on it is called Faithful and True, and in righteousness He judges and wages war... From His mouth comes a sharp sword, so that with it He may strike down the nations, and He will rule them with a rod of iron; and He treads the wine press*

of the fierce wrath of God, the Almighty. And on His robe and
on His thigh He has a name written, "KING OF KINGS, AND
LORD OF LORDS" (Revelation 19:11, 15-16).

Rather than despair, we need to remember the reason we are here
and the tremendous hope we have to share with a dying world. Yes, the
world looks bad, and it will most likely get worse as lawlessness increases,
but *we walk by faith, not by sight* (2 Corinthians 5:7) and should not be
shaken as long as Jesus Christ is our main focus.

Knowing the power of the Holy Spirit, many early church fathers,
particularly those within the Protestant Reformation, believed the
church could permeate every aspect of culture and continue salting
it and shining on it until culture resembled Christianity. In our age,
however, because of a general unwillingness to speak publicly, the world
ends up influencing us.

In 1997, Dr. D. James Kennedy (1930-2007), founder of Truth in Action
Ministries and Coral Ridge Presbyterian Church in Ft. Lauderdale, Florida,
preached a sermon entitled, "Will the Church Forget?" He explained
how God needs men and women who will speak on the pressing and
sometimes controversial issues of today, and he emphasized how "we
are literally seeing the end of Western Civilization." He also reminded
individual believers to become and remain active in this culture war.
Dr. Kennedy declared:

> We are involved in a great conflict for the soul of this nation,
> for the soul of the world – and many are spectators on the
> side. Ah, dear one, Christ wants you to be a soldier for Him.
> Pray that God will fill you with intensity to do whatever you
> can, to become involved, to get out of the bleachers and onto
> the playing field and become a participant in the greatest
> struggle in the history of the world – a struggle for goodness,
> a struggle for godliness, a struggle of Christ against Satan.
> That is the battle we are in.

If this is your heart as well, let's work to wake up and warn as many
of our brothers and sisters as possible. People need to hear the truth,
and we are running out of time. The message we proclaim is so simple

it takes us to complicate it: Christ crucified for the sins of the world. The great Charles Finney once said to church leaders and pastors that they were to "be thoroughly awake to our responsibility in respect to the morals of this nation."

Though pastors and teachers will be held to a much higher standard and stricter judgment (James 3:1), every one of us will be held responsible for delivering God's message and bearing good fruit. Let's never make it about us, our church, a pastor, or our own inadequacies. It's about Jesus who saved us from the wrath of God, so we may experience the love of God.

No more remaining silent about sin. No more caving in to pressure. Our struggle is not against people, and our enemy will not relent, so let us fight to advance the kingdom of God and bring as many with us as possible. Onward, forward, and steady. No retreat. No regrets. It is the least we can do for the One who called us into service.

> But thanks be to God, who gives us the victory through our Lord Jesus Christ. Therefore, my beloved brethren, be steadfast, immovable, always abounding in the work of the Lord, knowing that your toil is not in vain in the Lord (1 Corinthians 15:57-58).

Satan has increased his attacks on believers because he knows his time is short, but persecution may be exactly what we need. We are truly in the end times, my friend. The final countdown is underway. The clock is ticking away on America and this world. The good news for Christians is that our redemption is drawing near! This means the remaining prophecies in the Bible will soon be fulfilled.

CHAPTER 15

THEN THE END WILL COME

From now on I am telling you before it comes to pass, so that when it does occur, you may believe that I am He.
John 13:19

Behold, the former things have come to pass, Now I declare new things; Before they spring forth I proclaim them to you.
Isaiah 42:9

The end of all things is near; therefore, be of sound judgment and sober spirit for the purpose of prayer.
1 Peter 4:7

What I say to you I say to all, 'Be on the alert!'
Mark 13:37

BIBLE PROPHECY AND SIGNS OF OUR TIMES

It had to be God. He put it on my heart to end this book with the subject of prophecy. It seemed like such a daunting task. Then after praying about it, I realized three major things happen when we understand prophecy better: Our faith is strengthened, our hope in Christ is encouraged by the fulfillment of prophecy, and we are more excited to tell others! As for the theme of this book and the silence of Christians, we cannot confidently share what we don't know or understand.

Did you realize the most dominant subject in the New Testament next to salvation is the second coming of Jesus Christ? His return is our hope. The purpose of this chapter is to encourage you and deepen your understanding of Bible prophecy. Considering some of the sobering information you have read in this book, we tend to forget the best is yet to come!

To those who trust in Him and obey His commandments, God has promised a fulfillment to our hope in Christ and security in His presence for eternity. The entire Bible points to Jesus Christ, and prophecy should encourage us to dig deeper into the Word of God, marvel at its perfection, and trust its truth – particularly concerning what is yet to come.

According to scholars, there are 1,845 references to the return of Jesus Christ in the pages of the Bible. In fact, references to the second coming outnumber references to the first appearance of Jesus by an 8 to 1 margin! We easily get lost and overwhelmed by prophecies and their meaning until we take a closer, more concentrated look. At least one quarter of the Bible is prophecy (some suggest one third), so we must make a sincere effort to understand these Scriptures.

Jesus' return is highlighted in seventeen Old Testament books, and within the twenty-seven New Testament books, there are 321 mentions of the second coming. This latter number equates to one out of every thirty verses in which the return of Christ is mentioned.

Prophecy indicates believers who are alive when He returns will be ushered into the kingdom of heaven (1 Thessalonians 4:13-18). All of the promises in the Old Testament to Israel will be fulfilled as well as the New Testament promises to believers, and Christ will reign as King over the whole earth for one thousand years. This is the end of history as we know it: The earth will be completely destroyed (2 Peter 3:10), and the universe imploded and replaced by a new earth and new heavens in which we will be with Him forever.

Jesus prophesied saying, *Heaven and earth will pass away, but my words will not pass away* (Luke 21:33). Jesus made this statement over 2,000 years ago, way before the printing press was invented, and today His words remain accurate, trustworthy, and indisputable. The Bible is the best-selling book of all time, and hundreds of millions of Bibles and portions of Scriptures are distributed every year worldwide.

It amazes me with all the evidence and Scripture proving the existence, deity, and truth of Jesus Christ that many still refuse to believe. One reason for this may be the fact His birth and earthly life had one purpose, but His return will have a very different purpose – the final judgment of all mankind. It further amazes me that hundreds of prophecies were fulfilled by Jesus. From the beginning of time, no one else has fulfilled a single one. Let's stop limiting God in our minds or saying the entire Bible is not His holy Word just because human beings wrote it.

The "God-breathed" sixty-six books in the Bible were written by forty different authors; men *spoke from God as they were carried along by the Holy Spirit* (2 Peter 1:21 NIV). These messengers of God came from diverse backgrounds, and Scriptures were written in three different languages over a period of 1,500 years on three different continents! There are no contradictions or inconsistencies in the Word of God, and over 25,000 archeological finds support the fact that people, places, and events mentioned in the Bible are real and accurate. Skeptics who say they need more evidence simply do not *want* to believe – it is an act of the will.

What human being could have ever manufactured such an intricate plan – a masterpiece combining thousands of years of historical events, as well as prophecies, in perfect and specific detail? More importantly, what man could have created and insured the carrying out of such an elaborate story *in advance*, well before many of those written about were born, before nations were formed, and years before historical events had even taken place? Over a span of thousands of years, hundreds of prophecies were made by men living in different time periods and who had never met or communicated with one another!

> *The sum of Your word is truth, And every one of Your righteous ordinances is everlasting* (Psalm 119:160).

FULFILLED BY JESUS CHRIST

In the events surrounding His birth, Jesus Christ – Emmanuel, "God with us" – fulfilled prophecies about the Messiah no other person has fulfilled. Could these events have been manipulated? As for details surrounding the crucifixion and death of Jesus, at least twenty-eight prophecies were fulfilled. Jesus Himself fulfilled more than 300 prophecies. What are the odds? For those who have an open mind, evidence produced by an honest investigation of the life and death of Christ should astound even the most intellectual skeptics and mathematicians.

In his book, *Science Speaks: Scientific Proof of the Accuracy of Prophecy and the Bible,* Professor Peter Stoner (1888 – 1980) calculated the probability of one man fulfilling a handful of Messianic prophecies.[152] Stoner was Chairman of the Departments of Mathematics and Astronomy at Pasadena City College in California and Chairman of the Science Division at Westmont College in Santa Barbara. His research revealed the *mathematical probability of one person* fulfilling just eight of the prophecies was a mind-boggling one chance in 10^{17} (one, followed by 17 zeros)! The word *impossible* comes to mind.

The odds of one person fulfilling forty-eight prophecies equal 10 to the 157th power! Imagine the astronomical odds overcome as Jesus Christ successfully fulfilled hundreds of prophecies – which He has – and there are more to come when He returns.

God leaves nothing up to chance. Rather than provide a lengthy list here, let's take a look at just a handful of key Bible prophecies about Jesus Christ fulfilled by Him:

- The Messiah will be born in Bethlehem of a virgin; He will be called Immanuel and live in Nazareth (Isaiah 7:14; Micah 5:2; Matthew 2:23).

- He will be a prophet like Moses, enter Jerusalem triumphantly, *riding on a donkey* (Deuteronomy 18:15; Zechariah 9:9; John 12:12-19).

- He will be rejected by His own people and betrayed by one of His followers for thirty pieces of silver (Isaiah 53:1-3; John 1:11; Zechariah 11:12-13; Matthew 26:14-16).

- The Messiah will be mocked, taunted, spit upon, severely beaten, and flogged (Psalm 22:7-8; Isaiah 50:6; 53:5).

- He will be tried and condemned to die by crucifixion (Psalm 22:14-16; John 19:15-16).

- His hands and side will be pierced; His garments will be divided by casting lots, but His bones will not be broken (Zechariah 12:10a; Psalm 22:16-18; 34:20; John 19:36).

---

152 Peter Stoner, *Science Speaks: Scientific Proof of the Accuracy of Prophecy and the Bible*, 1944, Chapter 3, "Christ of Prophecy" http://sciencespeaks.dstoner.net/Christ_of_Prophecy.html.

- The Messiah will bear the sins of many and pray for those who kill Him (Isaiah 53:12b).

- He will suffer with sinners, die with criminals, and He will be buried with/by a rich man (Isaiah 53:12a; Matthew 27:38, 57-60).

- The Messiah will be raised from the dead (Psalm 16:10; 30:3; 1 Corinthians 15:4-8).

- He will make His enemies a footstool for His feet; He will be exalted and will sit at God's right hand (Psalm 110:1; Hebrews 12:2; Acts 2:32-36; Hebrews 10:12-13).

Why become more familiar with prophecy? If prophecies are inaccurate or wrong, the Bible would not be trustworthy. This, however, is not an issue nor has the Bible ever come close to being proved false. In rare cases of apparent inconsistencies, the problem always stems from our misunderstanding Scripture in context or our inability to properly interpret its meaning.

THE SIGNS OF OUR TIMES

Having written extensively about the decline of morality, the increase of sin, and the fact too many Christians have conformed to this world, we must again reinforce some key points as it relates to Bible prophecy and the end times. The earth today is filled with humanism, selfishness, violence, and every sin imaginable. Society is declining and practically all moral restraint has vanished. In the United States, violent crime has increased nearly 500 percent since the early 1960s, and interestingly enough, that was when God, the Bible, and prayer began to be eradicated from public schools. You tell me if there is any correlation.

> *Just as it was in the days of Noah, so also will it be in the days of the Son of Man. People were eating, drinking, marrying and being given in marriage up to the day Noah entered the ark. Then the flood came and destroyed them all* (Luke 17:26-27).

The implication here is people were living and carrying on as if nothing was wrong, completely ignoring their sin and rebellion against

God and His laws. There was an increase of sin in the land as people lived for the moment with no concern about spiritual things or the future. We have the same mentality in America today, don't we? Jesus predicted the increase of lawlessness would cause the love of some to grow cold, and false prophets would deceive many people (Matthew 24:11-12). Millions of people have gone hungry, millions live in poverty, and millions of lives have been aborted, as we have gone on with our lives while looking the other way.

Today, one obvious sign similar to the days of Noah is that many people continue to ignore warnings from those preaching the truth of Scripture. Apostasy and deception are commonplace in many churches and denominations as religious leaders are departing from the truth. Tolerance is elevated above the exclusivity of Christ and His teachings, while experience-based religion is more popular than Bible-based Christianity. In this new age of deception, relevance is more important than repentance.

Another interesting point occurred when Jesus told the disciples the temple in Jerusalem would be destroyed. They asked Him when that would happen and what would be the sign of His return. The first thing He said was, *See to it that no one misleads you* (Matthew 24:4). Jesus immediately went on to explain some of the signs to come, such as wars, rumors of wars, famines, earthquakes, false teachers, and the persecution of Christians. We are seeing all of these things today, including nations fighting nations, all of which He described as *the beginning of birth pangs* (Matthew 24:8).

A new level of evil has arisen as people justify more sinful behavior, bringing us to new heights of godlessness. Persecution of the godly will increase, and evil men will *proceed from bad to worse, deceiving and being deceived* (2 Timothy 3:12-13). Some believers have departed from the faith, and even Christians are being seduced by doctrines of demons. This is a wake-up call to the remnant!

Though many good churches exist in America and people are still being saved, it is only by the grace and mercy of God and the presence of active, committed believers, His true church, that the Holy Spirit's presence and power is restraining more evil in our land. I certainly would not want to be around when the church is gone and Christians are raptured.

Believe it or not, with all the warnings from Scripture and the signs we are beginning to witness, people will *still* be surprised and caught off guard when Christ returns (1 Thessalonians 5:2-5).

You may have heard the story about Ruth Graham responding to Billy Graham after she read a draft of a book he was writing. She said to her husband, "Billy, if God doesn't punish the United States of America, He's going to have to apologize to Sodom and Gomorrah!" Some sources indicate she made that statement in the mid-1960s, not long after the Bible and voluntary prayer to God were banned from government schools.

About three years ago, Billy Graham wrote "my heart aches for America," as he reflected on the spiritual condition of our nation. Recalling his wife's response, he said:

> I wonder what Ruth would think of America if she were alive today. In the years since she made that remark, millions of babies have been aborted and our nation seems largely uncon-cerned. Self-centered indulgence, pride, and a lack of shame over sin are now emblems of the American lifestyle.[153]

Thousands of years ago, the decay we see in this country and world-wide was predicted in Scripture. God is not surprised.

Other signs of the age include increased famines and earthquakes (Matthew 24:7), tropical storms, and chaotic weather patterns (Luke 21:25-26) we have been seeing for years. Record low temperatures have recently been seen across the country, and Michigan broke a century-old record for snowfall in mid-November 2014. In western New York, seven feet of snow fell as single-digit temperatures have caused many deaths, declared states of emergencies, and threats of roofs caving in due to the weight of the snow. Most winter areas do not see that much snow in an entire season. Two days later, rain was in the forecast, and flooding was a concern as temperatures were in the 50s and snow melted.

Another obvious sign of the end times is the increase and threat of

---

153   Billy Graham: 'My Heart Aches for America,' 7/19/2012, http://billygraham.org/story/billy-graham-my-heart-aches-for-america/.

deadly pestilence (Revelation 6:8) including plagues and diseases such as AIDS, Cancer, Ebola, Hantavirus, West Nile, Dengue fever, SARS, bird flu, and others.

ISRAEL AND JERUSALEM

On May 14, 1948, a most remarkable event took place when the nation Israel was born in one day, as prophesied in Isaiah 66:8. This is unprecedented in all of history: Over five million Jews have returned to Israel, and as predicted, the remnant was restored (Isaiah 11:11-12; Ezekiel 37:21-22; 38:8). Never before in history has a people been dispersed and scattered among the nations of the earth and then return to their homeland from the north, south, east, and west (Isaiah 43:5-6). Nearly a million Jews traveled south from Russia alone, tens of thousands have left France, and the emigration of Jews to Israel from other nations continues.

About the size of New Jersey, Israel is not just the center of the universe, but the center of attention politically, spiritually, and geographically. The Bible was proved true when Israel became a desolate wasteland for about 1,900 years, but today we see the fulfillment of several more prophecies, such as *Israel will bud and blossom, and fill the whole earth with fruit* (Isaiah 27:6; Isaiah 35:1-2 NIV). Israel now exports fresh produce to the world to the tune of 800 million dollars each year, including over 200 million dollars from flowers and plants.

Nearly uninhabited and desolate a century ago, this little nation exports well over 40 billion dollars' worth of goods. Tourism is one of Israel's major sources of income and economic growth, attracting a record 3.54 million foreign tourists last year. According to the World Bank, exports of total goods and other services Israel provided to the rest of the world were over $91 billion (USD). How is this possible? Some suggest it is because of the increased rainfall while others point to Israel's irrigation technology. Let's not forget God.

According to the prophets Amos and Joel, the mountains of Israel would one day flow with sweet wine, and God would restore the people so they could rebuild ruined cities (Amos 9:13-15; Joel 3:18). They would plant vineyards and gardens, enjoy the land, and God promised *they*

will not again be rooted out from their land which I have given them.
Amos and Joel are among the first biblically prophetic books written
sometime between 750 BC and 835 BC.

The prophet Isaiah also describes forests of trees filling the formerly
barren land and specifically mentions the cedar, acacia, myrtle, olive,
juniper, pine, and cypress trees (Isaiah 41:18-20). God fulfilled His
promise to open up rivers, springs, and fountains of waters so people
would know *the hand of the Lord has done this.* In the last hundred
years, approximately one billion trees have been planted in Israel. This
is all part of Bible prophecy!

Just as predicted, the city of Jerusalem had been destroyed, *trampled underfoot by the Gentiles* (Luke 21:24) since AD 70. According to
prophecies, Jerusalem would be – and was – rebuilt on its own ruins
(Jeremiah 30:18; Zechariah 12:6) and reestablished in 1948. The Jewish
people finally regained full control of the city during the Six-Day War
in 1967. On June 7 of that year, the Israeli army broke through and
returned Jerusalem to the Jewish people for the first time in 1,897
years! Israel has been attacked many times and even outnumbered, and
yet – somehow – this tiny nation has not only survived, it has thrived.

Another major prophecy that was fulfilled is the restoration and
revival of Hebrew as the spoken language (Zephaniah 3:9). According
to *Jewish News,* the process began in October 1881 as Eliezer Ben-
Yehuda and his friends agreed to exclusively speak Hebrew in their
conversations, leading to Hebrew becoming the national language of
Israel once again.[154]

Around that time a belief existed that "one of the criteria needed to
define a nation worthy of national rights was its use of a common language" in the society, but the language had not been spoken as a mother
tongue since the second century. Because of his goal to reestablish the
language, Ben-Yehuda is said to have raised his son to speak Hebrew
throughout his childhood while sheltering him from other languages.
One of the keys to its revival was the development of the first Hebrew

---

154 Daniel Bensadoun, "This Week in History: Revival of the Hebrew Language,"
     Jewish News, 10/15/2010, http://www.jpost.com/Jewish-World/Jewish-News/
     This-week-in-history-Revival-of-the-Hebrew-language.

schools in small communities during the early 1900s. Regardless of how man thinks it happened, we must acknowledge that God made it happen.

The burden of the word of the LORD concerning Israel. Thus declares the LORD who stretches out the heavens, lays the foundation of the earth, and forms the spirit of man within him, "Behold, I am going to make Jerusalem a cup that causes reeling to all the peoples around; and when the siege is against Jerusalem, it will also be against Judah. It will come about in that day that I will make Jerusalem a heavy stone for all the peoples; all who lift it will be severely injured. And all the nations of the earth will be gathered against it (Zechariah 12:1-3).

Similar to Old Testament times, the very existence of Israel and Jerusalem causes surrounding nations to tremble; their hatred of the Jews is almost irrational. In modern times, Hitler tried wiping out the Jews, as will the Antichrist during the tribulation. As news reports today are filled with the global conflict over Israel, many nations have formed an alliance against Israel (Psalm 83:4-8), particularly Muslim nations sworn to her destruction.

In Scripture, God declares the Jews to be His people and Jerusalem His city. However, the Vatican and the United Nations want to make Jerusalem an international city. The UN Security Council went so far as to pass a resolution against Israel in 1980, Resolution 476, stating Israel's claim to Jerusalem is invalid. (The United States did not vote.) The resolution declared,

[A]ll legislative and administrative measures and actions taken by Israel, the occupying Power, which purport to alter the character and status of the Holy City of Jerusalem have no legal validity and constitute a flagrant violation of the Fourth Geneva Convention.[155]

According to various sources, a majority (some sources say over 60 percent) of General Assembly resolutions passed since the UN was established in 1945 are against Israel. As prophesied, anti-Semitism has increased worldwide, along with the persecution of Christians.

---

155 UN Security Council Resolution 476; 6/30/1980, Jewish Virtual Library, http://www. jewishvirtuallibrary.org/jsource/UN/unres476.html.

How important is Jerusalem? At the return of Jesus Christ, He will enter the city through the now cemented and sealed Eastern Gate (Ezekiel 44:1-3; Nehemiah 3:29). This significant city gate is one of eight gates to Jerusalem and was walled up by Muslim conquerors in the 16th century. Just as the Bible teaches, the Eastern Gate to the city remains closed and will be sealed until the Messiah returns. The glory of the Lord will come *by way of the gate facing toward the east* (Ezekiel 43:4). The Eastern Gate is the only one that has been shut for 500 years.

This is both interesting and significant due to the fact the city walls and gates in Jerusalem have been torn down and rebuilt more than once. And when they were rebuilt, it was always on the same spots. The oldest city gate, the Eastern Gate was the only one not to be rebuilt by Suleiman the Magnificent around AD 1540. In addition, some of the massive stones in the wall were identified as masonry from the 6th Century BC, which is during the time the prophet Nehemiah rebuilt the city walls and gates.[156]

THE RETURN OF THE CHRIST

There are several views among believers as to the timing of the rapture in relation to the great tribulation prophesied in Scripture. Let me first emphasize the most important thing is the fact of Jesus' return! Two theories dominate: a pretribulation view and a post tribulation view. The church, meaning "believers in Jesus Christ," will either be taken up to heaven prior to the tribulation (a view a majority support) or we will not be raptured until the very end of the tribulation period. The rapture and the second coming of Jesus Christ may well be a single event (pretrib) rather than events occurring at different times (post trib).

Keeping this subject in perspective, salvation is the priority, and we must preach the gospel to ensure as many people as possible will turn to Christ and be saved. While we're told to beware of the Antichrist, Jesus exhorted His followers to watch for Him. If our Lord returns before the tribulation, praise God; we will miss the most terrible times ahead. If Jesus returns after the tribulation, praise God; we will be honored to suffer for the cause of Christ. The bottom line is, Scripture is full of promises

---

156   Biblical Archeological Review [BAR], Mar/Apr 1992, p. 40.

that we can confidently look for the *blessed hope and the appearing of the glory of our great God and Savior, Christ Jesus* (Titus 2:13).

According to Scripture, when Jesus returns, *His feet will stand on the Mount of Olives, which is in front of Jerusalem on the east* (Zechariah 14:4). So, when Jesus returns, we know from Scripture He will come from the east and will touch ground on the Mount of Olives. We can confirm this with the prophecy the angels spoke immediately after Jesus gave final instructions to His followers and ascended into Heaven, right before they all *returned to Jerusalem from the mount called Olivet.* The angels said:

> *This Jesus, who has been taken up from you into heaven, will come in just the same way as you have watched Him go into heaven* (Acts 1:11-12).

But let's not miss the fact that prior to His crucifixion, Jesus entered Jerusalem through this same Eastern Gate on Palm Sunday riding on a donkey (John 12:14). Written five centuries before the birth of Christ, the prophet Daniel predicted this exact event would take place. He also gave us the very date the Messiah would enter Jerusalem as King, allowing people to worship Him publicly for the first time (John 12:13-15).

> *So you are to know and discern that from the issuing of a decree to restore and rebuild Jerusalem until Messiah the Prince, there will be seven weeks and sixty-two weeks; it will be built again, with plaza and moat, even in times of distress* (Daniel 9:25).

There are many excellent books and resources available on this pivotal subject. While researching for this chapter, I read articles and talked to people who have studied Bible prophecy for years. I first met writer, Mary Danielsen, at one of the annual Great Lakes Prophecy Conferences held at Calvary Chapel in Appleton, Wisconsin. In an overview of Bible prophecy, she touched on the above Scripture passage from Daniel:

> The prophecy states that 69 weeks of years (69 "7s", or 69×7 = 483 years) would pass from the decree to rebuild Jerusalem until the coming of the Messiah. Since Daniel was written in Babylon during the Jewish captivity after the fall of Jerusalem, this prophecy was based on the Babylonian 360-day calendar.

Thus, 483 years x 360 days = 173,880 days. According to records found in the Shushan Palace and confirmed in Nehemiah 2:1, the decree to rebuild Jerusalem was issued by the Persian king, Artaxerxes Longimanus, on March 5, 444 BC.

Remarkably, 173,880 days later (adjusting for leap years), on March 30, 33 AD, Jesus rode into Jerusalem on a donkey (fulfilling Zechariah 9:9). Five days later, Jesus was crucified on a Roman cross just outside Jerusalem. (Crucifixion as a form of execution did not even exist when His last words were foretold hundreds of years earlier in Psalm 22, but the Romans would later adopt it.) Three days later, the New Testament declares Jesus rose from the dead, fulfilling other prophecies too numerous to mention here.[157]

Experts agree this prophecy in Daniel was not only fulfilled by the Messiah, but it appears to be so important God gave the date; and since this is a rare occurrence in Scripture we know it must be significant. In Nehemiah 2, care was given to note, *In the month of Nisan, in the twentieth year of King Artaxerxes ...* The reference is important because it establishes the date given to restore Jerusalem and rebuild the city walls.

Author and theologian, Sir Robert Anderson, was the chief inspector for Scotland Yard. He was greatly respected for his skill as an investigator. Sir Robert Anderson, a British astronomer and mathematician, also makes the strong case that Jesus fulfilled this prophecy exactly to the day, entering Jerusalem precisely 173,880 days from Nehemiah 2:1. (Anderson believes the date was April 6, 32 AD.) Regardless, soon the following prophecy will be fulfilled as well:

> *Lift up your heads, O gates, And be lifted up, O ancient doors, That the King of glory may come in! Who is the King of glory? The Lord strong and mighty, The Lord mighty in battle* (Psalm 24:7-8).

REVELATION

There are many good books and Bible studies on Revelation, but for the average Christian, we should have a basic understanding of the big

157 Mary Danielsen, *The Things to Come*, Prophecy 101, 8/10/2014, http://thethings2come. org/?p=1038.

picture of Revelation rather than attempting to know every little detail in the book. In addition, let us not make it more complicated than it really is by letting some of the symbolism intimidate us. First, when a lamb is referred to in Revelation, it is always Jesus – while references to the dragon refer to Satan. Many things cannot be fully discerned until certain events take place, but remember this amazing fact: The God of the universe chose to give us a glimpse of the future to warn and encourage us.

Translated in Greek, the word *revelation* is *apokalypsis*, which we know as apocalypse, meaning divinely inspired writings revealing truth about future events. *Prophecy* simply means "prediction," and by reading, hearing, and paying special attention (heed) to it, we will be blessed.

> *The Revelation of Jesus Christ, which God gave Him to show to His bond-servants, the things which must soon take place; and He sent and communicated it by His angel to His bond-servant John, who testified to the word of God and to the testimony of Jesus Christ, even to all that he saw. Blessed is he who reads and those who hear the words of the prophecy, and heed the things which are written in it; for the time is near* (Revelation 1:1-3).

Just as many of the New Testament letters were written to a specific church or body of believers in a particular city, the book of Revelation had historic meaning for first-century Christians. Though this book is for all believers to learn from, specific churches were warned and called out in chapters two and three. The purpose was and is to edify believers, strengthen their faith, and encourage them to stay strong in the face of persecution. John, the writer of Revelation, was exiled to the small island of Patmos *because of the word of God and the testimony of Jesus* (Revelation 1:9).

In his vision, John sees Jesus in the middle of seven golden lampstands, which is the first symbolism in the book. Jesus is holding seven stars in His right hand, and *out of His mouth came a sharp, two-edged sword*, which is a reference to the Word of God (Hebrews 4:12) that Jesus will wield and speak upon His return (Ephesians 6:17).

Jesus identifies Himself saying,

> *Do not be afraid; I am the first and the last, and the living One;*

and I was dead, and behold, I am alive forevermore, and I have the keys of death and of Hades. Therefore write the things which you have seen, and the things which are, and the things which will take place after these things (Revelation 1:17-19).

In the very next verse, the mystery of the seven stars in Jesus' right hand and the seven golden lampstands is revealed when He explains, *the seven stars are the angels of the seven churches, and the seven lampstands are the seven churches* (Revelation 1:20).

Why the number seven? The number seven is used in the Bible to indicate completion, a finished work, or divine perfection. It is used some 490 times in Scripture, so it must be significant. Revelation was a message for seven churches that were in Asia at the time, but these written words should be just as convicting to us.

American Christianity and today's church has been compared to several of those mentioned in chapters two and three. The church in Laodicea was reprimanded for being lukewarm (Revelation 3:16); the church in Ephesus left their first love and fell away from the faith (Revelation 2:4), and the church in Sardis was sternly warned to repent and "wake up" because they were relying on their good reputation and past works (Revelation 3:1-3).

These messages are particularly meaningful and relevant today to a comfortable, lukewarm, culture-conforming church in America that once had a solid reputation. The signs of the times indicate we have walked away from the true faith in the one true God, essentially leaving Jesus Christ outside many church walls by selectively preaching or by ignoring His word. Jesus admonishes those He loves to *be zealous and repent* (Revelation 3:19) and reminds us He disciplines and reproves us because He loves us. In fact, Jesus Himself is pictured standing at the door of the church knocking and waiting to be invited back inside (Revelation 3:20). I'll let you decide if these warnings apply to your particular church or denomination.

In essence, Revelation invites all believing Christians to peek into the future and choose between judgment and revival. Revival begins with prayer; with bold, passionate individuals pursuing their first love and seeking the things of God above all else. To do this, we need to cultivate an eternal perspective and encourage others to read the Word of God. If we fail to invest time with the Lord every day, we can easily get sidetracked by life and the things of this world. In so doing, we might miss those gems from the Bible, including Jesus' promise to His disciples that He would go on ahead and prepare a place for them in heaven when He declared:

> *If I go and prepare a place for you, I will come again and receive*
> *you to Myself, that where I am, there you may be also* (John 14:3).

Though we will not dig deeply into the mysteries of Revelation at this time, remember how comforting this book must be for families of those who have been killed for their faith as well as Christians throughout the world suffering mild to severe persecution today. At the time the book was written, many believers, including several of Jesus' disciples, had already been killed, and countless others would be martyred in the hundreds of years to follow. Imagine the joy surviving believers felt when they read this:

> *When the Lamb broke the fifth seal, I saw underneath the altar*
> *the souls of those who had been slain because of the word of God,*
> *and because of the testimony which they had maintained; and*
> *they cried out with a loud voice, saying, "How long, O Lord,*
> *holy and true, will You refrain from judging and avenging our*
> *blood on those who dwell on the earth?" And there was given to*
> *each of them a white robe; and they were told that they should*
> *rest for a little while longer, until the number of their fellow*
> *servants and their brethren who were to be killed even as they*
> *had been, would be completed also* (Revelation 6:9-11).

Jumping ahead to the last few chapters in Revelation, one of the most important things to remember is it is imperative we focus our lives on the Lord's business because the time is short. We have been warned – many times. We will all be judged based on our works and our testimony. If our names are written in the Lamb's Book of Life, we will be saved.

In the end, Satan will be bound for a thousand years. After that, *he must be released for a short time* (Revelation 20:2-3). During this thousand-year period, all believers who have died in the Lord, including martyrs and those who have kept the faith in the face of persecution, will return to reign with Christ. Also included in this first resurrection are *those who had not worshiped the beast or his image, and had not received the mark on their forehead and on their hand* (Revelation 20:4-5).

In the short time Satan is released, he will deceive the masses and gather many nations together for war against Jerusalem and surround *the camp of the saints and the beloved city,* but the fire of God will consume them all. The devil and false prophet will be "thrown into the lake of fire," and immediately the great white throne judgment will take place (Revelation 20:7-10).

> *And I saw the dead, the great and the small, standing before the throne, and books were opened; and another book was opened, which is the book of life; and the dead were judged from the things which were written in the books, according to their deeds. And the sea gave up the dead which were in it, and death and Hades gave up the dead which were in them; and they were judged, every one of them according to their deeds* (Revelation 20:12-13).

In light of chapter 20 and others, we can see how the entire plan of God fits together as well as how the Old Testament prophets compliment New Testament writings. If you take a close look at the striking similarities in the book of Daniel and Revelation, for example, recalling the fact Daniel was written approximately 500 years before Jesus was born, while John wrote Revelation some fifty years after Jesus died, rose from the grave, and ascended into heaven; you cannot help but see how masterfully the Holy Spirit spoke through men of God.

WHAT ABOUT ISLAM?

How does Islam fit in to the end times? Several years ago, author Joel Rosenberg said, "To misunderstand the nature and threat of evil is to risk being blindsided by it. A new evil is rising in the world." We can see evil be spoken of as good right before our eyes whether it is on our television screens or the Internet.

ISIS is beheading and persecuting Christians and "infidels" worldwide as was prophesied in Scripture (Matthew 24:9). The growing terror this generation is witnessing is part of the predicted end time lawlessness, and political correctness in America often gives the terrorists a pass. This should be another wake-up call for America, as we are in the midst of a dangerous combination of events. Ignorance is partly to blame while a complicit liberal media attempts to cover for Islam, but even Christian leaders have been complacent when it comes to discerning prophecy and world religions.

There are approximately 1.6 billion Muslims, accounting for 23% of the world's population. In America, estimates suggest 3.5 million; 250,000 of which may be classified as those committed to radical Islam. Until recently, most Americans have looked the other way, but with instant news and Internet access, we hear about Christians or Jews being killed on a weekly if not daily basis. (Please check out Voice of the Martyrs at persecution.com) We have been warned about this persecution in the pages of the Bible, and we are to have a reverent fear of God rather than a fear of man.

Jesus Christ died for the sins of the world, and the gospel is the power of God for salvation. God has purchased people from every tribe and nation with the blood of Christ (Revelation 5:9). As ISIS continues their murderous rampage, spreading terror in places like Syria, Iraq, Nigeria (Boko Haram), and elsewhere; there are also reports that more Muslims are hearing the truth about Jesus for the very first time and are coming to faith in Christ. Other followers of Muhammad are turning to the only living God and Savior because of the godless reign of terror. God is at work through the Holy Spirit in the most terrible times even when we don't see the results right in front of us.

Joel Richardson and Walid Shoebat are two who suggest the Antichrist will emerge from Turkey, Syria, or Iraq. Modern Turkey is practically immersed in what used to be the Assyrian Empire, and Turkey's role in the end times seems to be supported by the prophets Isaiah and Micah as they refer to Assyria's opposition to the Messiah. Many others who have studied Bible prophecy, such as Hal Lindsey and David Jeremiah, point to a European Antichrist (which is the standard view among

Christians), because it is doubtful the Jewish people would support an Islamic leader. How it plays out sure will be interesting.

A majority of Muslims would never work with any other global government or religion unless it included or endorsed Islam and Shariah Law. According to the Bible, the Antichrist will be of Roman descent and will rise to power in Europe. Can you imagine Muslims submitting to or supporting a European leader? Particularly those seeking a Caliphate (a form of Islamic state including religious and political control or leadership) will not rest until Islam dominates the nations. ISIS is unwilling to coexist with other religions or political systems, period.

We cannot deny the truth regarding the deception and oppression of Islam. Due in part to modern technology, some Christians in the West have reluctantly discovered the brutality of a people who show no mercy to those who oppose their agenda. In addition, since ancient times, Islamic forces have stormed through villages and cities in vicious killing campaigns, beheading and slaughtering the innocent they consider to be infidels. The fact this is happening today should be of no surprise to those who are informed.

One problem many of us in America have is we now find our country enabling Islam, the Muslim Brotherhood, Hamas, and other terrorist organizations either directly or indirectly. It is no longer any secret the Obama administration openly supports Islam – remember the president's 2009 speech in Cairo when he first signaled his loyalty to Muslim nations? Now, ever since the "Arab Spring" in early 2011, Sharia Law has been implemented in several Islamic countries, and the persecution of Christians has reached record levels as a result.

Dedicated followers of Islam have been seeking a caliph to carry on the prophet Muhammad's original vision of Islamic domination through conquest. Many believe they have their man in Abu Bakr al Baghdadi. "Abu who?" You may be asking. It shouldn't surprise us that American news consumers do not know who he is. Always protecting the president, few media outlets reported in 2010, one year after President Obama released Abu Bakr al Baghdadi from an Iraqi jail, Baghdadi formed ISIS, and they have been on a bloody rampage of terror, death, and evil ever since.

Some see the rapid advancement of Islam as part of the prophecy regarding the last days authority given to the beast for forty-two months to engage in war against the saints and overcome them (Revelation 13:5-7). Allegiance and worship is demanded by this "beast," and all those whose names are *not* written in the Lamb's Book of Life will follow him. Whether or not the final Muslim caliph is the Antichrist the Bible refers to remains unclear.

The fact is that pure Islam aims to dominate the world, and the hateful savagery of deceived, dedicated followers cannot remain hidden any longer. Be reminded, Islam means "submission," and a practicing Muslim disciple is one who has submitted his life to Allah. Let's be clear – their movement will continue to advance for a time. However, according to Ezekiel chapters 38 and 39, Islam will suffer at least a partial defeat when they come against Israel.

Many Muslims, particularly in America, appear to be moderate and do not follow all the tenets of Islam; but why don't they publicly renounce acts of terror in the name of Islam? Sadly, we cannot ignore or forget what a small number of Muslims did in the months and years leading up to September 11, 2001. They lived among us, assimilated our culture, and carried out a massive act of terrorism that changed America forever.

Some of what I've written may be misinterpreted as hate speech due to those who discriminate against *all* Muslims because of the actions of the radicals. That kind of discrimination is wrong, just like discriminating against all Japanese citizens in America was wrong when their country bombed Pearl Harbor in 1941. We must be discerning and loving, but we also need to be informed and never back down from the truth. There are Muslims worldwide working to implement Sharia Law in as many countries as possible to fulfill their goal of global conquest.

Though America doesn't even seem to be a blip on the radar of end times prophecy, Israel will be the one to stand its ground according to Scripture. Arab nations will come against Israel and will not succeed, but because they love bloodshed, they will be consumed by it, and their land will be desolate (Ezekiel 35:6-7, 15). (Some say this prophecy against Mount Seir has already been fulfilled.)

Author, evangelist, and prophecy expert Dr. David Reagan of Lamb Lion Ministries reminds us the future of all Arabs isn't as bleak. He writes:

> Like the Jews, a remnant of the Arabs will emerge from the Tribulation with their hearts turned to the one and only true God, Yahweh (Jeremiah 12:14-17). The most remarkable prophecy concerning the future salvation of an Arab remnant is contained in Isaiah 19:16-25. Isaiah says that when the Lord strikes Egypt and Assyria, they will turn to Him and He will have compassion on them and "heal them." Isaiah then presents an incredible picture of Egypt, Assyria, and Israel living together in peace, worshiping the same God![158]

There are obvious contrasts between Christianity and Islam, particularly relating to end times doctrines. Nowhere in the world are *Christians* persecuting unbelievers, threatening lives, attacking places of worship, chasing people out of their own homes and villages while killing any who resist. However, most of us have seen headlines and news stories telling about the gruesome slaughter of Christians in what are now Muslim-dominated cities and countries.

In Mosul, for example, the Christian population was over 100,000 a decade ago. Within a month of ISIS proclaiming leadership and slaughtering minorities, estimates have dropped from 5,000 to around two hundred Christians or fewer. In the summer months of 2014, a statement was issued by ISIS, the al Qaeda offshoot, to dwindling Christian populations where the Islamic State is taking over. They are implementing a "dhimma" contract, a historic practice under which non-Muslims were protected in Muslim lands in return for a special levy. The statement added:

> We offer them three choices: Islam; the dhimma contract – involving payment of jizya; if they refuse this, they will have nothing but the sword,[159]

In some cases, ISIS gives infidels three options: Convert to Islam,

---

158 Jan Markel, "Islam and God's End-Time Plan, 9/9/2014, http://archive.constantcontact.com/fs138/1101818841456/archive/1118460801509.html.

159 Reuters: "Convert, pay tax, or die," Islamic State warns Christians; 7/18/2014, http://www.reuters.com/article/2014/07/18/us-iraq-security-christians-idUSKBN0FN29J20140718.

pay exorbitant taxes, or be killed. Those of us in the West should not be shocked by the advancing evil in our time. Not only does the Bible predict it, but common sense says as man becomes more godless, evil will spread like disease. The fact remains evildoers need salvation through Jesus Christ.

Our reaction to terrorism and evil should be faith, love, and steadiness because it is for times such as these, Scripture is filled with the words "fear not." The Holy Spirit that God gives believers in Christ is a spirit of power, love, and a sound mind – not one of fear (2 Timothy 1:7). We are also encouraged to stand firm and *in no way be alarmed by your opponents* or adversaries even if it means we are called to *suffer for His sake* (Philippians 1:28-29).

In light of current world events including political upheaval, we must revisit these and other relevant Bible passages with a fresh perspective.

GLOBAL COMMUNICATIONS, ECONOMY, AND GOVERNMENT

From the upheaval in the Middle East to Tony Blair's push for a one-world religion to Vladimir Putin and Russia's role in the end times, world events are coming together at a furious pace as global instability is causing more people to consider options that were unthinkable a few decades ago. Modern communications appear to be opening up the door for some to consider global solutions to the problems of today. We should be amazed at the prophecies that are being fulfilled in this generation no one in Old or New Testament times could have imagined.

In Bible times, people either walked or traveled on horse or donkey, but today we can drive and fly anywhere, wherever we want to go. The prophet Daniel referred to this: *many shall run to and fro, and knowledge shall increase* (Daniel 12:4). We have centuries of knowledge on tiny microchips, and within a century our grandparents have seen the invention of automobiles and planes to human beings walking on the moon. How could the apostle John have known exactly how the nations would all be able to see the death of the "two witnesses" and rejoice over their dead bodies? (Revelation 11:9-10)

According to Scripture, certain future events will be seen by the entire world. John lived in an age of messenger by horse, not instant text messaging, Internet, or televised news. To me, this makes these prophecies even more amazing! What we live in today was unimaginable to them; so it had to be an omniscient, sovereign God speaking through them.

Think about the prophet Zechariah writing his apocalyptic and prophetic book over a span of forty years, completing it in 480 BC. He warned about a future "plague" of sorts that would be so intense people's flesh would dissolve, rot, or be consumed almost immediately as they were standing still (Zechariah 14:12). How could this be? We have the benefit, if you call it that, of understanding the use of nuclear weapons and how they can melt or dissolve matter in an instant.

How could any of these men of God have foreseen the rise of global communications and technological advances we take for granted? Remarkably, we now have all the technology necessary for a cashless society (How long have you had *your* debit card?) and are able to produce microchips so small they can be inserted into human beings, a necessary step to the Antichrist system (Revelation 13:17). We have three dogs, one of which has a microchip in the scruff of his neck for tracking should he get lost. In the Common Core chapter, we briefly touched on concerns many have about government mining or tracking our personal information. Radio frequency identification (RFID) technology is being used in society and ethical questions are being discussed.

Prophecy also supports the idea of a global economy (Revelation 13:16-17), a system that will unite world currencies in the hopes of saving or stabilizing things economically. As international leaders become more desperate to solve the current problems and economic failures, many will make a move to unite. Mary Danielsen explains:

> Connecting the world monetarily is crucial to their [globalists] goal, and the Bible says that one man will see to it that no one buys and sells without pledging allegiance to him spiritually. Everyone has heard of 666, but only in our time has the technology existed to make it a reality. The current digital payment systems that exist around the globe are part of a huge technological framework/infrastructure that has

been building since the days of the old IBM punch cards, the precursor to today's computers.[160]

In Europe, eighteen national currencies have been combined and replaced by the euro, which was introduced in 2002 as legal tender. In 1993, a treaty established the European Union (EU), and it has since developed a single market through which a common currency is used, as well as a standardized system of commerce laws and political guidelines member nations abide by. A total of twenty-eight sovereign states in and around Europe make up the membership of the EU, which includes the European Commission, Courts, Central Bank, and European Parliament.

Also predicted in the Bible is a move toward a global government (Daniel 2:40-44; Revelation 13:7-8). The former Roman Empire, which encompassed present-day Europe, would be revived and eventually dominate the world. Scripture supports the idea the world will be subdivided either into ten governing regions or the EU will have ten kings, as interpreted from this prophecy: *As for the ten horns, out of this kingdom ten kings will arise: and another will arise after them, and he will be different from the previous ones* (Daniel 7:24). EU nations with the largest populations are the UK, France, Spain, and Germany.

Naturally, after seeing economies and political systems "United in diversity" (The EU's motto), a global religion may not be that far off, especially when leaders of several denominations and faiths see ecumenism as a positive thing. According to prophecy, a one-world religion is just a matter of time (Revelation 13:8, 12; Rev. 17).

One recent meeting of interest was an Interfaith Conference at the Vatican in mid-November of 2014.[161] According to the Catholic News Service: Mormon, Jewish, Islamic, Buddhist, Hindu, Jaina Shasana, Taoist, and Sikh religions were present, as well as Roman Catholics, Baptists, and Protestants. Sponsored by the Pontifical Council for Interreligious Dialogue, this meeting included America's "Purpose Driven" Pastor,

---

160   Mary Danielsen, *The Things to Come*, Prophecy 101, 8/10/2014, http://thethings2come.org/?p=1038.

161   Heather Clark, "Russell More, Rick Warren to Join Pope Francis with Muslims, Buddhists for Interfaith Conference," 11/7/2014, http://christiannews.net/2014/11/07/russell-moore-rick-warren-to-join-pope-francis-with-muslims-buddhists-for-interfaith-conference/.

Rick Warren, who is quoted as saying, "Pope Francis is doing everything right," and "if you love Jesus, we're on the same team."

Joel Osteen felt the same way about Mitt Romney. Osteen stated during an interview that he believes Mormons are Christians. Countless people might love or respect Jesus because of what He did or taught, but they might not believe He is God, the Truth, the only Mediator between God and man; and they may not have placed their trust in Jesus Christ alone for salvation. Finding common ground is one thing, but tossing theological differences, idolatry, and false teachings out the window in order to unite for a cause sends a wrong message.

Someone once said, "God is always right and the rest of us are just guessing." That's how we can sometimes feel about prophecy, because there is plenty to study and watch for in the coming days. We keep our focus and keep the faith by remembering this life is temporary and every prophecy in Scripture will be fulfilled. We can be confident God's justice and His judgment will prevail. Malachi 4:1-3 states:

> "For behold, the day is coming, burning like a furnace; and all the arrogant and every evildoer will be chaff; and the day that is coming will set them ablaze," says the LORD of hosts, "so that it will leave them neither root nor branch." "But for you who fear My name, the sun of righteousness will rise with healing in its wings; and you will go forth and skip about like calves from the stall. You will tread down the wicked, for they will be ashes under the soles of your feet on the day which I am preparing," says the LORD of hosts.

God is concerned about reconciling the world to Himself and saving the souls of mankind, not about saving the United States or preserving the earth. The day of the Lord *will come like a thief,* and this world as we know it will pass away and be destroyed, which is why *we are looking for new heavens and a new earth, in which righteousness dwells* (2 Peter 3:10-13).

A basic understanding of prophecy is important because it strengthens our faith in the return of Jesus Christ, and the more we know and understand about the end times, the better we will be able to explain our secure hope to others. This brings us full circle in this book: We are called to trust Christ and his Word, love others, be prepared, and ready to defend the faith.

Understanding prophecy will also enable us to keep current events in perspective. With all the bad news, terror, and chaos in a shaky world today, we know how it all ends, and we can have an unshakable hope in a never-changing God. Let us worship Him with reverence and thankfulness because *we are receiving a kingdom that cannot be shaken* (Hebrews 12:28 NIV).

Yes, we are to obey Jesus' command to go and make disciples by the uncompromising preaching of the gospel. However, until we get our own houses in order, call the church back to repentance, and seek personal and corporate revival, our power and effectiveness will continue to be limited. God calls believers to holiness and obedience and says, *do not conform to the evil desires you had when you lived in ignorance* (1 Peter 1:14-16 NIV). The bride of Christ must cleanse herself from the pollution of the world and prepare for the return of the Bridegroom.

CONCLUSION

God is looking for men and women in the faith to be His messengers in these last days and to recommit our lives in wholehearted devotion to Christ. I admit my own past failures, including a lack of concentrated prayer and inconsistent service to our King. Have you admitted yours? Only with sincere confession, humility, and transparency before Him and each other will we be able to get back on track and do the work required of us with the joy of the Lord.

Let's hit our knees and cry out to Him for mercy, cry out for those who are not yet converted, and pray for a revival of His people. Let's encourage Christians to be fervent in spirit and ready to disciple others, because if a revival happens at any level, we know conversions to Jesus could rapidly increase.

If however, Christians do not see the need to repent, America has no chance of preservation. Has God ever allowed any nation to survive who had so much favor and the blessing of God only to turn its back on Him? Where are the watchmen warning the church about impending danger? Is today's church reliving history?

In the past, God would allow His people to be attacked so they might turn back to Him. Isaiah wrote to the Israelites: *your sins have hidden His face from you so that He does not hear* (Isaiah 59:2 NIV). Through the prophet Joel, the Lord told them to return to Him with all their heart, even after all their disobedience and sin, reminding them He is gracious and compassionate (Joel 2:12-13).

Our silence has had tragic consequences, but from now on, let's be prepared and useful to the Master (2 Timothy 2:21), encouraging people to return to Jesus Christ. These may be the final hours in which to take action and turn things around. A time is coming when we will no longer be able to speak.

Then comes the end; when He hands over the kingdom to the God and Father, when He has abolished all rule and all authority and power. For He must reign until He has put all His enemies

under His feet. The last enemy that will be abolished is death
(1 Corinthians 15:24-25).

*At that time many will fall away and will betray one another
and hate one another... But the one who endures to the end,
he will be saved. This gospel of the kingdom shall be preached
in the whole world as a testimony to all the nations, and then
the end will come* (Matthew 24:10, 13-14).

ABOUT THE AUTHOR

David Fiorazo is an author, writer, content contributor, public speaker, and radio personality who loves God and country. He has been involved in the broadcasting and entertainment industries for over thirty years and in Christian ministry for over twenty-five years. David loves and strives to defend and proclaim the truth of Jesus Christ without apology or compromise. He believes every life has a purpose and we are here for such a time as this.

Connect with David Fiorazo
Main site - http://www.davidfiorazo.com
Eradicate book – http://blottingoutgod.com
Facebook page – https://www.facebook.com/
EradicateBlottingOutGodInAmerica
Blog – http://davefiorazo.blogspot.com/
Twitter – https://twitter.com/fiorazo
LinkedIn - https://www.linkedin.com/in/davidfiorazo

Enemy forces continue to destroy this nation by attacking America's Judeo-Christian roots from within. This book will investigate government, media, Hollywood, public schools, our culture of death, and the push toward socialism and Marxism. You'll see how some churches and leaders are diluting the Word of God weakening the witness of believers. You may be outraged as this book exposes how sin is being openly promoted, yet encouraged because God is still in control. There's a remnant of committed Christians resisting evil and standing in the way. The choice is ours: who or what will we give our allegiance to, God or man; to Jesus Christ or to culture and politics? As Christians, our loyalties must not be divided any longer or America may be lost.

Available where books are sold

Arab Spring, Christian Winter will help you tie newspaper headlines to your scriptural knowledge of the Last Days. Ralph Stice draws a clear link between the Arab Spring and the rise of a worldwide power that appears to be ushering in the coming Antichrist.

This book will also show you what you need to watch for in tomorrow's news and guide you on how to fortify your faith for stormy days ahead. The Western Church has much to learn from Christian brothers and sisters in the Middle East. Familiar Scripture passages are unfolding with new clarity to believers everywhere.

Learn:

- Why the Arab Spring had to happen to fulfill scriptural prophecy

- How the Arab Spring led to the unleashing of pure Islam

- Which nation could be the crucial link between East and West and produce an Antichrist figure

- The responses of Middle Eastern Christians to intense persecution and what we Western believers can learn from them

Available where books are sold